Agency and Institutions in Sport

This book offers a unique insight into the role of individuals and organisations in shaping institutional arrangements within the context of sport. Institutional approaches can be used to examine the complex relationships between sport organisations and their broader environment and can help explain some of the most fundamental questions about the nature of how sport is organised including why are many sport organisations so similar? Why do they adopt practices that are seemingly irrational? And how can we explain how change occurs within sport organisations?

In drawing upon contemporary scholarship and empirical evidence collected by internationally recognised experts, this book provides a contemporary collection of studies that advances the understanding of agency in institutions through sport. In doing so, the chapters in this book bridge the theoretical divide between mainstream management and sport management to help facilitate a joint venture for future research. This book will be essential reading for advanced undergraduate or postgraduate students on sport or sport-related courses and researchers interested in institutional analysis and its potential application to sport.

The chapters in this book were originally published as a special issue of *European Sport Management Quarterly*.

Mathew Dowling is Senior Lecturer in Sport Management, Loughborough University, UK.

Jonathan Robertson is Senior Lecturer in Sport Management, Deakin University, Australia.

Marvin Washington is Professor of Management, University of Alberta, Canada.

Becca Leopkey is Associate Professor in Sport Management, University of Georgia, USA.

Dana Ellis is Associate Professor in Sport Management, Laurentian University, Canada.

Agency and Institutions in Sport

Edited by
Mathew Dowling, Jonathan Robertson, Marvin Washington, Becca Leopkey and Dana Ellis

LONDON AND NEW YORK

First published 2025
by Routledge
4 Park Square, Milton Park, Abingdon, Oxon OX14 4RN

and by Routledge
605 Third Avenue, New York, NY 10158

Routledge is an imprint of the Taylor & Francis Group, an informa business

Introduction, Chapters 1, 2, 4 and 5 © 2025 European Association for Sport Management.
Chapter 3 © 2023 Kyle A. Rich, Grace Nelson, Tammy Borgen-Flood & Ann Pegoraro. Originally published as Open Access.
Chapter 6 © 2023 Calvin Nite, Ajhanai Keaton, Patrick Neff and Craig Fulk. Originally published as Open Access.

With the exception of Chapters 3 and 6, no part of this book may be reprinted or reproduced or utilised in any form or by any electronic, mechanical, or other means, now known or hereafter invented, including photocopying and recording, or in any information storage or retrieval system, without permission in writing from the publishers. For details on the rights for Chapters 3 and 6, please see the chapters' Open Access footnotes.

Trademark notice: Product or corporate names may be trademarks or registered trademarks, and are used only for identification and explanation without intent to infringe.

British Library Cataloguing in Publication Data
A catalogue record for this book is available from the British Library

ISBN13: 978-1-032-82219-8 (hbk)
ISBN13: 978-1-032-82222-8 (pbk)
ISBN13: 978-1-003-50354-5 (ebk)

DOI: 10.4324/9781003503545

Typeset in Minion Pro
by Newgen Publishing UK

Publisher's Note
The publisher accepts responsibility for any inconsistencies that may have arisen during the conversion of this book from journal articles to book chapters, namely the inclusion of journal terminology.

Disclaimer
Every effort has been made to contact copyright holders for their permission to reprint material in this book. The publishers would be grateful to hear from any copyright holder who is not here acknowledged and will undertake to rectify any errors or omissions in future editions of this book.

Contents

Citation Information vi
Notes on Contributors viii

Introduction 1
Mathew Dowling, Jonathan Robertson, Marvin Washington, Becca Leopkey and Dana Ellis

1 'When we meet, we play football, it reminds me of home': emotions, institutional work, and sport-for-development and peace 8
Mitchell McSweeney, Landy Lu and Lisa Kikulis

2 Trained to be sexist: operationalizing institutional logics in the co-construction of gendered discourse in sport 34
Meredith Patricia Flaherty

3 Regional policy and organizational fields in multi-level sport governance 51
Kyle A. Rich, Grace Nelson, Tammy Borgen-Flood and Ann Pegoraro

4 Integrating emotions into legitimacy work: an institutional work perspective on new sport emergence 72
Jingxuan Zheng and Daniel S. Mason

5 Agency in institutionalized sport organizations: examining how institutions suppress agency 93
Brent D. Oja, Calvin Nite, Minjung Kim and Jasmine Hill

6 The legitimacy work of institutional disruption and maintenance: examining the rivalry between LIV golf and the professional golf association 113
Calvin Nite, Ajhanai Keaton, Patrick Neff and Craig Fulk

Index 134

Citation Information

The chapters in this book were originally published in the *European Sport Management Quarterly*, volume 24, issue 1 (2024). When citing this material, please use the original page numbering for each article, as follows:

Introduction
Agency and institutions in sport
Mathew Dowling, Jonathan Robertson, Marvin Washington, Becca Leopkey and Dana Ellis
European Sport Management Quarterly, volume 24, issue 1 (2024), pp. 1–7

Chapter 1
'When we meet, we play football, it reminds me of home': emotions, institutional work, and sport-for-development and peace
Mitchell McSweeney, Landy Lu and Lisa Kikulis
European Sport Management Quarterly, volume 24, issue 1 (2024), pp. 8–33

Chapter 2
Trained to be sexist: operationalizing institutional logics in the co-construction of gendered discourse in sport
Meredith Patricia Flaherty
European Sport Management Quarterly, volume 24, issue 1 (2024), pp. 34–50

Chapter 3
Regional policy and organizational fields in multi-level sport governance
Kyle A. Rich, Grace Nelson, Tammy Borgen-Flood and Ann Pegoraro
European Sport Management Quarterly, volume 24, issue 1 (2024), pp. 51–71

Chapter 4
Integrating emotions into legitimacy work: an institutional work perspective on new sport emergence
Jingxuan Zheng and Daniel S. Mason
European Sport Management Quarterly, volume 24, issue 1 (2024), pp. 72–92

Chapter 5
Agency in institutionalized sport organizations: examining how institutions suppress agency
Brent D. Oja, Calvin Nite, Minjung Kim and Jasmine Hill
European Sport Management Quarterly, volume 24, issue 1 (2024), pp. 93–112

Chapter 6
The legitimacy work of institutional disruption and maintenance: examining the rivalry between LIV golf and the professional golf association
Calvin Nite, Ajhanai Keaton, Patrick Neff and Craig Fulk
European Sport Management Quarterly, volume 24, issue 1 (2024), pp. 113–133

For any permission-related enquiries please visit:
www.tandfonline.com/page/help/permissions

Notes on Contributors

Tammy Borgen-Flood, Department of Recreation and Leisure Studies, Brock University, St. Catharines, ON, Canada.

Mathew Dowling, School of Sport, Exercise and Health Sciences, Loughborough University, Leicestershire, UK.

Dana Ellis, School of Sports Administration, Laurentian University, Sudbury, ON, Canada.

Meredith Patricia Flaherty, Sport Management Program, School of Human Movement, Sport, and Leisure Studies, Bowling Green State University, Bowling Green, OH, USA.

Craig Fulk, Department of Kinesiology and Sport Management, Texas A&M University, College Station, TX, USA.

Jasamine Hil, Texas A&M University, College Station, TX, USA.

Ajhanai Keaton, Department of Health and Sport Sciences, University of Louisville, Louisville, KY, USA.

Lisa Kikulis, Department of Sport Management, Brock University, St. Catharines, ON, Canada.

Minjung Kim, Texas A&M University, College Station, TX, USA.

Becca Leopkey, Department of Kinesiology, University of Georgia, Athens, GA, USA.

Landy Lu, School of Kinesiology, University of Minnesota, Minneapolis, MN, USA.

Daniel S. Mason, Faculty of Kinesiology, Sport, and Recreation, University of Alberta, Edmonton, AB, Canada.

Mitchell McSweeney, School of Kinesiology, University of Minnesota, Minneapolis, MN, USA.

Patrick Neff, Department of Kinesiology and Sport Management, Texas A&M University, College Station, TX, USA.

Grace Nelson, Department of Recreation and Leisure Studies, Brock University, St. Catharines, ON, Canada.

Calvin Nite, Department of Kinesiology and Sport Management, Texas A&M University, College Station, TX, USA; Center for Sport Management Research and Education, Texas A&M University, College Station, TX, USA.

Brent D. Oja, College of Applied Human Sciences, West Virginia University, Morgantown, WV, USA.

Ann Pegoraro, Gordon S. Lang School of Business and Economics, University of Guelph, Guelph, Canada.

Kyle A. Rich, Department of Recreation and Leisure Studies, Brock University, St. Catharines, ON, Canada.

Jonathan Robertson, Deakin Business School, Deakin University, Geelong, VIC, Australia.

Marvin Washington, College of Social Sciences & Humanities, University of Alberta, Edmonton, AB, Canada.

Jingxuan Zheng, Faculty of Kinesiology, Sport, and Recreation, University of Alberta, AB, Edmonton, Canada.

Introduction

Mathew Dowling, Jonathan Robertson, Marvin Washington, Becca Leopkey and Dana Ellis

ABSTRACT
Much like the social phenomenon which it seeks to explain, institutional theory has become an institutional and dominant theoretical research traditional within sport management. In the context of sport, institutional theory can be used to examine the complex relationship between sport organisations and their broader environment. Specifically, it explains how sport organisations are influenced by and in turn influence, broader social, political and economic forces, as well as how these institutional forces shape the behaviour and practices of athletes, coaches and fans. The five original contributions contained within this special issue seek to advance institutional scholarship and bridge the growing theoretical divide between sport management and management. Taken together, the papers in this special issue represent the potential for not only further illumination of how institutional theory can advance sport management, but also how sport management might hold the possibility for further articulation and advancement of institutional theory. In doing so, we set out a future research agenda that calls for a return to the original motivations and concepts of institutional theory and a further appreciation of the distinctiveness of the sport context for understanding institutional arrangements.

Much like the social phenomenon which it seeks to explain, institutional theory has become an institutionalised and dominant theoretical research tradition within sport management. The theoretical tradition emphasises institutions, which are broadly understood as 'cultural, normative, and regulatory structures and activities that provide stability and meaning to social behaviour' (Scott, 1995, p. 33). In the context of sport, institutional theory can be used to examine the complex relationships between sport organisations and their broader environment. Specifically, the approach can help explain how individuals (e.g. athletes, coaches and fans) and organisations (e.g. teams, leagues, companies) are influenced by, and in turn influence, broader social, political and economic forces within the sport industry. The utility and relevance of institutional theory are evident by the fact that nearly 200 studies have utilised institutional constructs to investigate sporting institutions (Robertson et al., 2022).

Rather than a singular theoretical perspective, institutional theory can be more accurately described as a research tradition, with several key concepts that can be employed and are particularly relevant to understand and explain the changing nature of sport. These perspectives include legitimacy, change, isomorphism, fields, logics and institutional work. Part of the reason why institutional theory has emerged as a research tradition is because there were so many different origin stories that emerged from varying strands of scholarship. The work of DiMaggio and Powell (1983) on isomorphism and fields, Meyer and Rowan (1977) on institutional myths, Zucker (1977) on legitimacy, and Tolbert and Zucker (1983) on diffusion contained a common thread. That is, while each of these scholarly contributions led to novel theoretical advances, they also each started with a range of simple empirical questions: what makes organisations become similar? Why do organisations adopt practices that are seemingly irrational? And how can we explain organisational change?

The phrase 'neo-institutionalism' was first articulated by Powell and DiMaggio (1991) in their 'orange book' and more recently further explicated by Greenwood and colleagues in *Organizational Institutionalism* (Greenwood et al., 2008; 2017). A central assumption underpinning early institutional approaches was that individuals and organisations are subject to, and therefore at the mercy of, broader institutional forces (e.g. Slack & Hinings, 1994). More contemporary institutional research has begun to challenge the underlying assumption of structural determinism that positions actors as 'cultural dopes' subject to the 'iron cage' of institutional forces (Powell & DiMaggio, 1991). Arguably, this shift in thinking, or 'agency turn', has marked a fundamental departure from earlier institutional studies by focussing on institutional work[1] which Lawrence and Suddaby (2006) define as 'the purposive action of individuals or organizations aimed at creating, maintaining and disrupting institutions' (p. 215). More recently the institutional work perspective has expanded to include scholarship on 'how, why, and when actors work to shape sets of institutions, the factors that affect their ability to do so, and the experience of these efforts for those involved' and the 'practices and processes associated with actors' endeavours to build, tear down, elaborate and contain institutions, as well as amplify or suppress their effects' (Hampel et al., 2017, p. 558). It is this latter, more contemporary inclusion of the role of agents in shaping institutional arrangements, which we use as the basis to advance and extend institutional scholarship in sport management within this special issue.

Contemporary uses of agency in institutional studies provide a distinctive opportunity for sport management researchers looking to leverage the sport setting to extend and develop theory. In its more basic sense, sports are ideal institutions to examine as all sports at their core are made-up systems of rules agreed upon by a field of stakeholders. In addition, sport also consists of institutions that matter to and are reflective of society, encompassing a range of normative systems and cognitive understandings around issues of development, governance, health, identity, inclusion, (in)equity, integrity, media, participation, socialisation and technology. Individuals and organisations collectively shape these institutions via their actions. Consequently, while sport management scholarship has an extensive history of institutional analysis, placing individuals at the heart of this analysis opens a range of interesting and exciting opportunities to advance our understanding of sport.

For this special issue, we are particularly interested in publishing a body of work that demonstrates clear theoretical contributions to advance our understanding of agency in institutions (e.g. multi-level studies, emotions, institutional work, novel methodological approaches). More specifically, our aim is to build upon and directly respond to the recent work of Robertson et al. (2022) and Nite and Edwards (2021) to begin to bridge the growing theoretical divide and 'time-lag' between mainstream management and sport management scholarship (Dowling et al., 2023). And, within this shared empirical context (sport) and theoretical tradition (institutional theory), help facilitate the development of a joint venture (Washington & Patterson, 2011) and a diffusion of ideas (Robertson et al., 2022) between the fields of management and sport management.

Contributions to the special issue

McSweeney et al. examined the relationship between (individual and collective) emotions elicited by forced migration, the institutional work of a sport for development and peace (SDP) organisation, and the ability of refugees to challenge the institution of social inequality in their host community. The authors partnered with Young African Refugees for Integral Development (YARID), an NGO based in Kampala Uganda, to undertake *participatory action research* (PAR) that allowed them to co-produce knowledge with participants and better understand their lived experience. Their findings suggest positive and negative emotions influence both the institutional work of an SDP organisation and the ability of the refugees to impact upon institutions of social inequality, stimulating both the maintenance and disruption of extant institutions. These findings contribute to our understanding of institutional theory by focusing on lived experience to illuminate how the strategic use of collective emotions can act as a catalyst for institutional work and subsequently facilitate the disruption of institutions.

Also employing a novel methodology to scholarship in sport management, *Flaherty* undertook an autoethnography to examine the co-construction of gendered institutional logics in her experiences coaching and playing elite US sport. Across four identified dominant logics (less than, conform socially, protect girls and vision of value) she narrated her experiences as both someone who was shaped by gendered discourse and practices, and someone who reproduced those same actions and assumptions. In doing so, she illustrates how micro-level understandings of behaviours, sensemaking and power structures impact the institutional work of co-constructing gendered logics.

Rich et al., examined multi-level, regional governance through an institutional lens by undertaking an instrumental case study. They sought to understand how regional policy impacts field structuration and policy implementation in the organisational field of amateur sport in Ontario, Canada. They found the dynamic positioning of sport within varying sectors impacted resourcing and planning which, in turn, offered implications for field structuration. They also found there to be an emphasis on economic accountability and self-sufficiency prescribed at the municipal and local levels which influenced field-level change and regional policy implementation. Theoretically, they contribute to our understanding of multi-level governance in organisational fields by highlighting how the agency of an ever-changing group of actors (regional government) can alter a field and the implementation of policy within it. Furthermore, they call attention to the role of policy in the translation of ideas and the need to balance competing logics at varying levels of governance within this framework.

Using the development of Mixed Martial Arts (MMA) as a case study, *Zheng and Mason* investigated the role of emotion in the emergence of new sports. Specifically, they examined the influence of discursive institutional work on negative emotions during the legitimation of MMA as a new sport. The authors identify various forms of emotion-specific discursive institutional work which aided in addressing negative emotions (substitution, pacification and disruption) and creating positive emotions (stimulation, cultivation and substitution) to bring about legitimation. In each of the three phases of MMA's development, differing combinations of these forms of work were recognised. Their study promotes the primacy of emotion alongside cognition in institutional legitimacy work. They note that emotions themselves can and should be the target of institutional work and ultimately be influenced by institutional change. With this in mind, and given the difficulty of altering emotions, the authors suggest that emotion-specific institutional work is vital in the overall work of maintaining and disrupting institutions.

Oja and colleagues expand our understanding about the dichotomy of structure and agency within sport organisations. More specifically, the authors examine how institutionalised work practices impact employee agency (i.e. their ability to make changes to practices and structures in their organisation) within the US college system (i.e. NCAA). Using a purposive data collection strategy, 13 interviews representing individuals in non-coaching positions across separate universities were amassed and analysed using a thematic analysis procedure. Findings revealed how workplace norms and bureaucracy impacted employee's abilities to create modifications and improvements in their organisation. Thus, raising the question of whether current work arrangements within sport are sustainable.

Finally, *Nite et al.*, dive into a relatively new sporting context by examining the rivalry between LIV Golf and the Professional Golf Association (PGA). Specifically, the authors are interested in the interplay between legitimacy work and emotions. Their research questions aimed to better understand how dominant organisations create messages to influence perceptions of legitimacy while at the same time examining how these messages provoke emotional responses from evaluators of newer, less dominant organisations or rivals. The authors engage with sociologically based framing theory (cf. Frederick et al., 2021; Tewksbury & Scheufele, 2009) to guide their emotional discourse analysis of 38 news articles to understand how the frames or messages in this case are packaged, constructed and understood. Findings demonstrated how the dominant PGA framed themselves as 'true golf' attempting to delegitimise their rival as posing threats to legacy and tradition, destruction of the game, and negating the meritocratic structures of the sport while playing on emotions rather than rationality. This novel study contributes to our understanding of how human emotion influences perceived legitimacy and institutional work.

Future research directions: advancing institutional scholarship through sport

Taken together, the papers in this special issue represent the potential for not only further illumination of how institutional theory can advance sport management, but also how sport management might hold the possibility for further articulation and advancement of institutional theory (Fonti et al., 2023). Like most special issues, when we put the call together, we had some suggestions for the type of research that could not only extend sport management studies, but also institutional theory. The papers in this special issue, address many of our original suggestions: the role of individuals in creating, maintaining and disrupting institutional sport settings, the role of emotions, and papers that combine institutional theory with other perspectives. However, in a similar vein, some topics were not addressed, including: the origins of sport institutions, or societal consequences for institutional arrangements in sport, as well as materiality and institutional work.

As a call for more research that could advance institutional theory, we suggest three future directions. First, we want to encourage scholars, in some ways, to return to the original motivation(s) of institutional theory. As previously mentioned, the original motivations of some of the seminal papers in institutional theory were an effort to make sense of an empirical phenomenon. For example, DiMaggio and Powell were concerned with why two totally different organisations resemble each other, Tolbert and Zucker sought to understand how various practices diffused even though the organisations adopting these practices did not have any use for them. Here is where we think sport management could help further develop contemporary institutional theory. As such, rather than starting with the question how does current institutional theory explain a sport phenomenon? Future researchers could instead seek to understand a problem or issue in the sport domain and then discuss how the answer to this problem or issue might extend to a variety of institutional questions that are present within current institutional scholarship. For example, how does temporality of major event cycles help (de)stabilise sport institutions (Reinecke & Lawrence, 2023)? How does the embodied world of concern of an athlete-activist animate broader institutional processes within society (Creed et al., 2022)? By virtue of its presence at the forefront of so many issues ranging from diversity, gender issues, to sustainability, sport has clear utility in advancing contemporary theory development (Fonti et al., 2023). Knitting together these conversations – as we have tried to within this special issue – will only continue to advance this body of knowledge.

Second, future research could (re-)connect concepts of neo-institutionalism to some of the original concepts, such as field-level contestation and institutional leadership (Zietsma et al., 2017). One of the common elements of most sport leagues and fields is that there is a 'leader' (often called commissioner, or president, or executive director). Asking how these leaders navigate their institutional environment and what their role is in shaping institutional settings provides a potentially fruitful path of integrating sport management and institutional theory work (Heinze et al., 2016). Similarly, leagues and mega-sport events (such as the Olympics) are always locations of conflict in sport (e.g. drug use in sport, sustainability, transgender issues) and as such, scholars could use sport to advance our concepts of organisational fields in general and field configuring events in particular (Lampel & Meyer, 2008).

Lastly, we feel that sport management scholars should return to the big question of why sport? What is it that makes it a unique (or at least a distinctive) context by which to explore institutional arrangements? We suggest that sport is well-positioned to explore the societal consequences or outcomes and the micro-level foundations of how actors navigate and shape institutional arrangements in sport. It also has significant potential to contribute meaningfully to contemporary theoretical debates surrounding materiality (sport is highly visible), plurality and hybridity (sport operates across and is nested within multiple institutional arrangements), and – as demonstrated by some of the articles with our special issue – emotion (sport is highly emotionally charged). Furthermore, there is a need to expand the theoretical plurality of institutional sport scholarship to explore how institutional theory can be utilised alongside a variety of other complimentary theoretical approaches (e.g. institutional theory and governance; institutional theory and corporate social responsibility; institutional theory and professionalisation) which largely remain unexplored.

As a final note, the guest editorial team would like to extend our sincere appreciation for all those who submitted and contributed to this special issue, including the many reviewers who gave up their time and contributed their expertise willingly to help produce this special issue, without their support this important body of work would not have been possible. We would also like to thank Paul Downward and Caron Walpole, who provided us with valuable guidance throughout the process.

Note

1. Here we include related (albeit distinct) concepts such as institutional entrepreneurship within our broader understanding of agentic approaches to institutional scholarship.

Disclosure statement

No potential conflict of interest was reported by the author(s).

ORCID

Mathew Dowling http://orcid.org/0000-0003-0741-9245
Jonathan Robertson http://orcid.org/0000-0003-1062-1145
Marvin Washington http://orcid.org/0000-0001-9893-3519
Becca Leopkey http://orcid.org/0000-0002-5870-8699
Dana Ellis http://orcid.org/0000-0002-7988-670X

References

Creed, W. D., Hudson, B. A., Okhuysen, G. A., & Smith-Crowe, K. (2022). A place in the world: Vulnerability, well-being, and the ubiquitous evaluation that animates participation in institutional processes. *Academy of Management Review*, 47(3), 358–381. https://doi.org/10.5465/amr.2018.0367

DiMaggio, P. J., & Powell, W. W. (1983). The iron cage revisited: Institutional isomorphism and collective rationality in organizational fields. *American Sociological Review*, 48(2), 147–160. https://doi.org/10.2307/2095101

Dowling, M., Robertson, J., Washington, M., Leopkey, B., Ellis, D., Riches, A., & Smith, L. (2023). 'Like ships in the night' and the paradox of distinctiveness for sport management: A citation network analysis of institutional theory in sport. *Journal of Sport Management* (Advance online publication). https://doi.org/10.1123/jsm.2022-0280

Fonti, F., Ross, J. M., & Aversa, P. (2023). Using sports data to advance management research: A review and a guide for future studies. *Journal of Management, 49*(1), 325–362. https://doi.org/10.1177/01492063221117525

Frederick, E., Pegoraro, A., & Sanderson, J. (2021). Sport in the age of trump: An analysis of Donald Trump's tweets. *International Journal of Sport Communication, 14*(3), 356–378. https://doi.org/10.1123/ijsc.2020-0287

Greenwood, R., Oliver, C., Lawrence, T., & Meyer, R. (2017). *The SAGE handbook of organizational institutionalism* (2nd ed.). SAGE.

Greenwood, R., Oliver, C., Sahlin, K., & Suddaby, R. (2008). *The SAGE handbook of organizational institutionalism*. SAGE.

Hampel, C., Lawrence, T., & Tracey, P. (2017). Institutional work: Taking stock and making it matter. In R. Greenwood, C. Oliver, R. Lawrence, & R. Meyer (Eds.), *The SAGE handbook of organizational institutionalism* (pp. 558–590). SAGE.

Heinze, K. L., Soderstrom, S., & Heinze, J. E. (2016). Translating institutional change to local communities: The role of linking organizations. *Organization Studies, 37*(8), 1141–1169. https://doi.org/10.1177/0170840615622068

Lampel, J., & Meyer, A. (2008). Field-configuring events as structuring mechanisms: How conferences, ceremonies, and trade shows constitute new technologies, industries, and markets. *Journal of Management Studies, 45*(6), 1025–1035. https://doi.org/10.1111/j.1467-6486.2008.00787.x

Lawrence, T., & Suddaby, R. (2006). Institutions and institutional work. In S. Clegg, C. Hardy, T. Lawrence, & W. Nord (Eds.), *Handbook of organization studies* (pp. 215–254). SAGE.

Meyer, J. W., & Rowan, B. (1977). Institutionalized organizations: Formal structure as myth and ceremony. *American Journal of Sociology, 83*(2), 340–363. https://doi.org/10.1086/226550

Nite, C., & Edwards, J. (2021). From isomorphism to institutional work: Advancing institutional theory in sport management research. *Sport Management Review, 24*(5), 815–838. https://doi.org/10.1080/14413523.2021.1896845

Powell, W., & DiMaggio, P. (1991). *The new institutionalism and organizational analysis*. University of Chicago Press.

Reinecke, J., & Lawrence, T. B. (2023). The role of temporality in institutional stabilization: A process view. *Academy of Management Review, 48*(4), 639–658. https://doi.org/10.5465/amr.2019.0486

Robertson, J., Dowling, M., Washington, M., Leopkey, B., Ellis, D., & Smith, L. (2022). Institutional theory in sport: A scoping review. *Journal of Sport Management, 36*(5), 459–472. https://doi.org/10.1123/jsm.2021-0179

Scott, R. (1995). *Institutions and organizations: Foundations for organizational science*. SAGE.

Slack, T., & Hinings, B. (1994). Institutional pressures and isomorphic change: An empirical test. *Organization Studies, 15*(6), 803–827. https://doi.org/10.1177/017084069401500602

Tewksbury, D., & Scheufele, D. A. (2009). News framing theory and research. In J. Bryantand & M. B. Oliver (Eds.), *Media effects: Advances in theory and research* (pp. 17–33). Routledge.

Tolbert, P. S., & Zucker, L. G. (1983). Institutional sources of change in the formal structure of organizations: The diffusion of Civil Service Reform, 1880-1935. *Administrative Science Quarterly, 28*(1), 22–39. https://doi.org/10.2307/2392383

Washington, M., & Patterson, K. (2011). Hostile takeover or joint venture: Connections between institutional theory and sport management research. *Sport Management Review, 14*(1), 1–12. https://doi.org/10.1016/j.smr.2010.06.003

Zietsma, C., Groenewegen, P., Logue, D. M., & Hinings, C. R. (2017). Field or fields? Building the scaffolding for cumulation of research on institutional fields. *Academy of Management Annals, 11*(1), 391–450. https://doi.org/10.5465/annals.2014.0052

Zucker, Lynne G. (1977). The role of institutionalization in cultural persistence. *American Sociological Review, 42*(5), 726–743. https://doi.org/10.2307/2094862

'When we meet, we play football, it reminds me of home': emotions, institutional work, and sport-for-development and peace

Mitchell McSweeney, Landy Lu and Lisa Kikulis

ABSTRACT
Research question: While there is a growing body of scholarship on institutional work in sport, less is known about the role of emotions by which institutions are affected. This study aims to explore the role of emotions in sport-for-development and peace (SDP)-related institutional work to challenge conditions of social inequality for refugees in Kampala, Uganda. Two core research questions are: (1) How do emotions related to forced displacement inform the institutional work of an SDP organization? (2) What emotions are mobilized by refugees and an SDP organization to challenge the institution of social inequality?
Research methods: Guided by a participatory action research approach, fieldwork was undertaken with a refugee-led organization in Kampala. Data collection included semi-structured interviews, photovoice, and photocollaging. Ethical consent was obtained from all individuals participating in the research and for the display of images.
Results and Findings: The findings demonstrate that a variety of emotions experienced as positive (e.g. love of sport) or negative (e.g. stress) stimulate SDP-related work to change relations between host communities and refugees. The findings also illustrate that emotions experienced positively (e.g. nostalgia, happiness) were generated via SDP activities, including creation of sport groups related to homelands and conflict resolution among refugees and host communities. Three mechanisms – diverting, bonding, peacemaking – are identified that enabled SDP-related practices to transform refugees' emotions. The resulting positive emotional state helped to undermine the institution of social inequality between the host community and refugees.
Implications: This study advances theoretical development of institutional theory in sport management by accounting for the lived experience and emotions that play a role in SDP-related institutional work.

Introduction

The displacement journeys that refugees go through are some of the most emotionally tolling processes humans can experience, given the combination of conflict in their homeland, continuous travel (e.g. to an asylum country), and resettlement in a new hostland. Further, upon resettlement, refugees are often confronted with formal institutional conditions such as resettlement programs and informal institutional conditions, including discrimination (Montgomery & Foldspang, 2008), social exclusion (Phillimore & Goodson, 2006), and unemployment (Jacobsen, 2002), all of which construct, maintain, and perpetuate the institution[1] of social inequality of refugees (Scheibelhofer, 2019).

While emotions have been conceptualized in varied ways (e.g. Ekman, 1999; Scheff, 2015), for this paper, we adopt a sociological conceptualization of emotions (Bericat, 2016; Turner & Stets, 2006) which acknowledges that while emotions are experienced by individuals, they are evaluative and socially conditioned responses to social relations and context (Creed et al., 2014; Zietsma & Toubiana, 2018). This conceptualization of emotions fits with the social constructionist perspective that is the foundation of an institutional approach (Berger & Luckmann, 1966; Friedland, 2018). A growing body of institutional theory literature explores the role of emotions (e.g. Farny et al., 2019; Moisander et al., 2016; Zilber, 2020). Such research reconceptualizes people as more than cognitively-driven creatures of habit (Hampel et al., 2017; Voronov, 2014) and instead views 'institutional processes as "lived"; as animated by persons with emotions, social bonds, and commitments, by persons to whom institutional arrangements matter' (Lok et al., 2017, p. 592). A recognition of how individuals feel (e.g. hopeful, disillusioned) about institutional practices addresses recent calls for more empirical analysis examining 'social and institutional change in response to disruption, division, and displacement' (Creed et al., 2022, p. 1535). Exploring how emotions are at the core of the intentional, purposeful institutional work of actors builds on the understanding that the processes and practices by which institutions are constructed, reified, and unsettled are enhanced and animated by the lived experience of human beings (Friedland, 2018; Lok et al., 2017).

In this study, a local, refugee-led organization implementing sport for development and peace (SDP) programs is explored to advance understanding of the role of emotions in institutional work of SDP. SDP is the intentional use of sport to achieve development goals (e.g. conflict resolution, social inclusion) (Kidd, 2008). Whilst research into SDP has exponentially grown since the early 2000s (McSweeney et al., 2021; Schulenkorf et al., 2016; Welty Peachey et al., 2020), there remains limited attention to the role of emotions and how they relate to the intentional and purposeful work taking place to contest institutional conditions such as social inequality for certain populations (e.g. forced migrants). Spaaij et al. (2019) noted that in studies of sport and forced migration, with some exceptions (Evers, 2010; Ley et al., 2018), emotions and 'sensory experiences' have been overlooked in favor of theories that emphasize cognitive perceptions. They suggest examining 'sensory experiences [including emotions] are essential if we are to truly understand the meaning of sport and physical activity in the everyday lives of refugees and forced migrants' (Spaaij et al., 2019, p. 14).

Given these research gaps, the purpose of this paper is to investigate the role of emotions in SDP-related institutional work aimed at challenging the conditions of social inequality for refugees in Kampala, Uganda. Social inequality as an institution is constructed, reinforced, and reproduced by various mechanisms (e.g. host community discrimination, social exclusion) related to forced migration. Understanding the way in which emotions play a key role in SDP-related institutional work allows for a closer examination of the lived experience of institutions and the agency of refugees who experience social inequality. Two research questions guided this study:

1. How do emotions related to forced displacement inform the institutional work of an SDP organization?
2. What emotions are mobilized by refugees and an SDP organization to challenge the institution of social inequality?

In the next section, literature related to institutional work in sport, the role of emotions in institutional work, and people and emotions in SDP is reviewed. This is followed by the methods and their justification, including data collection procedures and data analysis. Then, the findings of this study are presented followed by a discussion with the paper concluding with an outline of theoretical and practical implications.

Literature review

Institutional work in sport

Introduced by Lawrence and Suddaby (2006), institutional work represents a valuable theoretical approach to examining how action affects dynamic institutional processes such as creating, maintaining, and disrupting institutions. Lawrence and Suddaby (2006) proposed various types of practices aimed at creating institutions, including (a) political work intended to mobilize support and build rule systems and (b) cultural work seeking to reshape identities and belief systems. Following this framework, Dowling and Smith (2016) highlighted the role of Own the Podium, a not-for-profit sport organization, in shaping the rules and regulations of high-performance sport in Canada (i.e. political work) and in altering norms and beliefs in Canadian sport (i.e. cultural work). The work of maintaining institutions has inspired notable empirical investigation in sport, including in the context of the Olympic Games (Agyemang et al., 2018), intercollegiate athletics (Edwards & Washington, 2015; Nite, 2017), and ice hockey (Edwards & Stevens, 2019; Riehl et al., 2019). For instance, Nite et al. (2019) examined how the National Collegiate Athletics Association (NCAA) maintained its leading role in the field of intercollegiate athletics despite competing institutional logics (e.g. commercialism, amateurism), internal tensions (e.g. large vs. small member schools), and external challenges (e.g. the National Association of Intercollegiate Athletics). Institutional work related to disrupting an institution focuses on understanding practices aimed at undermining or discrediting the normative or cultural-cognitive pillars of institutions (Maguire & Hardy, 2009). In their extensive review of institutional work in sport management, Nite and Edwards (2021) point to a dearth of research on the efforts and actions of actors to disrupt institutions. In the field of SDP, McSweeney et al. (2019) identified the roles of symbolic (via the use of songs and dance) and relational work (via interpersonal interaction and interorganizational collaboration) in maintaining and disrupting the institution of Global North hegemony/Global South dependence in SDP.

In addition to the limited understanding of institutional work aimed at disrupting institutions in sport, this line of research has paid little attention to the lived and emotional experiences of individuals and/or collective actors as they engage in institutional work (Voronov & Vince, 2012), despite the possibilities that such research holds for advancing modern conceptions of institutional theory in general (McCarthy & Moon, 2018) and in sport management research more specifically (Nite & Edwards, 2021). As such, this study seeks to explore individual and/or collective emotions that enable actors to challenge social inequality of refugees.

Roles of emotions in institutional work

Emotions take on many different forms and types (Bericat, 2016; Jasper, 2011). While types of emotions often identify personal feelings, institutional practices are socially constructed (Berger & Luckmann, 1966). From this perspective, emotions are influenced by social interactions in a particular context (Friedland, 2018). It is this relational nature of emotions that has been highlighted by an expanding body of literature exploring institutional work (Farny et al., 2019; Lok et al., 2017).

On one hand, research has emphasized the role of 'high emotional investment' in values, norms, and practices as a motivator to defend or maintain current institutions (Gray et al., 2015; Voronov & Vince, 2012). Wright et al. (2017) found that when an emergency physician perceived the medical profession's value of representing patients' interests was at risk (e.g. due to delayed healthcare), the physician may experience moral emotions such as empathy for patients and frustration toward the violator. These emotions could drive the physician to take immediate action (e.g. sanctioning practices that are harmful to patients) to maintain the medical profession's institutionalized value. On the other hand, a 'weakened emotional attachment' to institutional prescriptions (Voronov & Vince, 2012, p. 69) may compel people to undermine, challenge, or even transform present institutions (Vince, 2021). In this vein, Jarvis et al. (2019) demonstrated that animal advocates' reactive emotions of 'shock, anger, and sorrow' (p. 1366) toward abusive practices in producing animals – combined with advocates' emotional commitment to protecting animals – propelled them to join the disruptive work to end factory farming.

In their review of the role of emotions in institutions, Lok et al. (2017) suggest a people-centred approach contributes to our understanding of how emotions can become an important source of resistance to and change in current institutional processes and practices (Giorgi et al., 2014). Numerous emotions may spur resistance, including dissatisfaction, frustration, shame, anger, resentment, and/or disdain (Evans & Moore, 2015; Lok et al., 2017). For instance, Heinze and Lu (2017) identified outrage and irritation over the National Football League's handling of concussions (e.g. denying the long-term consequences of concussions, prioritizing competition over player safety) which prompted various internal (e.g. current and retired players) and external (e.g. scientific community, media reporters, brain injury advocates, government officials) stakeholders to challenge the league's institutionalized concussion practices.

Lok et al. (2017) also outline a strategic approach to the role of emotions in institutional maintenance and change which views emotions as resources that can be tactically deployed to affect various types of institutional work. Previous studies suggest that emotions can be invoked to generate support and justify action (Farny et al.,

2019; Lu & Heinze, 2020). For example, Barberá-Tomás et al. (2019) explored how social entrepreneurs engaged in emotion-symbolic work to trigger strong emotions such as rage and despair to elicit emotional energy evoking enacting a response to plastic pollution. Identifying specific emotions and the relations of these emotions with people's investment or disinvestment in institutional practices (a people-centric approach) provides a foundation for understanding the strategic use of emotions (Lok et al., 2017). In the present study, we aim to combine the people-centric and strategic approaches to assess the role of emotions in SDP-related institutional work meant to challenge conditions of social inequality for refugees in Kampala, Uganda.

Emotions in sport for development and peace

As a sector of the sport industry that operates within the international development landscape, SDP is permeated with emotions given sport's ability to resonate with people in poignant ways. For instance, the emotional attachment people have with sport influences SDP recruitment and participation (Coalter, 2013). Additionally, people's 'love of sport' has been found to play a key role in volunteers' and practitioners' motivations for working within the SDP sector (Welty Peachey et al., 2014, 2018).

Scholars have also briefly touched on emotions in relation to the lived experience of SDP actors, including program participants and social entrepreneurs (e.g. Cohen & Welty Peachey, 2015; McSweeney & Hakiza, 2022; Oxford, 2019). For instance, Nols et al. (2019), in a study of critical pedagogy in SDP, found that humor, joy, respect, love, and care were key features for enabling a space of equality and no discrimination. These emotions were especially important for young people in the SDP program to feel at home, meet people from diverse backgrounds, and be 'temporarily freed from daily struggles such as discrimination' (Nols et al., 2019, p. 738). While this line of research has been informative and useful to illustrate that emotions are evident within the SDP sector, emotions have received limited theoretical attention, with some exceptions. For instance, Spaaij and Schaillée (2021) recently argued for the use of micro-sociological analyzes, particularly using interaction ritual theory, to better understand the embodied emotions that are experienced within SDP. In other work, Scott (2020) interrogated the emotion of confidence in SDP, providing an in-depth analysis into the way in which confidence mediated SDP participants lived experiences within and outside SDP activities. Still, both studies call for deeper investigation of the way in which emotions are experienced in SDP, especially to 'fully understand the influence SfD [sport for development] can have on peoples' lives' (Scott, 2020, p. 396). Applying Lok et al.'s (2017) framework for studying emotions and institutions will help to provide new insights by extending understanding of the role that emotions specifically play in the SDP sector, and how such emotions amplify and enhance the institutional work of actors striving to affect institutions.

Method

Context: Young African Refugees for Integral Development (YARID)

Young African Refugees for Integral Development (YARID) is a nonprofit, nongovernmental organization that was formally created in 2007 by three Congolese refugees who had been forcibly displaced to Uganda. When first displaced to Uganda, the current Executive Director (one of the organization's founders) and the other leaders of the organization saw that many refugees were left without leisure and recreational activities and also had limited social connections upon their migration. Thus, they began bringing together forced migrants to play football in Kampala. Initially, such activities were merely for having fun and bringing refugees together, but eventually ended up turning into a meeting place for migrants from various countries of origin and as a space to discuss the issues forced migrants faced within the host community of Kampala. Recognizing such issues, YARID was formed and became an official nonprofit organization, with four specific development programs that were cross-cutting, including: (1) education; (2) women's empowerment; (3) sport-for-development; and (4) innovations hub. In the next section, the method used for this study is outlined.

Participatory action research in institutional work and SDP

For this research, a participatory action research (PAR) approach was utilized (Kindon et al., 2007). PAR dictate's a commitment to emancipation whereby individuals involved in research benefit and are in some way actively engaged in challenging the unequal conditions in which they live (Kindon et al., 2007). Such an approach prioritizes collaborative knowledge production between researcher and participants and seeks to enable collective empirical study through processes of exploration, reflection, and action (McIntyre, 2007). Given that PAR views research participants as co-producers of knowledge, individuals involved in this study are referred to as co-researchers. Following Block et al.'s (2013) 'ethics of practice', Author 1 collectively worked with co-researchers to consider context dependent circumstances that shaped the design and process of the study. This included strategies to manage power imbalances such as: holding research orientations to clearly outline informed consent, which was reiterated throughout the study; creating a research advisory board for feedback and any alterations to the study; hiring a local community-based translator; and developing long-term relationships to construct action strategies based on the research (McSweeney et al., 2022).

There have been few studies of institutional work that have adopted a PAR methodology (Dover & Lawrence, 2010). However, PAR has been advocated for given the alignment the methodology has with the theoretical foundations of institutional work, including, in brief, heterogenous agency; an emphasis on practice; and the importance of situated knowledge (Dover & Lawrence, 2010). PAR has also been adopted for studies of SDP, particularly when global North researchers conduct empirical investigations in the global South (such as in this study) or Indigenous contexts in the global North (e.g. Hayhurst et al., 2015; McSweeney et al., 2023). While PAR does not automatically ensure research is reciprocal, and remains ripe with ethical complexities (see McSweeney et al., 2022 for an overview of such complexities in this research), the PAR approach utilized was appropriate given its focus on peoples' lived experiences based on their histories and social context (Crotty, 1998), which is required when exploring emotions and institutions (Lok et al., 2017).

Data collection

For this study, fieldwork was conducted in Kampala, Uganda by Author 1 from June to August 2019, using multiple data collection methods of semi-structured interviews, photovoice, and photocollaging. In total, 42 individuals participated in the research, including 21 males and 21 females, who were involved with YARID as program users ($n = 25$), staff ($n = 11$), and community members ($n = 6$). Individuals ranged from 18 to 45 years. Community members were not involved in photovoice and photocollaging due to time commitments and their current limited participation in YARID programs. Visual methods have been advocated for within PAR approaches as they aim to prioritize and engage participants in critical dialogue (Mitchell et al., 2017). For this study, photovoice and photocollaging were particularly useful for co-researchers to capture representations of their lived experiences and emotions; in fact, photovoice has been noted to facilitate 'emotional expression in ways that words alone could not' (Pickin et al., 2011, p. 71).

Co-researchers were either provided with a camera from Author 1 or used their cellular devices to take photos with the broad aim of capturing their experiences related to SDP, in order not to limit what co-researchers deemed important in their lives and wanted to photograph (Wang, 1999). Co-researchers were asked to take multiple photos to represent their experiences and to select one photo that was a benefit of SDP and one photo that was a challenge to SDP. Following photovoice activities, each co-researcher would participate in a semi-structured interview, which ranged from 30 to 120 min in length. Interview questions were focused on co-researchers' lived experiences, including history of migration and resettlement in Uganda, SDP participation, social entrepreneurship, and livelihoods. At the start or end of each interview, co-researchers had an opportunity to discuss their selected photos and explain their meaning, including how the photo is representative of their lived experience and why the photo is important to them – thus eliciting emotions (Wang & Burris, 1997).

Following photovoice and semi-structured interviews, photocollage sessions were held with co-researchers, which involves taking selected photos and posting these on a surface (in this case a poster board), writing captions for photos, and adding any drawings or other visuals deemed important by co-researchers (Castleden & Garvin, 2008). Photocollage sessions are particularly beneficial for engaging co-researchers in data analysis and enabling the co-production of knowledge (Castleden & Garvin, 2008). Following Wang and Burris (1997) three-stage process of selecting photos, contextualizing images and stories, and codifying by identifying patterns and themes, a form of preliminary analysis while in the field took place with co-researchers. During this process, co-researchers shared and engaged in dialogue in a group, taking turns to present their experiences and narratives and receiving feedback and commentary from others. Co-researchers thus reflected on their experiences and identified similar and different meanings they attached to their photos and narratives (Castleden & Garvin, 2008), with the most significant patterns being written on a large sheet of paper and confirmed with co-researchers. This preliminary analysis was then used to inform the analysis of visual and textual data upon Author 1 leaving the field, which is discussed next.

Data analysis

Phase 1: initial open coding

During this first cycle of coding, Author 1 familiarized themself with the entirety of the data and then, following Saldana's (2016) recommendations for initial open coding, began examining the data to reflect on the similarities and differences across co-researchers' lived experiences, including nuances within the content. For example, during this phase, it became apparent that virtually all refugees in the study experienced trauma and emotional suffering due to forced displacement, with such emotional trauma remaining a prevalent factor for numerous co-researchers upon resettlement. Moving from these experiences to interpretations of meaningful activities to counter such difficulties, an understanding of how co-researchers displayed positive reactions to SDP began to develop. For example, multiple co-researchers discussed their selected photovoice images regarding how they experienced joy, stress relief, and fun during SDP activities. Images were further analyzed during this phase by Author 1 moving back and forth between co-researchers semi-structured interview data related to images, the actual visual data, and their photocollage session presentations (Wang & Burris, 1997).

Phase 2: pattern coding

During the second cycle of coding, pattern coding was used as it is appropriate for examining patterns of human relationships and generating major themes from the data (Miles et al., 2013). Author 1 reviewed the initial codes and sought to assess their commonality while assigning pattern codes (Saldana, 2016). Included in this process was the search for common 'scripts' in the data based on multiple co-researchers' experiences – 'shared ways of knowing, interpreting, acting in the world' (Daiute, 2013). At this stage, narratives began to develop highlighting the emotions experienced by refugees in relation to their institutional context. For example, forced displacement and host community relations led to collective emotions (Farny et al., 2019) experienced by refugee such as loneliness, sadness, and shame, resulting in a low emotional state. In contrast, emotions elicited through SDP-related institutional work, such as nostalgia, peace, and forgiveness, were experienced as positive and stimulated a high emotional state.

At this stage of the coding process, Authors 2 and 3 were involved in data analysis by having meetings with Author 1 to discuss and review data interpretations, including agreements and disagreements about codes during initial coding. This process enabled a deeper reflection on the data following the 'insider/outsider' coding method (Corbin & Strauss, 2008) and re-coding of data as both Authors 2 and 3 were not involved in the initial coding or fieldwork. In addition, during this analytical step, all three authors discussed the data in relation to the guiding framework of Lok et al. (2017) to develop primary themes. Specifically, we began to abstract the data to the people-centric and strategic categories of Lok et al.'s (2017) framework given the relevance of the coded data to (1) emotions in response to institutions (i.e. people-centric) and (2) emotions as tools for institutional work (i.e. strategic). We also began to categorize the experiences refugees have of emotions as positive or negative specifically in relation to institutions and institutional work. In doing so, three forms of SDP-related institutional work were identified that created mechanisms to transform refugees' emotional state and seek to undermine the institution of social inequality experienced by forced migrants in Kampala.

Findings

In this section, we present our findings considering our research questions. Our first research question was explored by examining the way in which forced displacement and the resulting move to a new host community is ripe with certain emotions that amplify and maintain social inequality experienced by refugees. These emotions subsequently informed YARID and its members' SDP practices, particularly regarding implementing SDP for refugees as well as Ugandans to attempt to change perspectives and behaviors toward refugees. Following this and in response to the second research question, the strategic use of emotions for purposeful, SDP-related institutional work is discussed, with an emphasis on how the use of certain emotions in SDP have been utilized by YARID and its members to transform refugees' emotional state and undermine the experience of social inequality within Kampala. Three mechanisms in particular – diverting, bonding, and peacemaking – enabled SDP-related practices to transform refugees' emotions. Figure 1 provides an overview of our findings.

Displacement, host community relations, and the maintenance of social inequality

Fear, stress, insecurity, and loneliness: the emotional toll of forced displacement

Co-researchers in this study identified having an emotionally exhausting experience of forced migration due to push factors that led to displacement such as community and/or family conflicts, war, and political troubles within their homeland. Such displacement journeys were infused with a complexity of emotions, including *fear, stress, insecurity*, and *loneliness* (see Figure 1). Conflict within refugees' homelands often involved high risk situations with co-researchers' experiencing *fear* and *stress* about remaining in

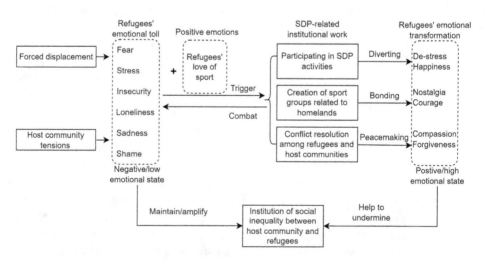

Figure 1. Overview of Findings.

their country of origin. For instance, Suzane (DRC, program user) expressed that 'Every time I think about the troubles I've gone through [...] I am living in a kind of life full of stress.' *Stress*, not only due to displacement but also living in a new host community and having little control over their futures, was a recurring emotion amongst co-researchers and was perpetuated by feelings of *insecurity*.

For instance, Merveille (DRC, program user) said even after relocating to Uganda, she still has 'that kind of fear, as if I am vulnerable, as if I am living in that [homeland] insecurity.' *Insecurity* was a common thread across refugees' narratives about forced displacement, with Michel (program user), saying: 'We left Congo because of the insecurity and war ... There are rebels.'

Initial displacement experiences had many effects on co-researchers' lives once they relocated to Kampala, including being separated from relatives and friends, leading to experiencing *loneliness* – an emotional disconnect from the people around them – upon resettlement. Pascal (DRC, staff) expressed how, 'It wasn't easy [migrating from the Congo] because I am alone ... I was really lonely because you don't have any member of the family who you can call.' *Loneliness* was also complicated by not knowing or hearing from family members after forced migration. Merveille (DRC, program user) selected a photo of her brother walking with his bicycle and described the distressing experience of being separated from most of her family (see Figure 2):

> OK, actually, at present, since I forsook my country, I have never heard of [from] my father, never heard of [from] my mother. And I've never heard of [from] my young sister because they went with my mother. She was still very young. I think right now, I really don't know if they are dead, if they are alive, what happened to them. [...] I and my brother, we are adopted in a new family.

Many refugees were in similar situations as Pascal and Merveille upon migrating – experiencing *loneliness* due to having limited social connections. Such challenges were further exacerbated through interactions with host community residents.

Shame and sadness: community tensions in Kampala

Co-researchers in this study discussed how host community relations were tense amongst Ugandan citizens and refugees. Many participants in this study felt that misplaced assumptions led to discrimination of forced migrants by host community residents, leading to *shame* and *sadness* (see Figure 1). For instance, during her photocollage session, Francine (DRC, staff) spoke to the impact of unfair assumptions on refugees, particularly for youth experiencing *loneliness*:

> The way that refugees are treated here in Uganda, the way I see it, for me it's not good. How can I explain this – some people in Uganda they don't treat refugees as human beings. When you go to their offices, some of them [teachers, employers] they consider them [youth refugees] as if they didn't go to school, as if they're uneducated people.

Such dehumanizing at worst and disrespecting at best experiences for refugees extended into day-to-day life, for example while attending University in Kampala:

> At school you may find whenever there is a presentation, something like that, they start laughing or people start saying 'banu acole' – refugees – which are making me feel that I am not part of this life, and that is really, really bad. (Pascal, DRC, staff)

Figure 2. Merveille's only remaining family member in Kampala.

The quote above indicates how relations between the host community and forced migrants often triggered a negative or low emotional state of refugees. Such a low emotional state is bolstered by interactions with the host community that amplify and maintain conditions of social inequality, such as social exclusion – where refugees are not seen as part of the local community but rather as someone different and who does not belong – buttressing their *loneliness*. Another co-researcher, David (DRC, program user), suggested that, based on assumptions that Congolese refugees are from a country laden with civil unrest and conflict, the host community perceives some forced migrants as criminals, adding to feelings of *shame*:

> And maybe they think that we may be suspect because remember, we [DRC refugees] are from a warrior country, they would think that maybe this man is having some criminal dealings … They will not feel comfortable when they see you work at night.

Though not all co-researchers discussed having difficulties with the host community, when taken together, forced displacement and resettlement elicit multiple complex emotions of individuals who must flee their homeland. Such emotions, including *fear, stress, insecurity, loneliness, shame,* and *sadness* were shared by most co-researchers in this study given their lived experience of forced migration, and thus exhibit collective emotions of co-researchers'. Whilst these emotions take a heavy toll on refugees and influence a low emotional state that is amplified by the host community via discrimination and social exclusion, such emotions also triggered SDP-related institutional work that sought to combat co-researchers' negative experiences of emotions and undermine the institutional conditions of social inequality.

Mobilizing emotions to facilitate SDP-related institutional work

For the love of sport: using emotions as a source for SDP-related institutional work

As stated earlier, the formation of YARID occurred in 2007, when informal football activities with forced migrants transformed into a space to discuss pressing issues related to refugees' lives. Moving forward, YARID integrated SDP as one of its primary four development program areas with a focus on using sport for social inclusion, conflict resolution, and livelihood activities, amongst other goals. Refugees' *love* of sport (see Figure 1) was a compelling reason – especially after having success in its early days of bringing people together via football – to adopt SDP as a program foci. As explained by Daniel (Uganda, staff):

> Because in Africa sports are like a disease, like a virus [laughter], that can affect so many people at once, eh? So it's not like say - if you call someone for a meeting and come for a meeting and mostly the turn out would not be so much. […] But if you call people that you come you have a football match and you have to play, and after that we are going to share ideas.

YARID saw the value in using sport because of its emotional pull to refugees: 'So I think we have the love for football and they [refugees] can easily be motivated to try and build a bigger career in that [sport] field' (Sheila, Uganda, staff). This love of football for some refugees also relates to feelings of hope. Multiple co-researchers emphasized that participating in SDP provided hope not only for a future career in sport (particularly football for males), but also could foster improved employability and communication skills to become community leaders and attain jobs.

Notably, YARID used people's love of sport to bring together both Ugandans and refugees from different homelands to influence change in perspectives and understanding of refugees by the host community as well as to foster social inclusion. Josue (DRC, staff) discussed one of his photovoice images and articulated the importance of sport for social inclusion and belonging (see Figure 3):

> It's [SDP] an exchange. An exchange between different people from different backgrounds, and I think this helps these [refugees and Ugandans] people. […] Remember in [English] class they don't have much time to talk, but during sports, it's almost them always talking, like give me the ball and so on. So it's a nice time to practice their language, but also to get in touch with different people.

The use of SDP to bring people together and foster social inclusion was seen as a success by most co-researchers. Joselyne (Uganda, staff) applauded the use of SDP for helping 'reduce the ignorance about refugees and the way they [host community residents]

Figure 3. Josue's photo of refugees playing football together and building social inclusion.

perceive them.' It is in this way that the emotions of both co-researchers *and* host community residents explained in the previous sections triggered resistance to discrimination and social exclusion of refugees and led to the intentional uptake of SDP activities that capitalized on people's *love* of sport to enable mechanisms that facilitated refugees' emotional transformation.

Feeling happy: participating in SDP for stress relief
The lived experience of forced displacement and resulting resettlement in a host community elicited emotions such as *stress, loneliness,* and *shame,* which are compounded by the fact that refugees often find themselves without many opportunities to engage in leisurely or recreational activities. Participating in SDP activities at YARID was intentionally aimed at diverting (see Figure 1) refugees' negative experiences of emotion by inducing positive experiences of other emotions such as *happiness, enjoyment, and calmness,* to enable stress relief. For example, Abdifatah (Somalia, community member), when asked about the importance of sport for members of YARID, said 'For refugees, first of all it is fun ... instead of staying at home they have fun there [playing football] and destress.' This notion of de-stressing was discussed by other co-researchers as well. David (DRC, program user) discussed the way in which SDP is used to purposely induce emotions that would remove the stress and depression associated with forced

displacement, and drew attention to how YARID coaches are important for shaping the energy of SDP participants: 'In our lives, we [refugees] are not getting anything to give us back the energy […] only the morale that we get from the coach is giving us back this energy.'

Indeed, a significant aspect of SDP at YARID is to involve refugees in activities that allow them to 'take their mind off of' and divert attention away from the challenges they face within life. Namono (Uganda, staff) discussed how sports are used as a lever for the purposes of emotional changes:

> […] cause like development is not only economic, it can be social. So if they [refugees] go for a sport activity they are making friends and that's a good thing. It can also be emotional if it distracts them from something that is not making them happy. Like sports is their [refugees] safe place.

Alongside the ability to have fun and relieve stress via participation in SDP was also the ability for co-researchers to experience *happiness*. David (DRC, program user) shared a photo he captured and explained: 'The other picture there you see is a picture that is showing that we are happy because our coach had finished giving us counselling' (Figure 4).

Figure 4. David and another co-researcher happy after SDP activities.

In addition, many co-researchers reported that their family members were happy about their involvement in SDP. For instance, Judith (DRC, program user) said that 'they're [husband and children] really happy for this [SDP] because they do tell me nothing except offer congratulating me.' The way in which the emotion of *happiness* was shared not only amongst participants of SDP but also in some cases, their families, once again illustrates the collective emotions which were experienced by forced migrants in this study. Further, YARID and its members also engaged in SDP-related institutional work focused on enhancing bonding opportunities for refugees.

Feeling nostalgic: creating sport groups to build an emotional attachment to home

In this study, a crucial way in which emotions were utilized in SDP to undermine conditions of social inequality such as discrimination and social exclusion was via the creation of sport groups related to co-researchers' homelands, which enabled bonding between refugees (see Figure 1). YARID and its members sought to form groups that would engage in sport (mostly football) once to multiple times a week, share resources amongst each other, and perhaps most importantly, foster a sense of belonging and home. Various co-researchers in this study lived in diaspora, which is generally defined as the way groups dispersed from their homeland remain connected through imagined and/or collective communities (Brubaker, 2005). An emotional connection to home fostered through the YARID sport groups prompted a sense of *nostalgia*. The groups are part of YARID's approach to SDP and seek to induce positive experiences of emotions associated with home such as *joy* that may respond to the emotions spurred by displacement, including *loneliness* and *sadness*.

Sport groups were both created by YARID and by organizational members. For instance, some sport groups were based on nationality to ignite memories of refugees' homeland and inspire relationship building amongst co-researchers'. Bebe (Burundi, community member) discussed how dancing would be incorporated into Burundian sport group meetings and that this 'makes me feel like I am back home.' This sense of *nostalgia* was shared by other co-researchers when discussing sport groups. Oscar (DRC, program user) captured a photo of the outside of a Congolese restaurant and discussed how eating food with the Congolese sport group fostered nostalgic memories (Figure 5).

Other groups included a women's sport savings group made up mostly of Congolese migrants. In this group, a mixture of religion, song, and storytelling would be used to elicit emotions such as *courage*: 'We sing the Congolese songs. The preaching will be in our own language. And the community, maybe with the friends will we narrate our stories back home. And it is bringing me to reconnect our courage' (Suzane, DRC, program user). Suzane explained that her and other women in the sport savings groups were feeling more secure in espousing their Congolese way of life in Uganda. Indeed, the sport groups were meant to provide spaces for refugees to share fond memories of home, offer support for one another, and to 'refresh': 'It's [women sport savings group] promoting people to enhance their mind, to refresh their mind, take out those conflicts and those troubles they face' (Helene, DRC, program user).

The sport groups at YARID and those formed by refugees themselves are a way to ignite a connection to refugees' homelands and induce *nostalgia*. In addition, the SDP-

Figure 5. Moise outside of a Congolese restaurant, producing feelings of nostalgia.

related work of creating sport groups related to homelands enabled bonding to occur amongst refugees and to positively experience emotions such as *courage*. Though such emotions are experienced as positive and potentially stymie the effect of negatively experienced emotions, such positive experiences of emotions may be temporary, lasting only during specific sport group activities. Still, YARID and its members sought to induce other emotions through their SDP-work.

Feeling peace: conflict resolution via SDP

At YARID, SDP activities as well as certain events were specifically implemented for the purposes of conflict resolution and peacemaking (see Figure 1). Some communities of forced migrants were in conflict with one another due to their histories. Antony (DRC, program user) explained that: 'So there is a very huge conflict among Rwandese and Congolese because when Congolese sees a Rwandese he says this is my enemy, this is our enemy.'

Recognizing the conflict between certain communities, YARID sought to utilize SDP to induce emotions such as *compassion* and *forgiveness* that play a key role in stimulating peacemaking. For example, Abdifitah (Somalia, community member) said that:

> Yeah, Somali's they have different tribes. And those tribes they used to fight back there [Somalia]. But here [YARID], when they play sport, you know forgive your brother [...] So you may have fought yesterday but today you play together, you spend the night together, doing things like that, so it's bringing the community together, especially the youth.

In this sense, participating in sport as a refugee with different ethnic communities sought to break down existing barriers such as conflict and instead bring together different ethnic groups and individuals to foster social belonging.

The intentional and purposeful way in which YARID focuses on peacemaking and conflict resolution also extends to their SDP events, illustrating how the organization is particularly interested in facilitating emotions such as *forgiveness* and *compassion* for one another amongst refugees. The Soccer for Peace event (see Figure 6) is 'a promotion of peace within the community' (Elvis, Uganda, staff) and involves participation of mixed ethnicity teams in a football tournament (both male and female teams), education about leadership, team building, conflict resolution, and community development, and lessons about refugee rights (Soccer for Peace Concept Note, 2016).

Patrick (DRC, staff) said that Soccer for Peace was useful for inspiring compassion and belongingness amongst different refugee communities and also Ugandans: 'And then when you are in sports, like you are playing soccer today, even if you are from Congo, some foreign lands, different communities, but when you are here we are one group. When we are playing we are together and there is no conflict.'

Indeed, SDP-related institutional work involving conflict resolution and emotions such as *compassion* and *forgiveness* enabled peacemaking to occur, thus resulting in a high emotional state for refugees which sought to undermine the conditions of social inequality. As stated by Simon (DRC, program user) 'sport is bringing people together or different nationalities together because when you are playing together or they are among you, peace must be seen … and a friendship also will be found and a different connection will be also started.'

Figure 6. Picture of Soccer for Peace event and trophy award ceremony to winning women's football team. (Photo is blurred as not all individuals in image participated in this study.)

Discussion

The purpose of this study was to investigate the role of emotions in SDP-related institutional work to challenge the institution of social inequality that refugees experience in Kampala, Uganda. Our key theoretical insight is that emotions – whether individual or collective – play a key role in stimulating SDP-related institutional work and are used in institutional work practices to undermine institutional conditions, bringing attention to the lived experience of institutions within sport management (Nite & Edwards, 2021). In the following sections, we discuss the theoretical implications of this study.

Emotions in SDP-related institutional work

Building on Lok et al.'s (2017) push for research that recognizes the complexity of emotions as a tool for institutional work, we explore the interplay between a people-centric and strategic approach to the role of emotions in SDP. Our research aligns with extant literature on emotions in institutional work, including that emotions may both mold institutional maintenance (Wright et al., 2017) and ignite challenges to present institutional conditions (Jarvis et al., 2019). Our study builds on this work by identifying the ways in which emotions in relation to forced migration amplify conditions of social inequality, particularly the way in which host community relations contributes to negative experiences of emotions by refugees. The findings generate insights into the people-centric approach identified by Lok et al. (2017) by illustrating that emotions in response to institutions stimulate intentional work of actors to resist institutions (see Figure 1). Indeed, the weak emotional attachment and emotions negatively experienced by refugees due to the institution of social inequality compelled YARID and refugees to undermine social inequality (Voronov & Vince, 2012). Further, contrary to Martin de Holan et al. (2019)'s finding that negative experiences of emotions constrain vulnerable actors' 'projective agency' (p. 920), our findings revealed that a mix of negative (e.g. fear, stress, insecurity) and positive experiences of emotions (e.g. love of sport) may trigger SDP-practices that seek to enable an emotional transformation.

Our findings also inform Lok et al.'s (2017) strategic approach by identifying the way in which emotions – such as happiness, nostalgia, and compassion – are strategically used in SDP-related institutional work to combat negative experiences of emotions of refugees and seek to undermine social inequality. Some of these findings relate to existing literature within SDP. For example, Welty Peachey et al. (2014, 2018) have found that 'love of sport' plays a significant role in volunteer and practitioner motivations, similar to the way in which people's emotional attachment to sport is used by YARID to bring refugees together. Scott's (2020) analysis of confidence revealed the way in which individuals make sense of their experiences in SDP. Our study builds on this analysis by considering a range of emotional experiences that refugees have when involved in SDP at YARID and their relationship to social inequality. Nols et al. (2019) have also reported that SDP allowed a temporary outlet for program participants from discrimination. Our findings echo this in the sense that while SDP enables emotional transformation of refugees and is associated with a positive emotional state, the realities of refugees' lives may return upon their exit from SDP activities.

Our study expands the above work by explicitly identifying the way in which emotions relate to institutions (Voronov & Vince, 2012). For instance, the findings indicate that SDP-related institutional work triggers and utilizes emotions in efforts to combat everyday issues such as discrimination and social exclusion refugees face. Such findings inform Spaaij and Schaillée's (2021) important research on interaction ritual within SDP, most especially the way in which co-researchers in this study mutually shared certain emotions (e.g. stress, love of sport) that enabled SDP-related institutional work to take place. In addition, this study advances new insights into how SDP – and the individuals participating in and leading SDP activities – influence 'micro-situational dynamics', such as experienced emotions, which may lead to positive SDP outcomes, such as the transformation of refugee's emotional states (Spaaij & Schaillée, 2021).

Our findings also revealed the mechanisms of diverting, bonding, and peacemaking that enable emotional transformation of forced migrants at an individual and collective level, challenging the institution of social inequality. This study thus illustrates the integral role that emotions have within institutional work (Farny et al., 2019; Voronov & Vince, 2012) and adds to the limited literature within sport management that discusses processes and practices of disrupting or challenging institutions (McSweeney et al., 2019). Importantly, the findings also extend insights into the experiential component of forced migration and sport (Spaaij et al., 2019), which has been explored in only a few studies (Evers, 2010; Ley et al., 2018).

Collective emotions and institutions

In both sport management (Lu & Heinze, 2020; Nite & Edwards, 2021) as well as broader institutional theory research (Toubiana & Zietsma, 2017; Voronov & Vince, 2012), scholars have increasingly emphasized that emotions require deeper scrutiny given they are a 'defining component of institutional processes' (Farny et al., 2019, p. 37). This study offers novel evidence on the collective emotions experienced by refugees, particularly regarding the emotional toll of forced displacement and their emotional transformation via SDP-related practices. Hence, the study expands the focus within SDP from individual experiences of emotions (e.g. Cohen & Welty Peachey, 2015) and builds on current conceptualizations within institutional theory focused on collective emotions within local institutional work (Farny et al., 2019; Zietsma & Toubiana, 2018). Furthermore, this research illustrates how collective and individual emotions both influence SDP-related practices and human experiences of institutions – particularly the institution of social inequality. This is significant for the field of SDP as emotions have been discussed primarily in relation to how programs have been formed and/or implemented (e.g. Nols et al., 2019), whereas the findings of this study reveal that institutional conditions elicit emotions that in turn trigger purposeful, intentional work that also seek to undermine institutional conditions (Lawrence & Suddaby, 2006; Lok et al., 2017). Thus, this study provides novel insights into synchronizations of emotion (Spaaij & Schaillée, 2021) whereby refugees in this study shared certain emotions and moods that led to strategical SDP-related institutional work.

Understanding collective emotions in SDP-related institutional work is particularly important given that most programs focus on certain populations who have experienced marginalization in some way. Thus, it is likely that SDP program participants – such as refugees in this study – have similar emotional experiences and a sense of familiarity with what others are going through. Indeed, Cohen and Welty Peachey (2015) highlighted that a social entrepreneur felt compassion to other SDP participants who had experienced homelessness. The findings of this study demonstrate that collective emotions spur SDP work – in fact, the emotions of refugees and their lived experiences prompted the creation of YARID itself. As said by Farny et al. (2019, p. 38), 'the elicitation and convergence of collective emotions constitutes a certain togetherness both justifying the appropriateness of action and motivating co-agents to engage in joint action.' Our findings align with this statement as the forced displacement co-researchers experienced elicited negative experiences of emotions that justified the use of SDP to combat unequal relations with host community residents and strive to undermine inequality. In addition, the emotional transformation that occurred through SDP-related institutional work via mechanisms of diverting, bonding, and peacemaking, utilized collective emotions that also related to the lived experience of forced migrants, such as nostalgia and sport groups related to homelands.

Conclusion

Practical implications

Beyond this study's theoretical implications, this study also holds relevance for SDP practice. First, SDP organizations and practitioners should purposefully seek to structure programs and activities that take into deeper consideration emotions of SDP participants (see Nols et al., 2019). While staff and leaders of SDP programs should seek themselves to be positive and upbeat to elicit positive responses from participants, this should not be done at the expense of acknowledging negative or painful experiences of emotions that SDP participants may face in their lives. SDP programs focused on supporting individuals who have experienced trauma should seek to utilize a trauma-informed approach that seeks to have SDP participants process both negative and positive experiences of emotions (see Ferreira Gomes et al., in press; van Ingen, 2016). Second, this study highlights how institutions – in this case social inequality – are influential in determining the emotions humans experience in their day-to-day life. The findings also indicate that institutions may be challenged or undermined by engaging in institutional work strategically with emotions. Thus, SDP organizations and practitioners must remain critical and identify those relations and institutional conditions that amplify inequality for certain populations. Overall, this study illustrates that SDP and sport managers more generally should be cognizant of and take time to explore the crucial role that emotions play in all facets of daily life and sport contexts.

Limitations and future research

A limitation of this study is that we were unable to collect data with Ugandan citizens who were SDP participants (although were able to conduct interviews with Ugandan staff at YARID). Such data would have offered additional insight into the way in which SDP at YARID has been prompted by host community relations in Kampala between Ugandans and refugees, as well as furthered understanding of how emotions have spurred institutional work that strives to change the behaviors of people (Lok et al., 2017), in this case host community residents. Still, this research does indicate that SDP was taken up specifically to influence change of perspectives of refugees and to create bonding opportunities between Ugandans and refugees. Future research should seek to investigate emotions and institutions with specific attention to the way in which resistance or behavior-change is prompted by certain institutional conditions, to expand understanding of such processes and practices. For example, the way in which unequal institutional conditions may prompt certain emotions that lead to diversity, inclusion, equity, and other social justice programs in both SDP and other sport settings would shed further light on institutional work and emotions.

A key facet of this study was the use of PAR and visual methods. The use of innovative methods has been called for within sport management (Hoeber & Shaw, 2017). Photovoice was particularly useful for co-researchers to elicit emotions through images and provided a catalyst for individuals to expand on their emotional experiences within semi-structured interviews. Indeed, photovoice has been said to enable a better understanding of people's emotions (Pickin et al., 2011) and foster critical consciousness of social issues (Carlson et al., 2006). Thus, future studies within sport management that examines social change, emotions, and institutions from the perspective of human agents, should consider using the photovoice method and other innovative methods to offer research participants opportunities to express themselves. We hope that this paper will spur future research and attention to the important role of emotions in the SDP sector, and lead to further understanding of the emotional dimensions of institutional work.

Note

1. We use Greenwood et al.'s (2008) definition of institution: 'more-or-less taken-for-granted repetitive social behaviour that is underpinned by normative systems and cognitive understandings that give meaning to social exchange and thus enable self-reproducing social order' (p. 4–5).

Disclosure statement

No potential conflict of interest was reported by the author(s).

Funding

This work was supported by a Social Sciences and Humanities Research Council of Canada Joseph-Armand Bombardier Canada Graduate Scholarship (CGS), a CGS-Michael Smith Foreign Study Supplement, and by funds received from the North American Society for Sport Management (NASSM) Doctoral Research Grant Program.

References

Agyemang, K. J., Berg, B. K., & Fuller, R. D. (2018). Disrupting the disruptor: Perceptions as institutional maintenance work at the 1968 Olympic Games. *Journal of Sport Management, 32*(6), 567–580. https://doi.org/10.1123/jsm.2017-0268

Barberá-Tomás, D., Castelló, I., De Bakker, F. G., & Zietsma, C. (2019). Energizing through visuals: How social entrepreneurs use emotion-symbolic work for social change. *Academy of Management Journal*, 62(6), 1789-1817. https://doi.org/10.5465/amj.2017.1488

Berger, P. L., & Luckmann, T. (1966). *The social construction of reality: A treatise in the sociology of knowledge*. Anchor.

Bericat, E. (2016). The sociology of emotions: Four decades of progress. *Current Sociology*, 64(3), 491-513. https://doi.org/10.1177/0011392115588355

Block, K., Warr, D., Gibbs, L., & Riggs, E. (2013). Addressing ethical and methodological challenges in research with refugee-background young people: Reflections from the field. *Journal of Refugee Studies*, 26(1), 69-87. https://doi.org/10.1093/jrs/fes002

Brubaker, R. (2005). The 'diaspora' diaspora. *Ethnic and Racial Studies*, 28(1), 1-19. https://doi.org/10.1080/0141987042000289997

Carlson, E. D., Engebretson, J., & Chamberlain, R. M. (2006). Photovoice as a social process of critical consciousness. *Qualitative Health Research*, 16(6), 836-852. https://doi.org/10.1177/1049732306287525

Castleden, H., & Garvin, T. (2008). Modifying photovoice for community-based participatory indigenous research. *Social Science & Medicine*, 66(6), 1393-1405. https://doi.org/10.1016/j.socscimed.2007.11.030

Coalter, F. (2013). *Sport for development: What game are we playing?* Routledge.

Cohen, A., & Welty Peachey, J. (2015). The making of a social entrepreneur: From participant to cause champion within a sport-for-development context. *Sport Management Review*, 18(1), 111-125. https://doi.org/10.1016/j.smr.2014.04.002

Corbin, J., & Strauss, A. (2008). *Basics of qualitative research: Techniques and procedures for developing grounded theory*. Sage.

Creed, W. D., Hudson, B. A., Okhuysen, G. A., & Smith-Crow, K. (2014). Swimming in a sea of shame: Incorporating emotion into explanations of institutional reproduction and change. *Academy of Management Review*, 39(2), 275-301. https://doi.org/10.5465/amr.2012.0074

Creed, W. D., Hudson, B. A., Okhuysen, G. A., & Smith-Crowe, K. (2022). A place in the world: Vulnerability, well-being, and the ubiquitous evaluation that animates participation in institutional processes. *Academy of Management Review*, 47(3), 358-381. https://doi.org/10.5465/amr.2018.0367

Crotty, M. J. (1998). *The foundations of social research: Meaning and perspective in the research process*. Sage.

Daiute, C. (2013). *Narrative inquiry: A dynamic approach*. Sage.

Dover, G., & Lawrence, T. B. (2010). A gap year for institutional theory: Integrating the study of institutional work and participatory action research. *Journal of Management Inquiry*, 19(4), 305-316. https://doi.org/10.1177/1056492610371496

Dowling, M., & Smith, J. (2016). The institutional work of own the podium in developing high-performance sport in Canada. *Journal of Sport Management*, 30(4), 396-410. https://doi.org/10.1123/jsm.2014-0290

Edwards, J., & Stevens, J. (2019). Institutional maintenance and elite sport: A case study of high-performance women's ice hockey in Canada. *Sport in Society*, 22(11), 1801-1815. https://doi.org/10.1080/17430437.2019.1644010

Edwards, J. R., & Washington, M. (2015). Establishing a "safety net": Exploring the emergence and maintenance of College Hockey Inc. and NCAA Division I hockey. *Journal of Sport Management*, 29(3), 291-304. https://doi.org/10.1123/jsm.2012-0122

Ekman, P. (1999). Basic emotions. In T. Dalgleish, & M. J. Power (Eds.), *Handbook of cognition and emotion* (pp. 45-60). Wiley. https://doi.org/10.1002/0470013494.ch3

Evans, L., & Moore, W. L. (2015). Impossible burdens: White institutions, emotional labor, and micro-resistance. *Social Problems*, 62(3), 439-454. https://doi.org/10.1093/socpro/spv009

Evers, C. (2010). Intimacy, sport and young refugee men. *Emotion, Space and Society*, 3(1), 56-61. https://doi.org/10.1016/j.emospa.2010.01.011

Farny, S., Kibler, E., & Down, S. (2019). Collective emotions in institutional creation work. *Academy of Management Journal*, 62(3), 765-799. https://doi.org/10.5465/amj.2016.0711

Ferreira Gomes, J., Hayhurst, L. M. C., McSweeney, M., Sinclair, T., & Darroch, F. (in press). Trauma- and violence-informed physical activity and sport-for-development for victims and survivors of gender-based violence: A scoping study. *Journal of Sport for Development*.

Friedland, R. (2018). Moving institutional logics forward: Emotion and meaningful material practice. *Organization Studies*, *39*(4), 515–542. https://doi.org/10.1177/0170840617709307

Giorgi, S., Guider, M. E., & Bartunek, J. M. (2014). Productive resistance: A study of change, emotions, and identity in the context of the apostolic visitation of U.S. women religious, 2008-2012. In P. Tracey, N. Phillips, & M. Lounsbury (Eds.), *Research in the sociology of organizations: Religion and organization theory* (Vol. 41, Pp. 259–300). Emerald Group. https://doi.org/10.1108/S0733-558 × 20140000041016

Gray, B., Purdy, J. M., & Ansari, S. (2015). From interactions to institutions: Microprocesses of framing and mechanisms for the structuring of institutional fields. *Academy of Management Review*, *40*(1), 115–143. https://doi.org/10.5465/amr.2013.0299

Greenwood, R., Oliver, C., Sahlin, K., & Suddaby, R. (2008). Introduction. In R. Greenwood, C. Oliver, R. Suddaby, & K. Sahlin (Eds.), *The Sage handbook of organizational institutionalism* (pp. 1–46). Sage.

Hampel, C. E., Lawrence, T. B., & Tracy, P. (2017). Institutional work: Taking stock and making it matter. In R. Greenwood, C. Oliver, T. B. Lawrence, & R. E. Meyer (Eds.), *The Sage handbook of organizational institutionalism* (pp. 558–590). Sage. https://doi.org/10.4135/9781526415066

Hayhurst, L. M., Giles, A. R., & Radforth, W. M. (2015). 'I want to come here to prove them wrong': Using a post-colonial feminist participatory action research (PFPAR) approach to studying sport, gender and development programmes for urban indigenous young women. *Sport in Society*, *18*(8), 952–967. https://doi.org/10.1080/17430437.2014.997585

Heinze, K. L., & Lu, D. (2017). Shifting responses to institutional change: The National Football League and player concussions. *Journal of Sport Management*, *31*(5), 497–513. https://doi.org/10.1123/jsm.2016-0309

Hoeber, L., & Shaw, S. (2017). Contemporary qualitative research methods in sport management. *Sport Management Review*, *20*(1), 4–7. https://doi.org/10.1016/j.smr.2016.11.005

Jacobsen, K. (2002). Livelihoods in conflict: The pursuit of livelihoods by refugees and the impact on the human security of host communities. *International Migration*, *40*(5), 95–123. https://doi.org/10.1111/1468-2435.00213

Jarvis, L. C., Goodrick, E., & Hudson, B. A. (2019). Where the heart functions best: Reactive-affective conflict and the disruptive work of animal rights organizations. *Academy of Management Journal*, *62*(5), 1358–1387. https://doi.org/10.5465/amj.2017.0342

Jasper, J. M. (2011). Emotions and social movements: Twenty years of theory and research. *Annual Review of Sociology*, *37*(1), 285–303. https://doi.org/10.1146/annurev-soc-081309-150015

Kidd, B. (2008). A new social movement: Sport for development and peace. *Sport in Society*, *11*(4), 370–380.

Kindon, S., Pain, R., & Kesby, M. (2007). *Participatory action research approaches and methods: Connecting people, participation and place*. Routledge.

Lawrence, T. B., & Suddaby, R. (2006). Institutions and institutional work. In S. R. Clegg, T. B. Lawrence, & W. R. Nord (Eds.), *The sage handbook of organization studies* (pp. 215–254). Sage. https://doi.org/10.4135/9781848608030.n7

Ley, C., Rato Barrio, M., & Koch, A. (2018). "In the sport I am here": therapeutic processes and health effects of sport and exercise on PTSD. *Qualitative Health Research*, *28*(3), 491–507. https://doi.org/10.1177/1049732317744533

Lok, J., Creed, W. D., DeJordy, R., & Voronov, M. (2017). Living institutions: Bringing emotions into organizational institutionalism. In R. Greenwood, C. Oliver, T. B. Lawrence, & R. E. Meyer (Eds.), *The Sage handbook of organizational institutionalism* (pp. 591–620). Sage. https://doi.org/10.4135/9781526415066

Lu, L. D., & Heinze, K. L. (2020). Examining institutional entrepreneurship in the passage of youth sport concussion legislation. *Journal of Sport Management*, *35*(1), 1–16. https://doi.org/10.1123/jsm.2019-0327

Maguire, S., & Hardy, C. (2009). Discourse and deinstitutionalization: The decline of DDT. *Academy of Management Journal, 52*(1), 148–178. https://doi.org/10.5465/amj.2009.36461993

Martin de Holan, P., Willi, A., & & Fernández, P. D. (2019). Breaking the wall: Emotions and projective agency under extreme poverty. *Business & Society, 58*(5), 919–962. https://doi.org/10.1177/0007650317745633

McCarthy, L., & Moon, J. (2018). Disrupting the gender institution: Consciousness-raising in the cocoa value chain. *Organization Studies, 39*(9), 1153–1177. https://doi.org/10.1177/0170840618787358

McIntyre, A. (2007). *Participatory action research*. Sage.

McSweeney, M., & Hakiza, P. (2022). Refugees, social entrepreneurship, and sport for development and peace. In M. McSweeney, P. G. Svensson, L. M. C. Hayhurst, & P. Safai (Eds.), *Social innovation, entrepreneurship, and sport for development and peace* (pp. 160–172). Routledge.

Mcsweeney, M., Hakiza, R., & Namukhula, J. (2022). Participatory action research and visual and digital methods with refugees in Kampala, Uganda: Process, ethical complexities, and reciprocity. *Sport in Society, 25*(3), 485–505.

McSweeney, M., Kikulis, L., Thibault, L., Hayhurst, L., & van Ingen, C. (2019). Maintaining and disrupting global-North hegemony/global-South dependence in a local African sport for development organisation: The role of institutional work. *International Journal of Sport Policy and Politics, 11*(3), 521–537. https://doi.org/10.1080/19406940.2018.1550797

McSweeney, M., Millington, R., Hayhurst, L. M., & Darnell, S. (2021). Becoming an occupation? A research agenda into the professionalization of the sport for development and peace sector. *Journal of Sport Management, 36*(5), 500–512. https://doi.org/10.1123/jsm.2021-0099

McSweeney, M., Otte, J., Eyul, P., Hayhurst, L. M., & Parytci, D. T. (2023). Conducting collaborative research across global North-South contexts: Benefits, challenges and implications of working with visual and digital participatory research approaches. *Qualitative Research in Sport, Exercise and Health, 15*(2), 264–279. https://doi.org/10.1080/2159676X.2022.2048059.

Miles, M. B., Huberman, A. M., & Saldana, J. (2013). *Qualitative data analysis: A methods sourcebook*. Sage.

Mitchell, C., De Lange, N., & Moletsane, R. (2017). *Participatory visual methodologies: Social change, community and policy*. Sage.

Moisander, J. K., Hirsto, H., & Fahy, K. M. (2016). Emotions in institutional work: A discursive perspective. *Organization Studies, 37*(7), 963–990. https://doi.org/10.1177/0170840615613377

Montgomery, E., & Foldspang, A. (2008). Discrimination, mental problems and social adaptation in young refugees. *European Journal of Public Health, 18*(2), 156–161. https://doi.org/10.1093/eurpub/ckm073

Nite, C. (2017). Message framing as institutional maintenance: The National Collegiate Athletic Association's institutional work of addressing legitimate threats. *Sport Management Review, 20*(4), 338–351. https://doi.org/10.1016/j.smr.2016.10.005

Nite, C., Abiodun, I., & Marvin, W. (2019). The evolving institutional work of the National Collegiate Athletic Association to maintain dominance in a fragmented field. *Sport Management Review, 22*(3), 379–394. https://doi.org/10.1016/j.smr.2018.05.002

Nite, C., & Edwards, J. (2021). From isomorphism to institutional work: Advancing institutional theory in sport management research. *Sport Management Review, 24*(5), 815–838. https://doi.org/10.1080/14413523.2021.1896845

Nols, Z., Haudenhuyse, R., Spaaij, R., & Theeboom, M. (2019). Social change through an urban sport for development initiative? Investigating critical pedagogy through the voices of young people. *Sport, Education and Society, 24*(7), 727–741. https://doi.org/10.1080/13573322.2018.1459536

Oxford, S. (2019). 'You look like a machito!': A decolonial analysis of the social in/exclusion of female participants in a Colombian sport for development and peace organization. *Sport in Society, 22*(6), 1025–1042. https://doi.org/10.1080/17430437.2019.1565389

Phillimore, J., & Goodson, L. (2006). Problem or opportunity? Asylum seekers, refugees, employment and social exclusion in deprived urban areas. *Urban Studies, 43*(10), 1715–1736. https://doi.org/10.1080/00420980600838606

Pickin, L., Brunsden, V., & Hill, R. (2011). Exploring the emotional experiences of foster carers using the photovoice technique. *Adoption & Fostering, 35*(2), 61–75. https://doi.org/10.1177/030857591103500207

Riehl, S., Snelgrove, R., & Edwards, J. (2019). Mechanisms of institutional maintenance in minor hockey. *Journal of Sport Management, 33*(2), 93–105.

Saldana, J. (2016). *The coding manual for qualitative researchers*. Sage.

Scheff, T. (2015). Toward defining basic emotions. *Qualitative Inquiry, 21*(2), 111–121. https://doi.org/10.1177/1077800414550462

Scheibelhofer, E. (2019). Conceptualising the social positioning of refugees reflections on socio-institutional contexts and agency with a focus on work. *Identities, 26*(3), 289–304. https://doi.org/10.1080/1070289X.2019.1589980

Schulenkorf, N., Sherry, E., & Rowe, K. (2016). Sport for development: An integrated literature review. *Journal of Sport Management, 30*(1), 22–39. https://doi.org/10.1123/jsm.2014-0263

Scott, D. S. (2020). The confidence delusion: A sociological exploration of participants' confidence in sport-for-development. *International Review for the Sociology of Sport, 55*(4), 383–398. https://doi.org/10.1177/1012690218814536

Spaaij, R., Broerse, J., Oxford, S., Luguetti, C., McLachlan, F., McDonald, B., Klepac, B., Lymbery, L., Bishara, J., & Pankowiak, A. (2019). Sport, refugees, and forced migration: A critical review of the literature. *Frontiers in Sports and Active Living, 1*, 1–18. https://doi.org/10.3389/fspor.2019.00047

Spaaij, R., & Schaillée, H. (2021). Inside the black box: A micro-sociological analysis of sport for development. *International Review for the Sociology of Sport, 56*(2), 151–169. https://doi.org/10.1177/1012690220902671

Toubiana, M., & Zietsma, C. (2017). The message is on the wall? Emotions, social media and the dynamics of institutional complexity. *Academy of Management Journal, 60*(3), 922–953. https://doi.org/10.5465/amj.2014.0208

Turner, J. H., & Stets, J. E. (2006). Sociological theories of human emotions. *Annual Review of Sociology, 32*(1), 25–52. https://doi.org/10.1146/annurev.soc.32.061604.123130

van Ingen, C. (2016). Getting lost as a way of knowing: The art of boxing within shape your life. *Qualitative Research in Sport, Exercise and Health, 8*(5), 472–486. https://doi.org/10.1080/2159676X.2016.1211170

Vince, R. (2021). Reflections on the role of bemusement in institutional disruption. *Journal of Management Inquiry, 30*(3), 273–284. https://doi.org/10.1177/1056492619872272

Voronov, M. (2014). Towards a toolkit for emotionalizing institutional theory. In N. M. Ashkanasy, W. J. Zerbe, & C. E. J. Hartel (Eds.), *Research on emotion in organizations: Emotions and the organizational fabric* (Vol. 10, pp. 167–196). Emerald Group Publishing.

Voronov, M., & Vince, R. (2012). Integrating emotions into the analysis of institutional work. *Academy of Management Review, 37*(1), 58–81. https://doi.org/10.5465/amr.2010.0247

Wang, C., & Burris, M. A. (1997). Photovoice: Concept, methodology, and use for participatory needs assessment. *Health Education & Behavior, 24*(3), 369–387. https://doi.org/10.1177/109019819702400309

Wang, C. C. (1999). Photovoice: A participatory action research strategy applied to women's health. *Journal of Women's Health, 8*(2), 185–192. https://doi.org/10.1089/jwh.1999.8.185

Welty Peachey, J., Lyras, A., Cohen, A., Bruening, J. E., & Cunningham, G. B. (2014). Exploring the motives and retention factors of sport-for-development volunteers. *Nonprofit and Voluntary Sector Quarterly, 43*(6), 1052–1069. https://doi.org/10.1177/0899764013501579

Welty Peachey, J., Musser, A., Shin, N. R., & Cohen, A. (2018). Interrogating the motivations of sport for development and peace practitioners. *International Review for the Sociology of Sport, 53*(7), 767–787. https://doi.org/10.1177/1012690216686856

Welty Peachey, J. W., Schulenkorf, N., & Hill, P. (2020). Sport-for-development: A comprehensive analysis of theoretical and conceptual advancements. *Sport Management Review, 23*(5), 783–796. https://doi.org/10.1016/j.smr.2019.11.002

Wright, A. L., Zammuto, R. F., & Liesch, P. W. (2017). Maintaining the values of a profession: Institutional work and moral emotions in the emergency department. *Academy of Management Journal*, *60*(1), 200–237. https://doi.org/10.5465/amj.2013.0870

Zietsma, C., & Toubiana, M. (2018). The valuable, the constitutive, and the energetic: Exploring the impact and importance of studying emotions and institutions. *Organization Studies*, *39*(4), 427–443. https://doi.org/10.1177/0170840617751008

Zilber, T. B. (2020). The methodology/theory interface: Ethnography and the microfoundations of institutions. *Organization Theory*, *1*(2), 2631787720919439. https://doi.org/10.1177/2631787720919439

Trained to be sexist: operationalizing institutional logics in the co-construction of gendered discourse in sport

Meredith Patricia Flaherty

ABSTRACT
Research Question: I enter the cultural processes of gender through operationalizations of the institutional logics that thread agency, structure, and the reproduction of dominant discourses. The research question that guided the design of my autoethnography was: How were gender logics co-constructed across my sport career?
Research Methods: Institutional logics as a method holds the potential to develop novel access points for deconstructing and disrupting dominant discourses. In an analytic autoethnography, I situate institutional logics as the organizing principles for the co-construction of gendered discourse in my story, as a former professional athlete and coach.
Results and Findings: I offer a selection of anecdotes written into a story, each operationalizing the co-construction of one of four dominant gendered logics: (a) 'less than', the primary overarching logic, (b) 'conform socially', (c) 'protect girls', and (d) 'vision of value', or projections of how my personality and potential should be harnessed.
Implications: The two most salient contributions to the literature from the autoethnography are (a) the nuance that emerged in the 'vision of value' logic, which evidenced a tension in how gendered visions of potential were imposed on talent that was valued for traditionally masculine characteristics, and (b) the disruptive and emancipatory potential of the proposed entry into the co-construction of sport discourse through the mechanisms of institutional theory.

Introduction

I was trained to be sexist. As an elite athlete, and later as a coach, across my career in sport, I was complicit in a system that is organized on the very premise that my own value was 'less than.'

I am a product of the US sport system, in which I was the success story. I was an elite youth player, recruited into the US's college system, and drafted as a goalkeeper into the first US professional women's soccer league, the Women's United Soccer Association (WUSA). My playing career launched me into a professional coaching career, where I was embedded at all levels of soccer in the US for two decades. As a youth athlete, I learned from the players, coaches, and parents on my teams that girls were weaker, less skilled, less athletic, and less competitive than boys. In elite soccer and in coaching, I was told that the differences in programming and disparate treatment of girls and women were justified based on that 'less than' logic. And, I was trained to know that anyone who questioned those ideological, naturalized truths was either foolish or *the problem*.

Institutional theory explains how cultural narratives are co-constructed to operate as naturalized truths around the value and abilities of girls and women in sport (Kerwin & Leberman, 2022; Messner, 2011; Washington & Patterson, 2011). Thornton et al. (2012) orient the institutional processes of cultural narratives around institutional logics, situating logics as the latent thread that binds agency and structure as the mechanisms of the co-construction of culture. Agency and structure are the foundational concepts in institutional theory and the processes of discourse, locked in a cultural exchange in which an individual's cognition and behavior, or agency, are constrained and enabled by structure, or the rules, norms, and truths (Friedland & Alford, 1991; Giddens, 1984; Greenwood & Hinings, 1996; Lawrence & Suddaby, 2006). Manifestations of the recursive relationship between agency and structure, in local iterations, are proposed by Thornton et al. (2012) as the source of the production and reproduction of discourses, carrying logics through the processes of culture.

Sport as a broad institution offers a unique analytical space for examining the boundaries of institutional theory and its concepts because of the prominent role sport occupies in the production and reproduction of cultural discourses (Cooper et al., 2017; Robertson et al., 2021). Sport-specific logics, such as naturalized sex-segregation and an embedded competitive ethic, platform sport as a cultural site where gender relations and normalized gender identities are contested and developed (Cooper et al., 2017; Messner, 2011; Shaw & Frisby, 2006).

Autoethnography pairs with institutional theory in both purpose and delivery through the processes of agency. Where autoethnography is a methodological tool for disrupting discourse through claiming agency over a story (Cooper et al., 2017), institutional theory provides conceptual and theoretical entry into those discourses (Lok & De Rond, 2013; Thornton & Ocasio, 2008). I use my story (white, cis-gendered female) to enter the cultural processes of gender through operationalizations of the institutional logics that thread agency, structure, and the reproduction of dominant discourses. The research question that guided the design of my autoethnography was: How were gender logics co-constructed across my sport career?

Agency is my assumed perspective in the story, conceptualized in Giddens's (1984) structuration theory as the capacity to act, or 'to make a difference to a pre-existing state of affairs or course of events' (p. 46). I enter the recursive cycle of agency and structure at sensemaking as an access point into the co-construction of discourses and the processes of institutional theory (Fairclough, 2005; Lok & De Rond, 2013; Weick et al., 2005). I situate institutional logics as the latent strand of discourse, carried by implicit and explicit structural messages about the rules, norms, and truths for girls and women in sport and, recursively, my reproductions of those (Lammers, 2011; Robertson et al., 2021; Thornton & Ocasio, 2008).

Methods

An autoethnography is both process and product, where each dimension carries emancipatory potential (Cooper et al., 2017; Ellis et al., 2011). Through the process of writing and reporting the co-construction of my socialization into gender rules, norms, and truths, I relocate my agency to an analytical level, where I actively reclaim the story and deploy it to intentionally disrupt gendered logics (Cooper et al., 2017; Lok & De Rond, 2013).

The product dimension of autoethnography is a narrative that: (a) proposes to 'understand a self or some aspect of a life as it intersects with a cultural context' (Ellis et al., 2011, p. 279), and (b) one that positions the reader 'to enter the author's world and to use what they learn there to reflect on, understand, and cope with their own lives' (Ellis et al., 2011, p. 280). My product is the autoethnographic account of the process of being trained to be sexist written to carry the theoretical development and application of the concepts central to the process of institutionalization of culture: sensemaking, agency, structure, and their co-construction of discourse.

Analytic autoethnography

Analytic autoethnography delivers assurances of validity through five specific elements: (a) complete member in-group status, (b) acknowledgement of reflexivity that co-constructs or co-constructed the context, (c) the centrality of the author to the story, (d) augmentative data sources, and (e) aiming to use empirical data to advance knowledge or theory (Anderson, 2006).

Anderson's condition on advancing theory is a prominent feature of my autoethnography. I use agency as a theoretical mechanism for entry into discourses and institutional work (Lok & De Rond, 2013; Thornton & Ocasio, 2008). My accounts of sensemaking, agency, and structural interactions compose a story that conceptually layers onto Thornton et al.'s (2012) model of micro foundations, which locates the process of culture in those co-constructions.

My personal narrative (64,282 words) was written and maintained through edits and revisions in Microsoft Word on a personal device. The narrative was triangulated by interviews ($N = 8$); historical markers, such as the passage of Title IX in the US and the subsequent proliferation of women's sport programs in the US college system; and the literature on gendered barriers to participation and leadership in sport (Burton, 2015; Shaw & Penney, 2003; Staurowsky et al., 2020).

Interviews were with actors from my story, including former coaches, teammates, coworkers, and direct-report supervisors. The interviews were unstructured, designed to elicit the participant's perspective of the language, behaviors, rules, norms, and truths that contrasted and complemented my version of the shared context (Anderson, 2006). I kept an audit trail that reads as journaling the process of autoethnography, documenting tensions in writing, such as feelings of shame for what the process illuminated, or rotating new perspectives gained through interview (Anderson, 2006; McIlveen, 2008).

The data corpus was analyzed as an analysis of discourse through iterations of editing the narrative and layering interview data into anecdotes that carried accessible descriptions of sensemaking and structural arrangements while preserving the ethos of the story

(Anderson, 2006; Fairclough, 2005). Though Ellis (2009) holds that, in autoethnography, there is a foundational tension between the author's agency over their own story and protecting the anonymity of the characters appearing in it, I have altered any identifiers due to the sensitive nature of some of the language and behaviors that were central to carrying the story.

The four dominant logics that thread my story were labeled qualitatively, modeled after how the 'less than' logic is conceptualized as an organizing principle in the literature on gender in sport (Shaw & Frisby, 2006). The qualitative labels represent the sets structural messages around gender that I interacted with: (a) 'less than', the primary overarching logic, (b) 'conform socially', (c) 'protect girls', and (d) 'vision of value.'

Writing agency: operationalizing institutional logics

Institutional logics are 'the socially constructed, historical patterns of cultural symbols and material practices, including assumptions, values, and beliefs, by which individuals and organizations provide meaning to their daily activity, organize their time and space, and reproduce their lives and experiences' (Thornton et al., 2012, p. 2). The socially constructed truths about gendered value in sport are commonly conceptualized as the 'less than' logic, purported as both an antecedent to and outcome of gendered access and treatment discriminations that transcend international rules, cultures, and systems (Shaw & Penney, 2003; Staurowsky et al., 2020; Wicker et al., 2022). The cultural reproduction of the 'less than' logic operates on the principles of discourse as co-constructed through language and behavior that is reflexive around structural messages (Cooky, 2009; Lok & De Rond, 2013; Messner, 2011): I was as much a perpetrator of the reproduction of sexism in sport as I was a victim.

I was raised in a system that rewarded me for knowing that girls and women were 'less than'. I reproduced the truths from the bench of a US Soccer sideline, when I told a team full of 17-year-old girls that, as a coach, I liked to have a female referee 'because women are easier to manipulate'. I said it in passing, as though it was common knowledge and nothing more than an industry insight. It was a narrative that had been taught to me ... by many of the men I had played for or coached with. I was taught that women referees were weaker, and *that* they were weaker was not necessarily a problem, it was just a *truth* – and one I should take advantage of as a coach ... to manage the game.

I didn't understand at the time, as a young coach, why and how I was reproducing the 'less than' logic for my team of young women. It wasn't until I transitioned out of coaching and became immersed in the literature on gender in sport that I understood how and why complicit discourses around gender and other power arrangements are produced and reproduced.

The less than logic

The 'less than' logic was a feature of every sport experience I had. My first organized sport was coach-pitch baseball at 6 years old on an all-boys' team in an all-boys' league. I was bad at baseball; or so I thought. I didn't play much – most of my memories of baseball are from the bench. When I did play, I played in right field. I did like baseball though; I loved fielding in practice. It was like fetch, and I just wanted to run. I was an over-active child who was tough to contain and always at full throttle ... atypical for a girl.

After my second baseball season, I was told that I was 'too weak to make the throws' and that I should I switch over to softball. My coaches said that I would be a better player and have a better experience playing with the girls. I was heartbroken that I was a bad baseball player. I hadn't yet encountered any sport in which I was not the fastest, strongest, and most intensely competitive among the boys in my neighborhood or the kids at my school. Those were the traits that made me who I was, innately.

The number of girls at softball tryouts only filled one diamond. The coaches had set up stations for batting and fielding. At the fielding station, a line of girls took turns handling ground balls that the coaches, all dads, gingerly hit to us to glove and throw to first base. The ground balls were routine for me, and the throws were easy. There was a palpable 'where did she come from?' sentiment among the coaches at the tryout because of the advanced skill I already had. I was the best athlete at softball, and maybe the best player, even among the girls who had played for years. I had gone from 'too weak' at fielding and throwing with the boys to exceptional at the same skills among the girls.

What I couldn't have known at the time was that ... I wasn't bad at baseball; I hadn't been too weak to make the throws. I got moved to softball because my coaches knew, as a truth, that a girl didn't belong in baseball ... she belonged in softball.

The Model of Micro Foundations

Taken-for-granted truths about the value of girls in women in sport as 'less than' are reproduced by everyday language and behaviors (Lok & De Rond, 2013; Shaw & Penney, 2003; Staurowsky et al., 2020). In their iteration of institutional logics, Thornton et al.'s (2012) model of micro foundations locates the production and reproduction of institutional logics, like the 'less than' logic, at the individual level, as those micro processes. They offer their model as a lens on institutional work through 'the role of language linking micro cognition to culture and institutional logics, and micro interactions in macro structures' (Thornton et al., 2012, p. 98).

The model of micro foundations explains how local interpretations of institutional logics, delivered through the language and behavior of individuals, shape meaning around the logic uniquely in-context (Fahlén & Stenling, 2019; Read et al., 2020; Thornton et al., 2012). The process lens of the model dictates that variance in local interpretations and productions of a logic aggregates to broader organizing principles of social patterns over time (Friedland & Alford, 1991; Lammers, 2011; Read et al., 2020). Those social patterns are the macro-level structures that operate, recursively, as cultural narratives (Lawrence & Suddaby, 2006; Shaw & Penney, 2003; Thornton et al., 2012); the model situates the agency/structure interactions as the manifestations of institutional logics that source cultural reproductions.

In my baseball anecdote, the series of contexts and associated messages are representations of how the 'less than' logic is reproduced through local, agentive interpretations and demonstrations. Where the coaches in baseball delivered the logic through exclusion, the coaches in softball, who were sure to coach us like the little girls we were, delivered it through caretaking. The variation in how the logic was delivered by the different men in different contexts in my story is the premise of the model of micro foundations as entry into the processes of dominant discourses in sport (Lammers, 2011; Thornton et al., 2012; Washington & Patterson, 2011).

My coaches in both sports had been abiding by the naturalized truths they were trained on; and the baseball coaches reproduced those truths for the boys in expelling me from the team. The messages I received: that I wasn't welcome on a boys' team, compounded with the level of competition and disheartening unseriousness I encountered in softball, was that I didn't belong anywhere. In softball, I was a problem child.

I was a strong-willed and fearless softball player with an undeveloped set of social skills, like how to talk to others with humility or how to know when my aggression was out of bounds (for a girl). In softball, I was a discipline case. However, I was also the best player, the best athlete, and I was vocal – I organized the plays, baited runners into stepping off base to tag or throw them out, I called pitches ... I had all the elements of the 'it factor' as a star athlete, but my hyper-competitiveness and difficulty navigating social constraints dictated that I was 'a problem child.'

I played softball throughout my school years, but as a kid, my heart was in American football. American football was by far my favorite sport to watch and play. I felt like I belonged in football more so than in any other space. When I put my pads and helmet on, I was able to be everything that made me *the me*.

The first season I registered for Pop Warner, (the governing body in youth American football) my registration got lost. The league told my mom that it had been confused with a registration for cheerleading. After the season had started, and we hadn't heard from the league, my mom took me out to the fields where the teams practiced ... to get a refund.

We wove our way between team sites to find my age group, where Coach Clyde was conducting his practice. After my mom described the situation, Coach Clyde looked down at me and asked: 'Do you want to play?' I very much wanted to play ... he was unconvinced.

He called the team over, about 25 or 30 boys, introduced me by name, and told them I wanted to join their team. I remember that I felt more comfortable in that moment than I ever felt trying to figure out how to appropriately mesh with my softball teammates. He told the team to line up on one of the chalked boundaries in the practice area – shoulder to shoulder. We were going to race. This was where I belonged.

I didn't feel anything that I probably should have been feeling ... I wasn't nervous, I didn't feel like everyone was looking at me with side-eye (though they were), and I wasn't uncertain. I was ready to race. It was who I was.

Mimicking the cadence of ready-set-go, Coach Clyde yelled: 'Down, Set, Hut' ... and I took off. I won the race by yards. It wasn't even close. I was much faster than the boys. Coach made us do it again. The second race had the same result. After the second race, he looked at my mom and said: 'OK, let's get her some pads.'

American football became my main sport through my primary school years into high school. I developed into a smart, disciplined, and flat out mean left defensive end after two years at linebacker; I was defense-oriented by nature because I loved to run and hit ... to blow plays up. The sport was made for me; I was never a problem child or discipline case in football.

I never made *friends* with the boys on my football teams, but I did fit in as a teammate. The game was always just the game, and the coaches rarely treated me different from the boys. The jokes and the shows of masculinity were just part of the culture of football – they taught me how to survive in the men's locker room.

Baked into my experiences in football were implicit and explicit lessons about how to show power through masculinity and about how boys became men through football. At one practice, in the 7th grade, the running back fumbled the football, and our new coach threw a fit; he wanted to make sure that we understood how valuable the ball was and how to hold the ball properly without fumbling or getting it stripped, and to make his coaching point, I couldn't be in the team circle. Coach called the team together after the fumble and told me to go stand in a spot about 30 yards away, by myself, isolated from the team. I had no idea what was going on, but I went and stood away from the guys as instructed.

About a minute later, we got back to practice drills. During a water break, I asked the boys what the circle was all about, but they just ducked and covered – they didn't want to tell me. After practice, one of the boys I got along with told me. Coach brought the guys together to explain that, when you hold a football, you hold it by the points with both hands, arms crossed around it, and close to your chest. The way he emphasized holding on to the points of the football was by likening it to holding onto 'a set of tits' – 'hold on tight to those because you don't ever want to let go'. That's why he didn't let me in the circle – his coaching point was how to hold the football like 'tits'.

Agency and sensemaking: negotiating gender identities

Hyper-masculinity and sexualizing women are mechanisms of the 'less than' logic (Kim & Sagas, 2014; Staurowsky et al., 2020). Feminized insults as behavioral control and 'locker room talk' that subjugates women are normalized as part of the cultural processes of boys learning to be men through sport (Messner, 2011; Shaw & Frisby, 2006). In youth football, gendered and sexualized language was explicit and frequent, but didn't affect play when the whistle blew – I was expected by my coaches and my teammates to be the dominant, hard-hitter that made me among the best players on the team. In contrast, in baseball, the gendered shows were implicit, demonstrated through exclusion, both on the field and as an organizing principle. Despite that the 'less than' logic was delivered differently in my early experiences across baseball, softball, and football, the message was that girls and women are less valuable in sport. And that I was an entirely different breed of girl.

Sensemaking is a conceptual pivot point for institutional logics, where logics transition from structural influences into cognition and behavior, which then reconstitute local discourses and cultural narratives through the principles of agency (Cooky, 2009; Giddens, 1984; Weick et al., 2005). Context-specific sets of rules and norms carry macro-level ideologies and field-level logics uniquely, and recursively affect sensemaking in the context; different messages are privileged in different spaces, and the co-construction of local discourses will vary from context to context (Scott, 2008; Thornton & Ocasio, 2008; Weick et al., 2005). Sensemaking holds a presence in the institutional theory literature as the micro-level process of reflexive monitoring, conceptualizing how messages are interpreted and internalized to ground what is reproduced through agentive language and behaviors (Scott, 2008; Weick et al., 2005)

As a sensemaking process, boys are socialized into a hyper-masculine proxy in sport and girls are trained that they must negotiate their femininity in opposition to an athlete identity (Messner, 2011; Nite & Edwards, 2021; Weick et al., 2005). As boys earn social rewards for shows of masculinity, girls learn how to behave within the imposed constraints around the meanings of *female* and *athlete*, affecting motivation and engagement across contexts and time (Burton, 2015; Hoeber & Frisby, 2001). The outcomes associated with the logic are that boys, who are most likely to advance in the sport system and ascend to leadership positions, come to know that girls and women hold less athletic value and that their sport is less serious (Hoeber & Frisby, 2001; Messner, 2011); girls learn internalized tensions around what their body, training, and behavior should look like as athletes (Cooky, 2009; Staurowsky et al., 2020).

The conform socially logic

My transition from football to soccer in high school opened the door to what would become my full athlete identity for decades: I became a goalkeeper. I chose soccer as my university sport because, as a goalkeeper, I had less pressure to reduce my competitiveness or intensity than I had in softball. Goalkeepers are notoriously *crazy* in soccer culture, so the position was a natural fit for me. I still got to hit, I just hit the ground more often than another player.

My senior year in high school, on the inside, and with my club soccer team, I was an unbound goalkeeper; however, the goalkeeper traits were not as appreciated among my peers. At our senior class assembly, I won 'biggest ego' in the class superlative competition, and was gifted an ornately fashioned, purple hand-held mirror that looked like it was purchased at a Dollar Store.

I still have the mirror.

After the mirror episode at the assembly, at which another classmate was awarded 'most athletic' (girls' division), I didn't want to be embarrassed again. When Senior Appreciation Night came around, the ceremony that celebrated the seniors and their school accomplishments and plans for after graduation, I pulled my name from being recognized. One of our football players had earned a scholarship to play in the first division of the National Collegiate Athletic Association (NCAA), the US college sport system, a basketball player was headed to play in the second division, and I had a scholarship to State, to play soccer in the premier women's conference of the NCAA's first division. But I was absolutely not going to walk across that floor in front of my peers to announce my award. I was not going to give anyone a chance to think I was 'showboating'. I watched from the bleachers as the two boys were celebrated for their athletic grants-in-aid.

My first college coach never saw me play as a goalkeeper, but recruited me to her top-tier college program based on a recommendation from a National Team coach, whom I had impressed at his TopFlight goalkeeper camps. TopFlight was a coed goalkeeper-only camp that employed college players in the summers to coach youth campers and train in a high-level environment to prepare for our college season.

My goalkeeper identity was celebrated at TopFlight, and I was in my element. The camps were competitive and intense, and were overwhelmingly attended by boys and staffed with men. Status at TopFlight was earned through the demos – the skill demonstrations the goalkeeper staff did to teach the campers. I was a monster in the demos. The summer before I was called into National Team camp for the first time, I won the staff extension dive demo – which was unimaginable.

At the next pre-camp staff meeting, two days after I reached legend status in the extension dive contest, the head coach of the camp blasted the staff over less-skilled coaches muddying up the demos. What he meant by 'less-skilled' was the women; coach didn't like that the women were overpopulating the most prominent feature of camp.

That head coach, the 'Green Condor' (his nickname), always started his camps by lining up the campers in military-style rows for an introductory set of calisthenics; one of the prescribed movements was to have all of the campers raise their hands above their heads and bounce up and down ... so that the men on staff, lined up in front of the camper blocks to oversee, could watch the girl campers' breasts bounce up and down.

Despite that I was old enough to know better by the time I was embedded in Top-Flight, unlike when my football coach had explicitly sexualized women as a coaching point, this feature of camp didn't register for me as a problem: I hadn't known to notice at the time. The 'Condor Warm-Up', as we called it, came up in interview. An interview participant I had played and coached for, who was also a member of the Top-Flight hierarchy, spoke to the sexualized feature of the warm-up as just one of the many grossly sexist practices that was passed off as lighthearted and meaningless. And where I had been trained that I didn't even need to notice it, she spoke to feeling silenced by it, because she didn't have enough clout to speak against it.

For girls and women, fitting in and belonging often comes at the expense of their voice, to be humble, grateful of opportunities, and to not make waves (Darvin, 2020; Shaw & Penney, 2003). However, that logic conflicted with what I needed to be as a National Team goalkeeper, and later in coaching: a dominant orator and director. The pressure to reduce myself and to navigate what degree of reduction was appropriate for which circumstance required an inordinate amount of emotional labor. Where my dominant personality was a characteristic of what was lauded as my all-star talent, that same characteristic was what made me a discipline case from youth softball through my professional playing career in soccer.

The protect girls logic

The 'protect girls' logic centered on the expectation that girls and women needed to be shielded from shows of intensity, competitiveness, aggression, or otherwise masculine demonstrations (Messner, 2011). I was taught that I must monitor and moderate my own language and behaviors around the fragility of girls in my space, and to reduce displays of competitiveness and individual success ... because those were threatening behaviors. As a dominant personality and player, I had been positioned as a leader on most of my teams; as a *female leader*, I was meant to sacrifice successes, individuality, and my voice in the name of team cohesion.

From my very first college season, I was an elite player. I won all-conference awards three out of the four years I played in college, was an All-American at two different universities, and was named the *most valuable* defensive player (MVP) of the Women's College Cup, when I won the college national championship in my final season. Despite my accolades, the four years I spent in my first college program were tumultuous. I had come in as an unknown and turned out to be an immense, but unpredictable talent.

My State coaches spent most of my four years with them trying to train me into their version of a leader ... by reducing me.

In my third year at State, I suffered a season-ending injury to my hand. When I returned for my fourth year, I had been through the rehab process and into the National Team. I started out my fourth season splitting time with the backup who had played while I was out; I played the hard games, and she played the easy ones. I didn't like it, but I understood it. At mid-season, we were still splitting time, so I went to my coach to ask her what I needed to show to get the games a number one gets. That was my season to play myself into the World Cup roster, and I was only playing a portion of the minutes.

She told me that the number two 'deserves to play'. She told me I was being selfish for questioning why I wasn't getting the games and that I needed to be a better leader for the team by supporting the back up. What I heard was that a starting line-up in the premier conference in the country – the highest level of women's soccer in the US at the time – was about feelings ... not merit or ability. And that I would be rewarded verbally, but not with playing time, for submitting. I was a National Team player who was sharing playing time because of my coach's sensitivity to the back up's feelings. The leadership my coach expected me to show was to take a back seat.

Agency in Institutional Work. The 'protect girls' logic carried a tension that reflected the processes of institutional work, or 'the purposive action of individuals and organizations aimed at creating, maintaining and disrupting institutions' (Lawrence & Suddaby, 2006, p. 215). My story happens on the edge of Title IX in the US, which linked sport to the US educational system, platforming girls to gain access to sport opportunities as equal treatment under the law. Changes to the meaning and delivery of sport created tensions in the US sport system around carving out space for girls as athletes within traditional cultural boundaries (Shaw & Penney, 2003; Staurowsky et al., 2020).

Siloing girls into softball as a reduced version of baseball is an example of a structural-level manifestation (in policy) of institutional work on the 'protect girls' logic. In contrast, my baseball coach's decision that I would have a better experience in softball, or my college soccer coach's insistence on leadership through reduction, demonstrate agency-level manifestations of institutional work on the logic. When situated in a power hierarchy, like coaching or mentoring, agentive interpretations and impositions of gendered logics operated as structural parameters that I then had to negotiate into my own sensemaking, language, and behaviors. Those cyclical interpersonal intersections illustrate institutional work stratified by power arrangements at the agency level, through micro processes (Lok & De Rond, 2013).

The vision of value logic: embedded boundaries

The 'vision of value' logic was the most complex and salient organizing principle in my process of being trained to be sexist; the logic did not on its own, or in the first degree, carry sexism. Within the logic's parameters, there was space for the traditionally masculine characteristics that I carried to be celebrated as talent or potential; however, the projections of how to shape the potential operated only in a female version of the value. I was rewarded for being different from other girls or women, but only under certain conditions or within certain boundaries; the authority chose the spaces in which I was rewarded for displays of gendered characteristics: masculine or feminine. The 'vision of value' logic imposed a gendered version of how hyper-competitive, intense, dominant talent could be nurtured and trained to assimilate.

The 'vision of value' logic was derived from the tension coaches or mentors in my story demonstrated in how they accommodated changing opportunities and expectations for girls and women in sport within the constraints of their training to be sexist, which defaulted to constraining or harnessing the behaviors associated with the changes (De Bock et al., 2021; Heinze & Soderstrom, 2023). The boundaries and reduction imposed on me by my coach at State were untenable; I transferred my final year of college eligibility to another top-tier college program, where I won the NCAA MVP and national championship. I never made a World Cup roster, but I did end up being drafted into the first women's professional soccer league, the WUSA.

The transition from playing to coaching overlapped, and I played in two different women's leagues after college as I simultaneously held coaching jobs, because I couldn't earn a living wage on a player's salary. I played my way into a coaching job at the Central City Kickers, a national soccer club that hosted a women's team and a fully professionalized youth system with a slate of technical Directors of Coaching (DOC) supported by an administrative staff. I would be a DOC with the Kickers for 12 years across two different franchises. Both franchises had professional staffs with eight to ten DOCs and at least two Technical Directors. I never worked with another woman DOC at Kickers because, without exclusion, there was only one woman on the technical staff in each of the clubs' franchises. A former colleague, from another franchise, explained in interview that having a woman on staff at Kickers was 'like checking a box' – that the club had to have one woman on staff as a DOC, who, other than me, was invariably placed with the youngest girls' age groups.

I was different, though. I was promoted out of the DOC Youth Girls (DOCYG) to the Director of our Elite Clubs League program and the Director of Goalkeeping (DOCG).

I was not like the *other women* coaches because I had what it took to survive coaching. In my office, it was known that women didn't want to put the hours in and that they tended to leave coaching to have children or for other jobs, because they couldn't handle the rigor of the coaching lifestyle. That was why women weren't worth the time to invest in as coaches, and only hired into the DOCYG position.

My technical directors thought I was an asset – they thought I was an excellent coaching talent. I delivered coaching as I had played: competitive, intense, and loud. I was told that I was given the opportunities to work with programs beyond the youth girls because of how I deployed my goalkeeper identity as a coach. I was 'Flaher' (my nickname) – different from other women because I could earn the job on merit.

Several years into my tenure with Kickers, I asked one of my technical directors if I could get a boys' team; he told me that I would be an excellent coach for the boys, but that he wouldn't assign me a boys' team because I better served the players and the club working with girls. The argument made sense: that I was worth more as a strong female role model to the girls than I was worth as just another coach with the boys. Where I was recognized as a talented coach, my merit only carried on the girls' side.

Siloing women to positions only on the girls' side of sport is purported as a contributing factor to the *pipeline leak*, or the pattern of women failing to advance through leadership pathways in the sport system (Darvin, 2020; Sagas & Cunningham, 2004).

Additionally, the gendered patterns in leadership in sport undermine the legitimacy of women in positions of authority, for those who are able to survive the sport system to ascend to leadership (Shaw & Frisby, 2006; Wicker et al., 2022). Constraints on a woman's appropriateness for a job or gendered job descriptions for her carry that female leaders belong in roles that are less rigorous, where they can maximize what they offer via their affective capacities in relationships (Burton, 2015; Shaw & Frisby, 2006). Burton (2015) explains that restricting women to leadership positions only in women's sport operates to preserve patriarchal hegemony in sport, and recursively, shapes women's expectations for treatment and their motivation to follow the leadership pathway.

A vein of my era with the Kickers was involvement in the Olympic Development Program (ODP), a national talent identification program for youth soccer players that was delivered through hierarchically organized local programs. Oscar, the Technical Director and DOC of my state, kept me close; Kickers technical directors' opinions of my potential were part of Oscar's intention to mentor me; I held several different assignments in his programs.

Oscar was a powerful, hard spoken coach whose experiences and reputation carried weight in US Soccer. My first run with Oscar was as his assistant coach for an older girls' team for our state. Oscar's style was commanding: he was explicit about where I sat on the bench in orientation to him, what type of information or analysis I should provide and how I should deliver it to him, and when I should speak to which players and why. Oscar told me that he was teaching me how to run a team and staff.

When Oscar hired me as the Girls' Program Director in my local ODP district, he was explicit about why he was hiring me and what he expected. On my first day as Program Director, the first day of District tryouts, Oscar walked me out to field 8 at the complex to have a talk about what he expected of me. He made sure I knew that he had my back, telling me that I might meet some resistance from the coaches from the rival club, but that it was my program, and I could manage the staff as I saw fit. Oscar followed up his proclamations of support by telling me that he expected me to step up for this job – that he was giving me a chance to prove myself as a coach. His words to me before the all-staff meeting I was about to conduct were

> You are a very attractive woman, but you can't get by on that. I am giving you a chance here – I'm giving you a chance to prove that you can coach. You aren't going to be able to get by on your looks or your smile – you have to earn your opportunities through your coaching ability. You are going to have to step up and lead this program.

I was absolutely elated and bursting with pride; I grew ten feet in that conversation. I was so thankful that Oscar was giving me a chance, and I was ready to take on the program – ready to prove to him and all the other coaches that I was a good coach and capable director. His comments about my appearance and 'getting by on my smile' didn't land as sexist – I didn't know to hear them in that way; those were truths for me at the time that all women coaches should know.

The jokes, the inappropriate gestures, and the disrespect and disregard for the *other women* slid right by me as part of it being *what it was*. I was the one who was the *chosen one*, the one with the talent and the ability to survive the jokes and harassment. How I handled the coach's locker room was something I prided myself on and I thought set me apart from other women. I prided myself on not being fazed by sexual advances or harassment, like it was a patch on my sash – I could survive, compete, and excel in those spaces in ways that put me above other women, who couldn't. I could talk their language – the men's language – and I could usually turn something in the scenario around into a joke that made me 'one of the guys' … as long as I kept up my own locker-room behavior that was dismissive of women and their value in sport.

After an era with the Kickers, I was discontented with the culture of coaching in the youth game and started to transition into college coaching, now with a robust resume for player development. I had hoped that, in the college game, there would be more structural constraints around abuse of power and athletes because of the heightened degree of governance. As an assistant coach, an entry level job, I was a steal in terms of my talent, potential, and resume.

In both of the NCAA assistant positions that I held before I sunsetted my coaching career, my role was siloed as the goalkeeper coach, and my input into team training or game tactics was constrained to what related to goalkeeping. The value I brought was that I could work with the two or three goalkeepers and I could relate to the players on the team in a way that kept problems out of the head coach's office. The capacities I had built to analyze and manage training or games across my professional coaching career were not a job requirement.

Conclusions and contributions: the utility of agency

My story is not unique; I played and coached at elite levels, but many other girls and women did, too. And just like many of the women out of that pool, I hit a ceiling and off-loaded from the coaching conveyer belt I had been trained for. The very nature of my story as familiar makes it an accessible space for the reader to enter the cycle of the co-construction of gendered discourse in sport (Cooper et al., 2017).

A condition for validity in analytic autoethnography is that the reader engages with some dimension of the story that they can then relate to broader cultural phenomena (Anderson, 2006). The 'less than' logic is presented as an overarching organizing principle that grounds taken-for-granted language and practices that the reader might recognize from their relationship with sport. A manifest purpose of the autoethnography was to contribute a window into the co-construction of gender in sport discourse, in order to expose the complicity in reproducing sexism through common access and treatment discriminations.

The operationalizations of the co-construction of the 'less than' logic and the 'conform socially' logic provide the reader a window into gendered structural messages and my interpretation and negotiation of those in unique variations across time and contexts. The accounts of how the 'protect girls' logic was co-constructed and of the gendered boundaries associated with the 'vision of value' logic positioned the story in evolving logics about the accommodation of girls and women into sport (i.e. institutional work; Lok & De Rond, 2013). The two logics were developed as functions of interpersonal power arrangements, where coaches' or mentors' interpretations and negations of dominant gendered logics were delivered as structural messages in my story. The reader might extrapolate those gender structures to mentoring relationships from their experiences (Darvin et al., 2019).

The omnipresent tensions and reorganization of gender discourse between myself and social actors in my story layer onto Thornton et al.'s (2012) conceptualization of agency-level entry into institutional processes and institutional work through the model of micro foundations.

Contributions

A point of tension and the fundamental critique of institutional theory is the primacy afforded to 'structure' in its recursive relationship with agency, reducing the conceptual power of 'agency' and reproducing institutions' resistance to change (Fahlén & Stenling, 2019; Lawrence & Suddaby, 2006). The model of micro foundations circumvents the critique, situating logics as supraordinate to both agency and structure, (a) theoretically: where dominant logics operate as organizing principles of cultural processes and (b) methodologically: as a construct that can be analyzed through the patterning of local iterations of a logic as micro processes (Lok & De Rond, 2013; Thornton et al., 2012). In an institutional logics perspective, primacy in the process of culture moves from structural manifestations, as simply a delivery mechanism, to institutional logics as the meaning or information that is carried by the manifestations (Fairclough, 2005; Lammers, 2011; Thornton & Ocasio, 2008).

Institutional theory and autoethnography pair neatly around agency as a mechanism for entry into discourses and analyses of logics; method and theory can align paradigmatically, and both orient around linking micro processes to cultural issues (Cooper et al., 2017; Lok & De Rond, 2013). The model of micro foundations is the theoretical basis for my entry into the processes of discourse and institutional work on gender, told through story as analytic autoethnography. The concepts of institutional theory ground the accounts of my sensemaking around structural messages about gender norms and identities in sport, and my agency in producing and reproducing gendered logics through language and behaviors. The model platforms those co-constructions as an access point into dominant discourses, oriented around agency as a concept.

Entering the cycle of the co-construction of discourses and institutional processes through agency offers an alternative lens in sport management research (Lok & De Rond, 2013; Robertson et al., 2021). The sport management literature framed in institutional theory reflects broader research trends that precipitated the turn towards agency in neo-institutional theory, where analytical access into institutional processes is predominantly located at the structural level, as field or organizational analyses (e.g. Fahlén & Stenling, 2019; Nite & Edwards, 2021; Read et al., 2020). Specifically, research on institutional logics in sport (e.g. Gammelsæter, 2010; Skirstad & Chelladurai, 2011; Southall et al., 2008) can escape the *iron cage* of structural determinism through the model of micro foundations that locates logics as supraordinate to structure, theoretically.

Sport is an optimal space for building out the model of micro foundations and the theoretical boundaries of agency in a system of power that has historically been a catalyst for cultural change (Cooper et al., 2017; Robertson et al., 2021). Introducing an agency lens into the processes of institutional work platforms the visibility of story in the sport management literature, particularly those voices from marginalized communities (Lok & De Rond, 2013).

The paramount limitation of my autoethnography was that the sensemaking and structural interactions around gender are inextricably linked to my positioning as a white, cis-gendered woman (Shaw & Frisby, 2006). The 'less than' logic operates on the assumption of sex and gender as binary, and my story is bound by white and able-bodied privileges. Though I use my story to intentionally disrupt common language and practices that reproduce sexism in sport, I can only access those cultural reproductions as I have interacted with them. Stories and scholars who carry intersecting race, sexuality, or other historically marginalized identities are platformed through the model of micro foundations to access sport discourse. Agency as a theoretical mechanism into cultural processes positions story as a methodological carrier for the reproduction or disruption of dominant discourses (Cooper et al., 2017; Thornton et al., 2012).

Disclosure statement

No potential conflict of interest was reported by the author(s).

References

Anderson, L. (2006). Analytic autoethnography. *Journal of Contemporary Ethnography*, 35(4), 373–395. https://doi.org/10.1177/0891241605280449

Burton, L. J. (2015). Underrepresentation of women in sport leadership: A review of research. *Sport Management Review*, 18(2), 155–165. https://doi.org/10.1016/j.smr.2014.02.004

Cooky, C. (2009). Girls just aren't interested": The social construction of interest in girls' sport. *Sociological Perspectives*, 52(2), 259–283. https://doi.org/10.1525/sop.2009.52.2.259

Cooper, J. N., Grenier, R. S., & Macaulay, C. (2017). Autoethnography as a critical approach in sport management: Current applications and directions for future research. *Sport Management Review*, 20(1), 43–54. https://doi.org/10.1016/j.smr.2016.07.003

Darvin, L. (2020). Voluntary occupational turnover and the experiences of former intercollegiate women assistant coaches. *Journal of Vocational Behavior*, 116, 1–17. https://doi.org/10.1016/j.jvb.2019.103349

Darvin, L., Taylor, E., & Wells, J. (2019). Get in the game through a sponsor: Initial career ambitions of former women assistant coaches. *Journal of Issues in Intercollegiate Athletics*, 12, 590–613.

De Bock, T., Scheerder, J., Theeboom, M., De Clerck, T., Constandt, B., & Willem, A. (2021). Sport-for-All policies in sport federations: An institutional theory perspective. *European Sport Management Quarterly*, 1–23. https://doi.org/10.1080/16184742.2021.2009897

Ellis, C. (2009). Telling tales on neighbors: Ethics in two voices. *International Review of Qualitative Research*, 2(1), 3–27. https://doi.org/10.1525/irqr.2009.2.1.3

Ellis, C., Adams, T. E., & Bochner, A. P. (2011). Autoethnography: An overview. *Historical Social Research*, 36(4), 273–290. https://doi.org/10.12759/hsr.36.2011.4.273-290

Fahlén, J., & Stenling, C. (2019). (Re) conceptualizing institutional change in sport management contexts: The unintended consequences of sport organizations' everyday organizational life. *European Sport Management Quarterly*, 19(2), 265–285. https://doi.org/10.1080/16184742.2018.1516795

Fairclough, N. (2005). Peripheral vision: Discourse analysis in organization studies: The case for critical realism. *Organization Studies*, 26(6), 915–939. https://doi.org/10.1177/0170840605054610

Friedland, R., & Alford, R. R. (1991). Bringing society back in: Symbols, practices, and institutional contradictions. In W. W. Powell, & P. J. DiMaggio (Eds.), *The New institutionalism in organizational analysis* (pp. 232–263). University of Chicago Press.

Gammelsæter, H. (2010). Institutional pluralism and governance in "commercialized" sport clubs. *European Sport Management Quarterly, 10*(5), 569–594. https://doi.org/10.1080/16184742.2010.524241

Giddens, A. (1984). *The constitution of society: Outline of the theory of structuration*. University of California Press.

Greenwood, R., & Hinings, C. R. (1996). Understanding radical organizational change: Bringing together the old and the new institutionalism. *Academy of Management Review, 21*(4), 1022–1054. https://doi.org/10.2307/259163

Heinze, K. L., & Soderstrom, S. (2023). Leveling the playing field: Exploring how community embeddedness shapes institutional translation in youth sport. *European Sport Management Quarterly*, 1–22. https://doi.org/10.1080/16184742.2023.2185273

Hoeber, L., & Frisby, W. (2001). Gender equity for athletes: Rewriting the narrative for this organizational value. *European Sport Management Quarterly, 1*(3), 179–209. https://doi.org/10.1080/16184740108721896

Kerwin, S., & Leberman, S. (2022). Exploring the complicated and complex factors of evaluating a structured gender equity programme. *European Sport Management Quarterly*, 1–19. https://doi.org/10.1080/16184742.2022.2067207

Kim, K., & Sagas, M. (2014). Athletic or sexy? A comparison of female athletes and fashion models in sports illustrated swimsuit issues. *Gender Issues, 31*(2), 123–141. https://doi.org/10.1007/s12147-014-9121-2

Lammers, J. C. (2011). How institutions communicate: Institutional messages, institutional logics, and organizational communication. *Management Communication Quarterly, 25*(1), 154–182. https://doi.org/10.1177/0893318910389280

Lawrence, T. B., & Suddaby, R. (2006). Institutions and institutional work. In R. Clegg, C. Hardy, T.B. Lawrence, & W.R. Nord (Eds.), *The Sage handbook of organization studies* (2nd ed., pp. 215–254). Sage.

Lok, J., & De Rond, M. (2013). On the plasticity of institutions: Containing and restoring practice breakdowns at the Cambridge University Boat Club. *Academy of Management Journal, 56*(1), 185–207. https://doi.org/10.5465/amj.2010.0688

McIlveen, P. (2008). Autoethnography as a method for reflexive research and practice in vocational psychology. *Australian Journal of Career Development, 17*(2), 13–20. https://doi.org/10.1177/103841620801700204

Messner, M. (2011). Gender ideologies, youth sports, and the production of soft essentialism. *Sociology of Sport Journal, 28*(2), 151–170. https://doi.org/10.1123/ssj.28.2.151

Nite, C., & Edwards, J. (2021). From isomorphism to institutional work: Advancing institutional theory in sport management research. *Sport Management Review, 24*(5), 815–838. https://doi.org/10.1080/14413523.2021.1896845

Read, D., Skinner, J., Lock, D., & Houlihan, B. (2020). Field-configuring events as temporary sites for institutional change in sport: A case study of the Lausanne conference on anti-doping. *European Sport Management Quarterly, 23*(1), 227–249. https://doi.org/10.1080/16184742.2020.1845763

Robertson, J., Dowling, M., Washington, M., Leopkey, B., Ellis, D. L., & Smith, L. (2021). Institutional theory in sport: A scoping review. *Journal of Sport Management, 36*(5), 459–472. https://doi.org/10.1123/jsm.2021-0179

Sagas, M., & Cunningham, G. B. (2004). Does having "the right stuff" matter? Gender differences in the determinants of career success among intercollegiate athletic administrators. *Sex Roles, 50*(5/6), 411–421. https://doi.org/10.1023/B:SERS.0000018895.68011.fa

Scott, W. R. (2008). *Institutions and organizations: Ideas and interests* (3rd ed.). Sage.

Shaw, S., & Frisby, W. (2006). Can gender equity be more equitable?: Promoting an alternative frame for sport management research, education, and practice. *Journal of Sport Management, 20*(4), 483–509. https://doi.org/10.1123/jsm.20.4.483

Shaw, S., & Penney, D. (2003). Gender equity policies in national governing bodies: An oxymoron or a vehicle for change? *European Sport Management Quarterly, 3*(2), 78–102. https://doi.org/10.1080/16184740308721942

Skirstad, B., & Chelladurai, P. (2011). For 'love' and money: A sports club's innovative response to multiple logics. *Journal of Sport Management, 25*(4), 339–353. https://doi.org/10.1123/jsm.25.4.339

Southall, R. M., Nagel, M. S., Amis, J. M., & Southall, C. (2008). A method to march madness? Institutional logics and the 2006 National Collegiate Athletic Association Division I men's basketball tournament. *Journal of Sport Management, 22*(6), 677–700. https://doi.org/10.1123/jsm.22.6.677

Staurowsky, E. J., Watanabe, N., Cooper, J., Cooky, C., Lough, N., Paule-Koba, A., … Snyder, M. (2020). *Chasing equity: The triumphs, challenges, and opportunities in sports for girls and women.* Women's Sports Foundation.

Thornton, P., & Ocasio, W. (2008). Institutional logics. In R. Greenwood, C. Oliver, R. Suddaby, & K. Sahlin-Andersson (Eds.), *The SAGE handbook of organizational institutionalism* (pp. 99–129). Sage.

Thornton, P. H., Ocasio, W., & Lounsbury, M. (2012). *The institutional logics perspective: A new approach to culture, structure, and process.* Oxford University Press.

Washington, M., & Patterson, K. D. (2011). Hostile takeover or joint venture: Connections between institutional theory and sport management research. *Sport Management Review, 14*(1), 1–12. https://doi.org/10.1016/j.smr.2010.06.003

Weick, K. E., Sutcliffe, K. M., & Obstfeld, D. (2005). Organizing and the process of sensemaking. *Organization Science, 16*(4), 409–421. https://doi.org/10.1287/orsc.1050.0133

Wicker, P., Feiler, S., & Breuer, C. (2022). Board gender diversity, critical masses, and organizational problems of non-profit sport clubs. *European Sport Management Quarterly, 22*(2), 251–271. https://doi.org/10.1080/16184742.2020.1777453

Regional policy and organizational fields in multi-level sport governance

Kyle A. Rich, Grace Nelson, Tammy Borgen-Flood and Ann Pegoraro

ABSTRACT

Research Questions: Broadly, we sought to explore the role of regional policy in sport institutions and understand their implications for organizational fields in multi-level sport governance systems. Our research questions were (1) how do changes in regional policy impact the way that organizational fields are structured within multi-level governance structures? and (2) how does regional policy impact sport policy implementation?

Research Method: We used an instrumental case study methodology of regional policy in the Province of Ontario. Data were collected using document analysis. We collected 88 policy documents produced between 1995 and 2021. Data were analyzed using a critical policy analysis approach.

Results and Findings: Our findings demonstrate the ways that administrative arrangements and the ideas and beliefs underpinning regional policy had important implications for sport policy implementation in Ontario. The location of sport in successive provincial administrations had implications for the expected role of sport in the province. Ideas and beliefs related to what regional government should do, and who should be responsible for the delivery of services also impacted the way that sport was delivered in the province through the period studied.

Implications: Our work examines the agency of regional policymakers in the structuration and change of organization fields in sport institutions. We also critically examine the linkages between organizations in multi-level sport governance. Future work is required to understand the range of regional pressures that impact sport policy implementation in multi-level sport governance systems.

There is a growing body of literature drawing from institutional theory to understand how sports institutions work (Nite & Edwards, 2021; Robertson et al., 2022). Rooted in sociology and analyzing institutions as processes, practices, and ideas, institutional theory provides a framework through which to examine how institutions govern action (Washington & Patterson, 2011). Wooten and Hoffman (2017) posited that institutional theory offers a lens to examine how social choices are shaped, mediated, and channeled by the institutional environment. Thus, 'organizational action becomes a reflection of the perspectives defined by the group ... out of which emerge the regulative, normative, and cultural-cognitive systems that provide meaning for organizations' (Wooten & Hoffman, 2017, p. 55). While early work focused on legitimacy, change, and isomorphism, sports scholars have diversified their conceptual framing to examine constructs of logics, fields, and institutional work (Robertson et al., 2022). The shift represents an important attempt to recognize how actors can exercise agency within sports institutions (Nite & Edwards, 2021).

Sports scholars (Cousens & Slack, 2005; Kitchin & Howe, 2013; Robertson et al., 2022) have noted that understanding concepts such as organizational fields and institutional logics enable researchers to examine a community of organizations linked by shared meaning, governance systems, and patterns of relationships. Canadian sport is structured as a system of multi-level governance (Thibault & Harvey, 2013), and the public policy landscape in Canada is highly regionalized (Savoie, 2019); thus, institutional theory provides a tool to examine regional policy and the agency of policymakers, as well as their implications for sport policy implementation in Canada.

In this paper, we theorize amateur sport in Canada as an institution with clearly defined structures, actors, and fields that can be analyzed and as such, we add to the literature through an investigation of agency in this institution. To date, scholarly attention has focused on sport policy at the national level (Barnes et al., 2007; Parent et al., 2018; Thibault & Babiak, 2005; Thibault & Harvey, 2013) and on the managerial and policy-related issues experienced by Community Sport Organizations (CSOs, Doherty et al., 2014; Misener & Doherty, 2013; Rich & Misener, 2019) and municipal recreation organizations (Llewellyn & Rich, 2023; Oncescu & Fortune, 2022a, 2022b). Although provincial governments and sport organizations are important actors in the institution of sport in Canada, less is known about the impact of policy at the provincial level and how it shapes institutional arrangements and the implementation of policy between levels of governance. In this context, we understand policy as any 'course of action or inaction chosen by public authorities to address a given problem or interrelated set of problems' (Pal, 1992, p. 2). In the study of sport institutions, organizational fields, which can be defined as the complex networks of social relationships in which actors are positioned (Kitchin & Howe, 2013), have received less scholarly attention than other constructs (Roberston et al., 2022). Therefore, within multi-level sport governance frameworks, the role of provincial governments and the agency of policymakers within these organizational fields represent an under-explored element of the policy system. Therefore, in this paper, we consider the role of regional actors and the influence they have on the broader institution of sport. We examine regional policy as a powerful constituent within organizational fields of the Canadian amateur sports system. Therefore, our analysis seeks to understand how political changes (at the regional level) impact the structuration and change of fields related in that region, and how these changes impact the translation of ideas and implementation of policy.

The purpose of this paper is to examine provincial (henceforth referred to as regional) policy and the agency of policymakers, in order to explore their implications for institutions and sport policy implementation in Canada. Specifically, we examine regional policy as a constituent of organizational fields to understand how the actions of regional policymakers impact the structuration and change of fields and implementation of sport policy in the province of Ontario, Canada. In doing so, we provide an exploration of the mechanisms that explain the workings of multi-level sport governance in Canada. The following research questions guide this work: (1) how do changes in regional policy impact the way that organizational fields are structured within multi-level governance structures? and (2) how does regional policy impact sport policy implementation? As organizational fields represent important contextual considerations for understanding policy implementation, our work contributes to the discussion of the relationships between agencies and the institutional structures of amateur sports in Canada.

Literature review and theoretical framework

To frame this study, we review literature related to sport policy and regional development/governance in Canada. Next, we frame our contribution theoretically by examining organizational fields.

Policy and multi-level governance in Canada

In Canada, sport is governed through a federated, multi-level governance system. The federal branch of government (Sport Canada) is responsible for sport and federal sport policy, which is implemented through organizations at the provincial and community level (Parent et al., 2018; Shilbury et al., 2013, 2016). Through Sport Canada, policies and programs are established which guide decisions related to participation in both recreational and elite sports (Rich & Misener, 2019; Thibault & Harvey, 2013). However, these policies are implemented throughout a complex network of organizations including national sport organizations (NSOs), provincial and territorial sport organizations (PTSOs) who are generally organized around one or a small number of sports, and CSOs who deliver a large proportion of sport participation opportunities in Canada. Therefore, there are many actors involved and multiple steps before policy finds its way to the grassroots level. Multi-sport service organizations such as Canadian Sport for Life, Canadian Women in Sport, and the Aboriginal Sport Circle also enact and support government policies, programs, and objectives across sports and organizations (Rich & Misener, 2019). Building on these understandings, we theorize amateur sport in Canada as an institution with clearly defined structures, actors, and fields that can be analyzed.

The *Canadian Sport Policy* (*CSP*, Government of Canada, 2012) was formalized in 2002, with policy renewal processes in 2012 and 2022. This federal policy outlines the direction for Canadian sport and identifies desired outcomes (Thibault & Harvey, 2013). In addition to the networks of NSOs, PTSOs, and CSOs, Sport Canada has entered into bilateral agreements with regional governments to develop programs related to physical activity and sport (Thibault & Harvey, 2013). These agreements are designed around objectives related to increasing sports participation:

1. To support projects that strengthen physical literacy and children and youth participation that are compatible with the first three stages of Sport for Life or programming at comparable stages that exist across jurisdictions.
2. To support projects that provide opportunities for persons from under-represented and/or marginalized populations to actively participate in sports including in roles as athletes, coaches, officials, and volunteer leaders.
3. To strengthen Indigenous Capacity and Leadership for the Provincial/Territorial Aboriginal Sport Bodies (PTASBs).
4. To increase culturally relevant sport programming for Indigenous children and youth at the community level. (Government of Canada, 2021, para 6).

Therefore, while sport and physical activity fall under federal administrative structures, each province and territory has exclusive jurisdiction within its territory over significant aspects of the delivery of sport participation opportunities. Given the influence of provincial and territorial governments and policy on municipalities and their governance, these relationships and formalized agreements are an important element of public policy designed to increase sport participation. Each province and territory therefore has the power to adopt tailored policies and programs, provided they do not contravene the federal government's jurisdiction (Rose, 2006; Thibault & Harvey, 2013). For example, the Government of Ontario supported the development of local sports programs in Indigenous communities with the 2009–2011 *Sport for More* bilateral agreement.

Municipalities also play an important role in delivering sport participation opportunities, which often occurs through facilities and programming in municipal parks and recreation organizations. Indeed, the recreation sector is identified in *CSP* as one of the most prominent stakeholders implicated in the sport system (Canadian Heritage, 2012). Municipalities provide resources such as low-cost infrastructure and subsidies to CSOs (generally private sector organizations) which assist in developing and delivering participation opportunities. These provisions are also supported through policy and funding provided by both Federal and Provincial governments. For example, in 2006, the federal *Recreation Infrastructure Program* and the provincial *Ontario Recreation Program* provided more than $380 million for 758 recreation facility projects in the province of Ontario (Government of Ontario, 2009). Thus, the implementation of sport policy in Canada involves stakeholders at the national, provincial/territorial, and municipal levels. The resulting complex system of multi-level governance requires an interrogation of the relationship and influence of actors at different levels (Nite & Edwards, 2021) to develop a robust understanding of policy implementation.

Scholars have provided thorough historical overviews of sport policy in Canada (Thibault & Harvey, 2013) as well as comparative studies of sport policy between Canada and other nations (Bergsgard et al., 2007; Green & Houlihan, 2005; Green & Oakley, 2001). However, this work is often focused on sport policy at the national level. A more comprehensive understanding of implementation processes can be achieved by examining the complex nexus of factors that influence policymaking and implementation at different levels of governance: institutional theory offers the theoretical tools through which these relations can be understood. For example, Parent et al. (2018) examined how environmental changes (specifically related to updated federal legislation for not-for-profit corporations) impacted governance structures and processes in Canadian NSOs. These changes led to operational practices which emphasized accountability, transparency, and performance outcomes. Comeau (2013) drew from a historical institutionalism perspective to examine the evolution of *CSP* and how past policy decisions continue to impact sport policy formulation. The analysis highlighted that during policy orientation there was a focus on participation and health promotion, which later evolved to the promotion of excellence to foster national unity and finally the emergence of neoliberalism, where the responsibility of participation was placed on the individual (Comeau, 2013). These shifts were informed by changing political ideologies and orientations which underpinned policy development. Collectively, these studies demonstrate the complexity of relationships and influence within multi-level sports governance systems.

Recently, scholars have further highlighted how – despite a rhetoric of sport for all – institutional ideas, beliefs, and arrangements have been detrimental to the pursuit of equal opportunities to participate in sports for equity-deserving groups (Skille, 2011; Tink et al., 2020). These discussions often attribute these trends to tensions associated with neoliberalism – a political ideology that emphasizes the value of free market principles, with core tenets of individuality, efficiency, and accountability (Cureton & Frisby, 2011; Silk & Andrews, 2003). Within a neoliberal framework, administrations aim to govern at a distance by conceiving individuals as autonomous citizens capable of regulating their lifestyle choices to maximize their health and productivity and limit their potential harm to society (Lupton, 2013). In Canada, Oncescu and Fortune (2022a) noted how privatization and neoliberal ideology have impacted practitioners' conceptualizations and administration of recreation services. Drawing from Woolford and Nelund (2013), they elaborated how under neoliberal governmental agendas

> responsibilization is a set of techniques and methods used by the government to cultivate action on the part of individuals and community organizations in the private and non-profit sectors that they take active responsibility in relation to government and society at large (Oncescu & Fortune, 2022b, p. 2).

These techniques place the responsibility of tasks previously associated with the government on local organizations (Fahlén et al., 2015). Scholars have demonstrated that CSOs are increasingly expected to achieve social outcomes, be entrepreneurial, and operate with less support from the government (Bjärsholm & Norberg, 2021; Fahlén et al., 2015; Green & Houlihan, 2006; Oncescu & Fortune, 2022a, 2022b). Therefore, understanding the role of political, social, and economic contexts is an important consideration for an examination of agency, organizational fields, and sport policy implementation.

Regional development and governance systems in Canada

Among industrialized market economies, Canada is one of the most highly regionalized and fragmented. Savoie (2019) claimed that '[g]eography explains virtually everything Canadian, and it is central to understanding the workings of Canadian democracy' (p. 16). The relevance of regional policy and jurisdiction is recognized in the 2012 iteration of the *CSP*, which was conceptualized as a 'road map' and stated that 'each government will determine which of the goals and objectives of the Policy they plan to pursue, taking into account their relevance to jurisdictional mandate and priority' (Government of Canada, 2012, p. 3). Despite this recognition, little academic research has examined regional policy and its implications for sport policy implementation.

Economic and regional development scholars have highlighted the importance of regional differences and the need for flexible public policy structures that emphasize local contexts and encourage regional collaboration (Vodden et al., 2019). In the context of neoliberalism, the decentralization of governments, and skepticism about top–down development models, new ways of thinking about regions and regional development have gained prominence in both theory and practice. In the context of multi-level governance systems, changes in regional development practice are motivated by changing dynamics of power within and between public and private sector actors (Conteh, 2021). Departing from top–down approaches to development, *new regionalism* is espoused by incremental and place-based development approaches as well as thinking about the fluid and emergent nature of how regions are defined to encourage regional collaboration instead of competition (Conteh, 2012; Vodden et al., 2019).

There are clear synergies between the trends in new institutionalism and new regionalism. These shifts recognize shortcomings in top-down approaches and a need to acknowledge the agency of actors at the community or organizational level. These trends also resonate with calls in sports literature for participant-centered and asset-based approaches to sports development (Bates & Hylton, 2021; Misener & Schulenkorf, 2016; Rich, Moore, et al., 2022; Rich, Nicholson, et al., 2022). In this paper, we examine regional policy as a constituent and empirical evidence of an organizational field. To address the dearth of research at the regional level, we explore how regional policy (and the agency of policymakers) influences organizational fields and how changes in regional policy impact policy implementation in the context of multi-level governance.

Organizational fields

Fields can be understood as the arenas or institutional environments in which an actor operates. DiMaggio and Powell (1983) noted that fields 'constitute a recognized area of life: key suppliers, resource and product consumers, regulatory agencies, and other organizations …' (p. 148). Common languages, understandings, and ideologies may also describe the boundaries of an organizational field (Washington & Patterson, 2011). Building on Bourdiuesian Theory, Kitchin and Howe (2013) explained fields as complex networks of social relationships in which actors are positioned. Additionally, Wooten and Hoffman (2017) propose that an organizational field 'is as much about the relationship between the actors as it is about the effect of the field on the actors' (p. 63). These networks frame the way that actors compete or maneuver for resources. Ultimately, fields are richly contextualized spaces where actors engage in a common rule structure and shared normative understandings regarding matters that are consequential for field-level and organizational activities. Fields, therefore, construct the logics that inform actors' activities, as these positions and competitions require logics that underpin what is and isn't valuable as well as acceptable ways of achieving objectives (Kitchin & Howe, 2013). As key components of the field, logics are understood as diverse belief systems that differ fundamentally in their content, ordering principles, and nature of central assumptions (Washington & Patterson, 2011). Existing as both material and symbolic, institutional logics offer formal and informal rules of behavior and interaction, which guide and limit decision-makers in achieving the organization's tasks (Skirstad & Chelladurai, 2011). Institutional logics determine what is acceptable or not acceptable in a field and are considered the frame of reference that helps actors within their respective fields make decisions and act according to these principles, norms, and rules (De Bock et al., 2021). Within the field, actors are carriers of the dominant logics and governance structures (Cousens & Slack, 2005).

As the concept of field involves understanding the extent to which they are institutionally defined (DiMaggio & Powell, 1983), it is important to examine elements of field structuration. Structuration in organizational fields refers to the 'recursive interdependence of social activities and norms' (Scott, 1995, p. 106) continuously being produced and reproduced over time. Sports researchers are beginning to focus on the structuration processes to understand how the structuring of fields contributes to intra- and inter-organizational processes. For example, drawing on Bourdieu's conceptualization of the field, Wright (2009) examined how institutional change and formation occurred in first-class County cricket in England. Bourdieu's concept of field highlights that fields are sites of struggle for capital among relationally positioned actors and are constituted at multiple levels (Wright, 2009). As such, Wright (2009) suggested that first-class County cricket emerged in England as a field of restricted cultural reproduction, through an interplay between societal, organizational, and individual levels of the field. However, findings also suggest that the conception of the organizational field is formed empirically, inviting a reframing of the organizational field, which is dynamic, multi-level, and nuanced. In this research, we consider the organizational field of amateur sport in Ontario, within the broader institution of amateur sport in Canada. While the institution of amateur sport has specific structures, practices, and ideas that govern actions of actors and organizations more broadly, this regional field is bound both geographically and politically and has socially recognizable structures for actors within and outside of sports organizations in the province.

Institutional theorists have conceptualized the organizational field as the 'domain where an organization's actions were structured by the network of relationships within which it was embedded' (Wooten & Hoffman, 2017, p. 56), and the activities producing and reproducing these structures (Robertson et al., 2022). Within sports, studies have examined the interdependence of these social activities and structures and how they relate to institutional change (Cousens & Slack, 2005; Fahlén & Stenling, 2019; Nite & Edwards, 2021; Spaaij et al., 2018). For example, Gerard et al. (2017) examined multi-level institutional change in the International Paralympic Committee and suggested that field-level logics are simultaneously shaped by societal pressures coming from the top (i.e. from society to field) and from the bottom–up (i.e. organizations influencing the broader field). The researchers posit that at the field level, logic gradually moved from a rehabilitation-focused logic to a sport-focused logic resulting from both top–down and bottom–up pressures. They ultimately demonstrated that institutional change processes result from an interplay between the societal, field, and organizational levels. Also examining the nature of field-level change, Cousens and Slack (2005) analyzed changes in four facets of organizational fields over time, specifically: 'communities of actors, their exchange processes, their governance structures, and their beliefs and institutional logics of action' (p. 13). Their analysis demonstrated a shift in dominant logics from embracing sport-specific qualities to stressing the entertainment value of major league sport, resulting from changing governance models brought about by the deregulation of cable television. These researchers acknowledged that the organizational field informed institutional logics and vice versa, which is important for understanding the complex ways change happens in organizational fields.

Actors within an organizational field are exposed to a range of pressures, practices, logics, ideas, and beliefs through their engagements with other actors. Through the process of translation, the meanings associated with organizational practices can change 'as individual field members incorporate these items into their own organization' (Wooten & Hoffman, 2017, p. 67). Field members determine how to adapt an existing organizational practice such that it will hold meaning for their own organization, with the field playing a key role in facilitating this translation process. Robertson et al. (2022) noted that 'translation primarily investigates how ideas travel' (p. 5). This concept explains how organizations can import new institutional elements into their organization, to respond to internal and external pressures (Robertson et al., 2022). For example, organizational elements such as 'Organizational accountability, formalization of structure, focus on goal definition and emphasis on managerialism will impact how organizations respond to internal/external pressures in society while maintaining their own organizational goal(s)' (Krücken & Meier, 2006, p. 248). These organizational elements are important because internal/external pressures (e.g. political ideologies) will challenge these elements (Krücken & Meier, 2006). For example, Skille (2011) examined translation in a Norwegian football club and demonstrated that sports club policy is shaped by internal and external influences (e.g. team/club leader's interests, other sports clubs) and results in translations of ideas from similar football clubs that are viewed as legitimate. Therefore, policies and the translation of new organizational elements are important for maintenance and legitimacy within an organization's field.

In this research, we sought to examine regional policy as a constituent of organizational fields. Within the institution of amateur sport in Canada, we conceptualize the organizational field as an amateur sport in the Province of Ontario, a regional field that is bounded geographically, as well as politically as regional policy has implications for the actors and their operation within the field. Specifically, we sought to examine how political changes and the actions of regional policymakers impact the structuration and change of fields in the province. Therefore, these research questions guided our work: (1) how do changes in regional policy impact the way that organizational fields are structured within multi-level governance structures? and (2) how does regional policy impact sport policy implementation?

Methodology

We utilized an instrumental case study methodology to examine regional policy in the Canadian Province of Ontario. As we understand policy as any course of action or inaction used to address a single or interrelated set of problems (Pal, 1992), we focused on regional policy related to the public management of sport, which can be understood as a set of complex and interrelated (or wicked) problems (Sam, 2009). Case studies are a useful approach to understand a specific phenomenon within a naturalistic context (Baxter & Jack, 2008). Instrumental case studies are employed to 'get insight into the [research] question by studying a particular case' (Stake, 1995, p. 3). That is, the case is instrumental in building an understanding of something else (i.e. a phenomenon) or for building theory. As we were interested in understanding how regional policy (and changes therein) impacts sport policy implementation and the way that organizational fields are structured, we examined regional policy in the Province of Ontario with an instrumental case study.

Data were collected using document analysis. We systematically searched for documents related to the policy and decision-making processes of the Government of Ontario. Targeted searches on each provincial administration were conducted through Google, our Institutional Library, as well as the Archives of Ontario. Search terms included 'Sport', 'Recreation', 'Physical Activity', and 'Sport Policy', and were limited to documents published and pertaining specifically to policy at the provincial level. Additional search terms included the name of each premier (elected head of the provincial government) and year, to help differentiate sport policy and decision-making during different administrative terms (e.g. 2006 AND McGuinty AND Sport). Given that we were interested in the implementation of sport policy, we limited our search to documents published and produced from 1995 onward. Although sport policy was formalized at the federal level in 2002, the Government of Ontario at the time (i.e. the Harris Government) was elected in 1995. Therefore, to capture documents related to the work of this Government, documents were collected pertaining to the 36th Parliament (of Ontario) forward.

The collected documents were organized chronologically for analysis allowing the research team to explore the administrative terms of different premiers (i.e. Harris, McGuinty, Wynne, and Ford), and how policy and ideas were translated based on the structure and actions taken by the provincial governments over time. The search turned up 88 unique documents including policy documents, websites, and publications published between 1996 and 2021. Specifically, these included strategies and action plans, mandate letters for provincial ministers, press releases, academic publications examining provincial policy, as well as websites and policy documents related to provincial ministries and their programs. All data were stored and analyzed using NVIVO data analysis software.

Data analysis was conducted using a critical policy analysis approach (Jedlicka et al., 2022). This analytical approach highlights the institutions, ideas/beliefs, key actors, networks/administrative arrangements, and contexts/key events in policymaking processes. Informed by the literature on institutional theory broadly (Robertson et al., 2022) and organizational fields specifically (Wooten & Hoffman, 2017), we coded data deductively based on the constructs of critical policy analysis (i.e. institutions, ideas/beliefs, key actors, networks/administrative arrangements, and contexts/key events in policymaking processes). Following an initial round of coding, recurring codes associated with these constructs were identified and discussed by the research team collectively. For example, codes associated with ideas/beliefs included *economic growth* and *self-reliant organizations*. Subsequently, initial codes were grouped thematically. For example, codes such as *investing in games* and *hosting events* were grouped as *sport creates tourism*. Codes and thematic groups were then organized into higher-order themes and titled. Finally, the research team discussed these higher-order themes and selected examples from the data which best illustrated the identified themes.

Findings

The results of our critical policy analysis identified two key themes that are implicated in the administrative arrangements as well as the ideas and beliefs (Jedlicka et al., 2022) related to sport in regional policy. These two key themes: *The Changing Role of Sport* and *Accountability and Responsibilization* both illustrate the implications of regional policy and the actions of regional governments on sport policy implementation and the structuration of organizational fields.

The changing role of sport

Sports policy at the federal level has become increasingly centralized and professionalized since the formalization of the *CSP* in 2002. This is evident in the centralization of the National Coaching Certification Program and the implementation of the Long-term Athlete Development Framework.[1] Although provincial governments imported ideas and beliefs from federal sports policy (in many cases using language directly), the location of sport within provincial government administration changed several times in Ontario, and these changes had important implications for how sport was understood within the province. The first theme examines the implications of the changing location of sport within regional government. The theme was constructed from codes such as *enhancing health outcomes, supporting societal well-being,* and *sport enhances the economy*.

Sport was not explicitly recognized in the title of a provincial ministry until 2011. However, prior to this, sport was associated with the roles and responsibilities of various ministries. Sport's contribution to the economy was underscored by all administrations. As highlighted in a press release: 'Building a more active province can directly contribute to positive economic and social outcomes such as increased labor force productivity, improved student achievement and the social strength of individuals and communities' (Government of Ontario, 2013). However, ministerial responsibility for sport had implications for the extent to which this association was emphasized. Prior to 2002, sport was explicitly associated with economic growth and providing value to taxpayers. This was a recurring theme that arose throughout the documents analyzed, in which sport was identified as a tool to enhance economic outcomes or the productive state of the economy:

> Competitive amateur sport stimulates broad-based participation... at all levels and in all regions in Ontario. This results in significant public benefits: To the economy of the province and its communities through a wide variety of associated expenditures by individuals and families (Government of Ontario, 1996, p. 2).

Revenue-generating opportunities were therefore an integral part of sport and largely, sport-related policy was a means for the government to be accountable to the taxpayer.

However, in June 2005, the responsibility of sport was transferred to a newly created provincial Ministry of Health Promotion by Premier Dalton McGuinty (Rose, 2006). This is when more specific sport action plans were introduced such as the *Ontario Sport Action Plan* and the *ACTIVE2010* Strategy, which aimed to achieve enhanced participation, excellence, capacity, and interaction (goals identified in the *CSP*). For example, through *ACTIVE2010*, the government promised an investment of $5 million per year to improve awareness of the benefits of physical activity and motivate people to get active (Government of Ontario, 2004). This funding included a campaign to promote lifelong fitness to adolescents (10–14 years old) and one to educate adults (45–-65 years old) on the benefits of exercise (Government of Ontario, 2004). These action plans guided much of the decision-making, sport strategies, and funding in this period. Although this may appear to be distinct from previous (economic) associations within provincial administration, documents demonstrated that sport, tourism, and health outcomes remained in some ways interrelated. For example, a 2008 press release indicated:

> A successful Pan/Parapan American Games will be a catalyst for new and improved sports and recreation infrastructure for all Ontarians to lead healthier, active lives. These are some of the fundamental reasons the Pan/Parapan American Games bid is so important to our Province (Government of Ontario, 2008, para. 5).

The formalization of the relationship between sport and health resulted in increased funding opportunities (e.g. through the Communities in Action Fund), strategies (e.g. *ACTIVE2010*), and policies (e.g. *Access to Recreation for Ontarians Policy Framework*). With the recognition of the interdependencies of sport and health, government ministries also partnered to create initiatives (e.g. Healthy Kids Panel) to enhance health outcomes generally and specifically to address specific health outcomes (e.g. reducing obesity rates) in Ontario: 'Overweight and obesity are threatening our children's future and the future of our province... If our children are not healthy, then our society will not flourish' (Healthy Kids Panel, 2013, p. 2).

In 2011, the role of sport shifted again when sport was then added to the portfolio of the Ministry of Tourism, Culture, and Sport (Government of Ontario, 2011). The repositioning of sport alongside culture and tourism represents a realignment with economic development priorities. As indicated in a government press release, '[a]ligning tourism, culture and sport will help the ministry take a leading role in enhancing economic growth and business across the province' (Government of Ontario, 2011, para. 2). The responsibility of sport remained with this ministry until 2019, when it was renamed the Ministry of Tourism, Culture, and Sport *Industries* by the Ford Government – further emphasizing how economic development priorities remain implicated in sport-related policy in the province.

Despite these changing administrative arrangements, sport's potential to contribute to the economy was identified throughout the time period studied, regardless of the government in power. In many cases, identifying sport as a value to the taxpayer came up before identifying or discussing other health or social benefits, as highlighted in a press release related to hosting the Pan/Parapan American Games:

> Hosting the Games is part of the McGuinty government's plan to create jobs and strengthen the economy. It will also provide new sport venues for athletes to train and compete at home and recreation centres for Ontario families to lead healthier lives (Government of Ontario, 2012, para. 5).

Importantly, the shifts outlined here are also associated with changes to reporting and accountability measures for sport organizations and ultimately how legitimacy is framed and understood by actors within these networks. The intentions of the Provincial

Government to impact accountability measures are made clear in the mandate letter for the Minister of Tourism, Culture, and Sport:

> As Minister of Tourism, Culture and Sport, you will support festivals and events that build a strong economy and vibrant communities, attract tourists and contribute to job creation. You will continue to measure the contributions of these events and festivals and ensure that all decisions relating to them are supported by sound economic analysis (Government of Ontario, 2014, p. 2).

Considering the association of sport with different sectors (e.g. health and tourism), and the influence this has on funding, resources, and decision-making, it is important to consider how the role of sport is framed and articulated in regional policy. This framing ultimately illustrates how the actions of provincial policymakers dictate the relationships, support, and resources available to sport organizations – which also have implications for the structuration and change of organizational fields.

Accountability and responsibilization

The second theme examines the ideas and beliefs that underpinned changes in regional policy. Specifically, we identified an emphasis on accountability and responsibilization of individuals and organizations by regional actors. This theme was constructed using codes such as *self-reliant organizations, sport as value to the taxpayer,* and *sport enhances productivity.*

Prior to 1996, the province relied on the *National Recreation Statement* and the *Community Recreation Policy Statement* to guide its involvement with sport (Rose, 2006). The *Community Recreation Policy Statement* identified the role of municipalities in recreation and sport delivery: 'Municipalities are creations of the province through the *Municipal Act* and The Ministry of Tourism and *Recreation Act*, they are endowed with the responsibility for the provision of recreation services, programs, and facilities' (Ministry of Tourism and Recreation, 1987, para. 5). Throughout the period studied, the increasing prevalence of neoliberal rhetoric within regional policy also had important implications for the organization of sport. This rhetoric was evident in documents related to the Harris government (1995–2002) and their *Common Sense Revolution* (Sancton, 2000) which saw a proliferation of language related to accountability and the value of sport to the taxpayer (particularly through private sector partnership and tourism development). These beliefs illustrate the desire of the Provincial Government for sports organizations to be self-sufficient, decrease dependence on government funding, and be accountable for public spending. As indicated in the *Ontario Amateur Sport Strategy:*

> Government is prepared to support only those activities which are consistent with its goals and are provided in an effective and efficient manner, representing value to the tax payer. This approach to support will also take into account the responsibilities of other stakeholders and participants. Government is prepared to work together with sport organizations to help them move towards the ultimate goal of self-reliance where the organizations are able to depend on their own resources. (Ministry of Citizenship Culture and Recreation, 1996, p. 2):

The emphasis on accountability continued with subsequent governments. For example, a mandate letter from the Wynne Government to the Minister of Tourism, Culture, and Sport in 2014 (Wynne & Coteau, 2014) stated, 'It is of utmost importance that we lead with responsibility, act with integrity, manage spending wisely and are accountable for every action we take' (p. 3).

Initially, these trends led to a local services realignment which ultimately downloaded many of the responsibilities and costs arising from local services (previously held by the Province) to municipalities without providing extra financial support (Siegel, 2003; Tindal, 2015). As a result, services were drastically reduced. These financial reforms impacted the municipal capacity for delivering a range of services. For example, new funding criteria for eligible sport organizations to receive funding stipulated in the *Strategy for Amateur Sport in Ontario* (Ministry of Citizenship, Culture & Recreation, 1996) identified that, to receive funding from the province, organizations needed to be affiliated with a PSO or NSO and have a minimum number of prescribed registrants. These changes affected unorganized, recreational sport opportunities such as pick-up sport, after-school sport, and drop-in programs. The responsibility to support these organizations was downloaded to municipalities, who through the local services realignment, had limited resources to support new services. With the *Municipal Act, 2001* (legislated in 2003), municipalities were given more scope and autonomy for service provisions, including recreation; however, they had to rely mainly on their tax base and service charges for service delivery (Siegel, 2003). These changes had direct implications for the delivery of grassroots sport and recreation programs and participation opportunities.

Currently, the role of recreation service delivery remains with municipalities. As indicated in the 2018 Financial Information Return (Eidelman et al., 2018), parks and recreation expenditures by municipalities in Ontario were funded 98% through municipal revenues. The remaining 2% was funded through provincial and federal transfer payments. Through these processes, the focus of policy appears to be on increasing accountability, which – in the context of other changes – means the accountability of local (i.e. Municipal) governments. For example, *The Strategy for Amateur Sport in Ontario* (Ministry of Citizenship, Culture & Recreation, 1996) stated: '[t]he Ministry will also be turning its attention to the need for strategic directions in the areas of recreation and active living. Support to provincial recreation organizations will be focused on increasing self-sufficiency for recreation organizations' (p. 3). The diminished role of the provincial government is reflected in their withdrawal of responsibility for the delivery of sport and recreation. The shifting locus of control places the responsibility of sport at the local level, where organizations have varying levels of understanding and capacity to implement programs and initiatives associated with broader policy frameworks. Furthermore, it frames accountability for sport and recreation as an issue for municipal governments.

The policies of the Government of Ontario also promoted accountability by engaging with national sport policy accountability measures. NSOs and PTSOs in Canada are required to adhere to the objectives in the *Sport Funding and Accountability Framework* (*SFAF*, Canadian Heritage, 1995), as a requirement to receive funding from the federal government (Comeau, 2013). The *SFAF* provides a detailed framework for decisions concerning the funding of sports and outlines strict guidelines emphasizing accountability and efficiency. Cost-sharing agreements, transfer payments, and disbursements to the provinces follow similar principles (Comeau, 2013; Rose, 2006). These principles were also translated into policy at the regional level. As a founding framework for Ontario's investment in sport, the *Amateur Sport Strategy for Ontario* (Ministry of Citizenship, Culture & Recreation, 1996, pp. 7–8) stipulated that 'Ontario's support to amateur sport organizations will be tied to results, with support for administrative components tied directly to strategic activities' and 'As a condition of funding, PSOs will be expected to prepare business plans and to negotiate performance contracts with the ministry'. The assessment stages of the *SFAF* included evidence-based evaluation, the use of performance indicators to assess performance in the areas of high performance and sport participation, and accountability agreements with each organization which are tied to the goals of the federal government (Thibault & Harvey, 2013, p. 110). Both policies, therefore, identify qualification requirements related to results and/or performance indicators.

Notably, a strategic plan for the Sport Alliance of Ontario (a provincial sport development organization that lost funding and declared bankruptcy in 2015) indicated one of the main goals of the organization was to 'develop and provide quality programs and maximize business services' through the objective of 'operating efficient, well-run services that meet or exceed the needs/expectations of members' (Sport Alliance of Ontario, 2010, p. 2). Importantly, these parameters for funding eligibility and strategic planning goals indicated that accountability and efficiency were key components for monitoring, evaluation, and reporting structures. Sports organizations were at risk of losing or not obtaining funding if they did not adhere to these criteria. For example, a representative from the province commented that they pulled funding from the Sport Alliance of Ontario citing:

> a review found 'financial, governance and operational issues that were affecting its ability to adequately deliver our sport programs. In response to the report's findings and as part of our work to modernize and improve Ontario's sport system, a decision was made not to renew our funding agreement' (Gillespie, 2015, p. 1).

Although the documents examined indicated the requirement to measure financial accountability and efficiency, discussions of measuring participation numbers, health benefits, or other non-financial outcomes were notably absent. As such, ideas and beliefs underpinning the notion of accountability appear to be firmly grounded in economics rather than principals of health promotion or political will to increase the quantity or quality of sport participation opportunities in the province.

Discussion and conclusion

Our analysis highlights the role of regional policy in shaping organizational fields and policy implementation. In doing so, we examine the agency of regional actors and their implications for institutional elements of amateur sport. Although provincial governments in Ontario took leadership from federal levels on the language and content of their sport-related policy, the ideas and beliefs that underpinned their actions and the administrative arrangements that shaped their implementation had important implications for how policy was implemented within the province. Below, we discuss the implications of our findings for institutional theory and policy implementation in sports.

Regional policy and the structuration of organizational fields

Collectively, our work contributes important nuances to understanding the structuration and change of organizational fields by focusing on regional policy and its implications for sport policy implementation. As highlighted above, fields are the complex networks of social relationships in which actors are positioned to construct the logics that inform organizational activities and practices (Kitchin & Howe, 2013). Our analysis shows regional policymakers influence the ideas, beliefs, and administrative arrangements that underpin sport in regional policy, which has implications for the ways that actors compete and maneuver for resources within the province. Although *CSP* was influential in shaping structures and nature of relationships between sport organizations (Barnes et al., 2007), regional policy was influential in determining the resources (e.g. funding, facilities, etc.) available to actors who fall directly under their jurisdiction (e.g. Municipalities, sport development organizations). Policy documents provided insight into the logics that underpin changes in these organizational fields and how the actions of regional policymakers have implications for the broader institution of sport. As such, regional policy provided empirical evidence that can be helpful in mapping out the structure of and changes in organizational fields. Further, given that regional governments are regularly changing, examining regional policy offers important insights into how different actors (particularly those outside of sports organizations) exercise agency and ultimately political power that influence changes to organizational fields in multi-level governance frameworks.

Our analysis highlighted that, even in successive governments formed by the same political party (e.g. the McGuinty and Wynne governments), sport can be positioned differently – which suggests that tensions related to competing logics (Skirstad & Chelladurai, 2011; Stenling & Fahlén, 2009) are not only present for actors in sport organizations. Although leadership and broader policy orientation are established at the federal level, analysis of policy that is subject to an assessment of 'relevance to jurisdictional mandate and priority' (Government of Canada, 2012, p. 3) must consider the role of regional government and the agency of regional policymakers in implementation processes. This may be particularly relevant when the political orientations of governments at the federal and regional levels do not align. We suggest that regional governments are powerful actors within organizational fields and sport institutions more broadly and require further investigation by sport scholars. While flexible public policy systems are important for highly regionalized policy contexts (Vodden et al., 2019), we must continue to analyze the complex power dynamics that are inherent in multi-level governance systems (Conteh, 2021) to better understand the ways that actors exercise agency in structuring organizational fields. In this context, our analysis provides a foundation for further exploration into how institutional elements shape policy implementation processes – and ultimately outcomes – in different regions within multi-level governance.

Regional policy and sport policy implementation

Although investments in sport are legitimatized as investments in health and social outcomes at the federal level, as a result of actions taken by regional policymakers, this framing did not appear to have a durable presence within regional policy. Rather, after a short time associated with the Ministry of Health Promotion (following the formalization of the *CSP*), sport was re-coupled with tourism and associated more clearly with an economic development imperative. While sport's various contributions (i.e. to health, tourism, economic development, and community development) were recognized by all governments, the administrative arrangements surrounding sport served to frame which of these contributions were important and what practices were perceived as legitimate for sport actors and organizations in the province. In this way, our findings demonstrate the ways that ideas, beliefs, and administrative arrangements intersect with organizational fields and the logics that underpin them. These findings have implications for theoretical understandings of the structuration and change of organizational fields (Kitchin & Howe, 2013; Robertson et al., 2022) as well as methodological approaches to sports policy analysis (Jedlicka et al., 2022) and policy implementation in sport institutions (Fahlén, 2017; Skille, 2008; Stenling, 2014).

Our findings also illustrate the role of regional policy in the translation of ideas between organizations in multi-level governance frameworks (Robertson et al., 2022). Despite the many potential contributions of sport, a regional policy that dictated measures of funding and accountability framed how organizations needed to operate to remain viable and legitimate. As such, regional policy represents a powerful constituent of organizational fields that is likely to impact the practices of sport organizations and the way that policy is implemented as it moves through the sport system. In this way, we contribute to the small body of literature that has examined the influence of regional-level actors in Canadian amateur sport (Edwards et al., 2009) as well as the nature of the relationships between actors at different levels of multi-level governance frameworks.

The ideas and beliefs underscoring regional policy also had important implications for sport policy implementation. The simultaneous downloading of responsibility to municipal governments and moves to increase accountability within sport and recreation organizations effectively diminished the role of provincial governments in sport. Rather, an increase in focus on economic development and self-sufficiency of organizations emerged within regional policy, as this is aligned with the broader orientation of successive government visions for sport. The findings of our work contribute to the literature which has explored the roles of accountability (Fahlén, 2017) and commercialization of community sport (Stenling & Fahlén, 2009). Further, these findings highlight the role of regional governments in perpetuating neoliberal rhetoric that has been widely critiqued in the context of sport and recreation organizations in Canada (Cureton & Frisby, 2011; Oncescu & Fortune, 2022a, 2022b; Tink et al., 2020). Our analysis points to changes across a range of policy contexts (e.g. the local service realignment) and the implications they have for CSOs in Ontario. As such, regional policy and the agency of regional policymakers appear to be an important consideration for understanding how sport policy is implemented in Canada and within multi-level governance frameworks.

Our findings suggest a need for continued work to understand how changing political ideologies and actions at the regional level are key to understanding effective ways to craft and implement sports policy within complex power relationships inherent in the structures of multi-level governance frameworks. Therefore, our work contributes a theoretical understanding of how organizational fields are structured and changed and how regional policy impacts institutional elements and sports policy implementation processes. Importantly, our work contributes an understanding of the linkages between actors at different levels within multi-level governance frameworks. In conclusion, we offer reflections on the limitations of this study and possible directions for future research.

Our analysis provided exploratory insights into the role of regional policy in multi-level sport governance in one region (Ontario). Future research should interrogate policy in multiple regions to understand convergences and divergences of policy orientations and outcomes. These comparative analyses will provide more nuance to the discussions we have initiated here, as well as insights into best practices for policy makers. Future analyses may interrogate a range of external factors at the regional level that shape the agency of actors involved in sport policy implementation. For example, demographic changes associated with (ex)urbanization, migration, and economic restructuring may have implications for the way that regional governments understand sport and craft policy related to it. Highly regionalized contexts may provide the opportunity to examine the role of regional culture and local context in sport institutions and policy implementation. These future lines of inquiry may provide a robust understanding of the factors shaping organizational fields, their role in policy implementation, and how their influence(s) may vary across regions. Finally, the insights available from data collected through policy documents is limited. Future research should examine the agency of regional policymakers (and other regional-level actors) through methods that account for and critically examine their experiences (e.g. interviews and/or observations).

Note

1. These programs were notable outcomes of the 2002 Canadian Sport Policy objectives related to enhancing capacity within the sport system and interaction between sport stakeholders. They represented centralized frameworks that were established to apply to all sports.

Disclosure statement

No potential conflict of interest was reported by the author(s).

Funding

This work was supported by Social Sciences and Humanities Research Council of Canada [grant number 430-2021-00177].

References

Barnes, M., Cousens, L., & MacLean, J. (2007). From silos to synergies: A network perspective of the Canadian sport system. *International Journal of Sport Management and Marketing, 2*(5/6), 555–571. https://doi.org/10.1504/IJSMM.2007.013967

Bates, D., & Hylton, K. (2021). Asset-based community sport development: Putting community first. *Managing Sport and Leisure, 26*(1-2), 133–144. https://doi.org/10.1080/23750472.2020.1822754

Baxter, P., & Jack, S. (2008). Qualitative case study methodology: Study design and implementation for novice researchers. *The Qualitative Report, 13*(4), 544–559.

Bergsgard, N. A., Houlihan, B., Manset, P., Nødland, S. I., & Fommetvedt, H. (2007). *Sport policy: A comparative analysis of stability and change*. Routledge.

Bjärsholm, D., & Norberg, J. R. (2021). Swedish Sport Policy in an Era of Neoliberalism: An Expression of Social Entrepreneurship. *Frontiers in Sports and Active Living, 3*, 715310.

Canadian Heritage. (1995). *Sport funding accountability framework*. https://www.canada.ca/en/canadian-heritage/services/funding/sport-support/accountability-framework.html

Canadian Heritage. (2012). *The Canadian sport policy 2012*.

Comeau, G. S. (2013). The evolution of Canadian sport policy. *International Journal of Sport Policy and Politics, 5*(1), 73–93. https://doi.org/10.1080/19406940.2012.694368

Conteh, C. (2012). Public management in an age of complexity: Regional economic development in Canada. *International Journal of Public Sector Management, 25*(607), 464–472. https://doi.org/10.1108/09513551211260649

Conteh, C. (2021). Strategic adaptation of city-regions in federal systems: Comparing Canada and the United States. *Territory, Politics, Governance, 9*(1), 56–75. https://doi.org/10.1080/21622671.2019.1617772

Cousens, L., & Slack, T. (2005). Field-level change: The case of North American Major League professional sport. *Journal of Sport Management, 19*(1), 13–42. https://doi.org/10.1123/jsm.19.1.13

Cureton, K., & Frisby, W. (2011). Staff perspectives on how social liberal and neo-liberal values influence the implementation of leisure access policy. *International Journal of Sport Policy and Politics, 3*(1), 3–22. https://doi.org/10.1080/19406940.2010.544665

De Bock, T., Scheerder, J., Theeboom, M., De Clerck, T., Constandt, B., & Willem, A. (2021). Sport-for-all policies in sport federations: An institutional theory perspective. *European Sport Management Quarterly*, 1–23.

DiMaggio, P. J., & Powell, W. W. (1983). The iron cage revisited: Institutional isomorphism and collective rationality in organizational fields. *American Sociological Review, 48*(2), 147–160. https://doi.org/10.2307/2095101

Doherty, A., Misener, K., & Cuskelly, G. (2014). Toward a multidimensional framework of capacity in community sport clubs. *Nonprofit and Voluntary Sector Quarterly, 43*(2), 124S–142S. https://doi.org/10.1177/0899764013509892

Edwards, J. R., Mason, D. S., & Washington, M. (2009). Institutional pressures, government funding and provincial sport organisations. *International Journal of Sport Management and Marketing, 6*(2), 128–149. https://doi.org/10.1504/IJSMM.2009.028798

Eidelman, G., Hachard, T., & Slack, E. (2018). *In it together: Clarifying provincial-municipal responsibilities in Ontario.* Ontario 360. https://on360.ca/policy-papers/in-it-together-clarifying-provincial-municipal-responsibilities-in-ontario/#:~:text=In%20It%20Together%3A%20Clarifying%20Provincial-Municipal%20Responsibilities%20in%20Ontario,In%20It%20Together%3A%20Clarifying-Provincial-Municipal%20Responsibilities%20in%20Ontario

Fahlén, J. (2017). The trust-mistrust dynamic in the public governance of sport: Exploring the legitimacy of performance measurement systems through end-users' perceptions. *International Journal of Sport Policy and Politics, 9*(4), 707–722. https://doi.org/10.1080/19406940.2017.1348965

Fahlén, J., Eliasson, I., & Wickman, K. (2015). Resisting self-regulation: An analysis of sport policy programme making and implementation in Sweden. *International Journal of Sport Policy and Politics, 7*(3), 391–406. https://doi.org/10.1080/19406940.2014.925954

Fahlén, J., & Stenling, C. (2019). (Re) conceptualizing institutional change in sport management contexts: The unintended consequences of sport organizations' everyday organizational life. *European Sport Management Quarterly, 19*(2), 265–285. https://doi.org/10.1080/16184742.2018.1516795

Gérard, S., Legg, D., & Zintz, T. (2017). Multi-level analysis of institutional formation and change: The case of the Paralympic movement. *Sport, Business and Management, 7*(5), 515–541. https://doi.org/10.1108/SBM-10-2016-0068

Gillespie, K. (2015, April 8). Ontario Sport Alliance loses funds, heading for bankruptcy. *The Toronto Star.* https://www.thestar.com/news/gta/panamgames/2015/04/08/ontario-sport-alliance-loses-funding-headed-for-bankruptcy.html

Government of Canada. (2012). *Canadian sport policy.* https://sirc.ca/wp-content/uploads/files/content/docs/Document/csp2012_en.pdf

Government of Canada. (2021). *Sport participation.* Retrieved October 12, 2021, from https://www.canada.ca/en/canadian-heritage/services/sport-participation.html

Government of Ontario. (1996). *A strategy for amateur sport in Ontario.*

Government of Ontario. (2004, October 25). *New physical activity strategy means healthier Ontarians: ACTIVE2010 creates more fitness opportunities, helps get Ontarians moving.* [Press release]. https://news.ontario.ca/en/release/4443/new-physical-activity-strategy-means-healthier-ontarians#

Government of Ontario. (2008, October 2). *October 2008: Pan Am bid officially launched* [Press release]. https://news.ontario.ca/en/release/1220/october-2008-pan-am-bid-officially-launched

Government of Ontario. (2009, June 26). *Recreation facilities score funding for upgrades* [Press release]. https://news.ontario.ca/en/backgrounder/7569/recreation-facilities-score-funding-for-upgrades

Government of Ontario. (2011, December 7). *Ontario adds sport to tourism and culture* [Press release]. https://news.ontario.ca/en/release/19759/ontario-adds-sport-to-tourism-and-culture

Government of Ontario. (2012, July 10). *2015 games boosting Ontario's economy: McGuinty Government creating new jobs and sport facilities for communities* [Press release]. https://news.ontario.ca/en/release/21517/2015-games-boosting-ontarios-economy

Government of Ontario. (2013, January 15). *Government of Ontario providing more opportunities for sport and recreation: McGuinty government building strong, fit communities* [Press release]. https://news.ontario.ca/en/release/23076/ontario-providing-more-opportunities-for-sport-and-recreation

Government of Ontario. (2014). 2014 *Mandate letter: Tourism, culture and sport: Premier's instructions to the Minister on priorities for the year 2014*. https://dr6j45jk9xcmk.cloudfront.net/documents/3685/mandate-letter-2014-mtcs.pdf

Green, M., & Houlihan, B. (2004). Advocacy coalitions and elite sport policy change in Canada and the United Kingdom. *International Review for the Sociology of Sport, 39*(4), 387–403. https://doi.org/10.1177/1012690204049066

Green, M., & Houlihan, B. (2006). Governmentality, modernization, and the "disciplining" of national sporting organizations: Athletics in Australia and the United Kingdom. *Sociology of Sport Journal, 23*(1), 47–71. https://doi.org/10.1123/ssj.23.1.47

Green, M., & Oakley, B. (2001). Elite sport development systems and playing to win: Uniformity and diversity in international approaches. *Leisure Studies, 20*(4), 247–267. https://doi.org/10.1080/02614360110103598

Healthy Kids Panel. (2013). *No time to wait: The healthy kids strategy*. https://www.health.gov.on.ca/en/common/ministry/publications/reports/healthy_kids/healthy_kids.pdf

Jedlicka, S. R., Harris, S., & Houlihan, B. (2022). Policy analysis in sport management" revisited: A critique and discussion. *Journal of Sport Management, 36*(6), 521–533. https://doi.org/10.1123/jsm.2021-0193

Kitchin, P. J., & Howe, P. D. (2013). How can the social theory of Pierre Bourdieu assist sport management research? *Sport Management Review, 16*(2), 123–134. https://doi.org/10.1016/j.smr.2012.09.003

Krücken, G., & Meier, F. (2006). Turning the university into an organizational actor. In G. S. Drori, J. W. Meyer, & H. Hwang (Eds.), *Globalization and organization: World society and organizational change* (pp. 241–257). Oxford University Press.

Llewellyn, J., & Rich, K. A. (2023). Youth development in municipal recreation policy: A case study of Ontario, Canada. *International Journal of Sport Policy and Politics*, online first.

Lupton, D. (2013). *Risk* (2nd ed.). Routledge.

Ministry of Citizenship, Culture & Recreation. (1996). *Strategy for amateur sport in Ontario*.

Ministry of Tourism and Recreation. (1987). *A community recreation policy statement*.

Misener, K., & Doherty, A. (2013). Understanding capacity through the processes and outcomes of interorganizational relationships in nonprofit community sport organizations. *Sport Management Review, 16*(2), 135–147. https://doi.org/10.1016/j.smr.2012.07.003

Misener, L., & Schulenkorf, N. (2016). Rethinking the social value of sport events through an asset-based community development (ABCD) perspective. *Journal of Sport Management, 30*(3), 329–340. https://doi.org/10.1123/jsm.2015-0203

Nite, C., & Edwards, J. (2021). From isomorphism to institutional work: Advancing institutional theory in sport management research. *Sport Management Review, 24*(5), 815–838. https://doi.org/10.1080/14413523.2021.1896845

Oncescu, J., & Fortune, M. (2022a). Neoliberalism's influence on recreation access provisions: Municipal recreation practitioners' perspectives. *Journal of Leisure Research*, 1–20. Advance Online Publication. https://doi.org/10.1080/00222216.2022.2044942

Oncescu, J., & Fortune, M. (2022b). Keeping citizens living with low incomes at arm's length away: The responsibilization of municipal recreation access provisions. *Leisure/Loisir*, 1–23. https://doi.org/10.1080/14927713.2022.2032806

Pal, L. (1992). *Beyond policy analysis: Public issue management in turbulent times*. Thompson.

Parent, M. M., Naraine, M. L., & Hoye, R. (2018). A new era for governance structures and processes in Canadian national sport organizations. *Journal of Sport Management*, 32(6), 555–566. https://doi.org/10.1123/jsm.2018-0037

Rich, K., & Misener, L. (2019). Playing on the periphery: Troubling sport policy, systemic exclusion and the role of sport in rural Canada. *Sport in Society*, 22(6), 1005–1024. https://doi.org/10.1080/17430437.2019.1565387

Rich, K. A., Moore, E., Boggs, J., & Pegoraro, A. (2022). Mapping women's community sport participation to inform sport development initiatives: A case study of Row Ontario. *Frontiers in Sports and Active Living*, 129, https://doi.org/10.3389/fspor.2022.836525

Rich, K. A., Nicholson, M., Randle, E., Staley, K., O'Halloran, P., Belski, R., Kappelides, P., & Donaldson, A. (2022). Participant-Centered sport development: A case study using the leisure constraints of women in regional communities. *Leisure Sciences*, 44(3), 323–342. https://doi.org/10.1080/01490400.2018.1553124

Robertson, J., Dowling, M., Washington, M., Leopkey, B., Ellis, D. L., & Smith, L. (2022). Institutional theory in sport: A scoping review. *Journal of Sport Management*, 36(5), 459–472. https://doi.org/10.1123/jsm.2021-0179

Rose, M. (2006). *Sport policy and multi-level governance: A case study of Ontario and Quebec* [Unpublished masters thesis]. University of Ottawa.

Sam, M. P. (2009). The public management of sport: Wicked problems, challenges and dilemmas. *Public Management Review*, 11(4), 499–514. https://doi.org/10.1080/14719030902989565

Sancton, A. (2000). Amalgamations, service realignment and property taxes: Did the Harris Government have a plan for Ontario's municipalities? *Canadian Journal of Regional Science*, 23(1), 135–156.

Savoie, D. J. (2019). *Democracy in Canada: The disintegration of our institutions*. McGill-Queen's Press-MQUP.

Scott, W. R. (1995). *Institutions and organizations*. SAGE.

Shilbury, D., Ferkins, L., & Smythe, L. (2013). Sport governance encounters: Insights from lived experiences. *Sport Management Review*, 16(3), 349–363. https://doi.org/10.1016/j.smr.2012.12.001

Shilbury, D., O'Boyle, I., & Ferkins, L. (2016). Towards a research agenda in collaborative sport governance. *Sport Management Review*, 19(5), 479–491. https://doi.org/10.1016/j.smr.2016.04.004

Siegel, D. (2003). Recent changes in provincial – municipal relations in Ontario: A new era or a missed opportunity?. In R. Young & C. Leuprecht (Eds.), *Municipal-federal-provincial relations in Canada* (pp. 181–197). McGill-Queens University Press.

Silk, M. L., & Andrews, D. L. (2012). *Sport and neoliberalism: Politics, consumption, and culture*. Temple University Press.

Skille, E. Å. (2008). Understanding sport clubs as sport policy implementers: A theoretical framework for the analysis of the implementation of central sport policy through local and voluntary sport organizations. *International Review for the Sociology of Sport*, 43(2), 181–200. https://doi.org/10.1177/1012690208096035

Skille, E. Å. (2011). Sport for all in scandinavia: Sport policy and participation in Norway, Sweden and Denmark. *International Journal of Sport Policy and Politics*, 3(3), 327–339. https://doi.org/10.1080/19406940.2011.596153

Skirstad, B., & Chelladurai, P. (2011). For 'love'and money: A sports club's innovative response to multiple logics. *Journal of Sport Management*, 25(4), 339–353. https://doi.org/10.1123/jsm.25.4.339

Spaaij, R., Magee, J., Farquharson, K., Gorman, S., Jeanes, R., Lusher, D., & Storr, R. (2018). Diversity work in community sport organizations: Commitment, resistance and institutional change. *International Review for the Sociology of Sport, 53*(3), 278–295. https://doi.org/10.1177/1012690216654296

Sport Alliance of Ontario. (2010). *Strategic plan 2010–2013.*

Stake, R. E. (1995). *The art of case study research.* SAGE.

Stenling, C. (2014). Sport programme implementation as translation and organizational identity construction: The implementation of drive-in sport in Swedish sports as an illustration. *International Journal of Sport Policy and Politics, 6*(1), 55–69. https://doi.org/10.1080/19406940.2013.766900

Stenling, C., & Fahlén, J. (2009). The order of logics in Swedish sport–feeding the hungry beast of result orientation and commercialization. *European Journal for Sport and Society, 6*(2), 121–134. https://doi.org/10.1080/16138171.2009.11687833

Thibault, L., & Babiak, K. (2005). Organizational changes in Canada's sport system: Toward an athlete-centred approach. *European Sport Management Quarterly, 5*(2), 105–132. https://doi.org/10.1080/16184740500188623

Thibault, L., & Harvey, J. (2013). *Sport policy in Canada.* University of Ottawa Press/Les Presses de, l'Université, d'Ottawa.

Tindal, R. (2015). *Unit 1: Introduction to local government: Municipal administration program.* Association of Municipal Clerks and Treasurers Ontario.

Tink, L. N., Peers, D., Nykiforuk, C. I. J., & Kingsley, B. C. (2020). Moving beyond ideology: Contemporary recreation and the neoliberal discourses of new public health. *Leisure Studies, 39*(6), 767–781. https://doi.org/10.1080/02614367.2020.1778772

Vodden, K., Douglas, D. J., Markey, S., & Minnes, S., & Reimer, B. (Ed.). (2019). *The theory, practice and potential of regional development: The case of Canada.* Routledge.

Washington, M., & Patterson, K. D. (2011). Hostile takeover or joint venture: Connections between institutional theory and sport management research. *Sport Management Review, 14*(1), 1–12. https://doi.org/10.1016/j.smr.2010.06.003

Woolford, A., & Nelund, A. (2013). The responsibilities of the poor: Performing neoliberal citizenship within the bureaucratic field. *Social Service Review, 87*(2), 292–318. https://doi.org/10.1086/671072

Wooten, M., & Hoffman, A. (2017). Organizational fields: Past, present and future. In R. Greenwood, C. Oliver, T. B. Lawrence, & R. E. Meyer (Eds.), *The SAGE handbook of organizational institutionalism* (pp. 55–74). SAGE Publications.

Wright, A. L. (2009). Domination in organizational fields: It's just not cricket. *Organization, 16*(6), 855–885. https://doi.org/10.1177/1350508409337582

Wynne, K., & Coteau, M. (2014). *Mandate letter: Tourism, Culture and Sport Premier's instructions to the Minister on priorities for the year 2014.* Premier of Ontario.

Integrating emotions into legitimacy work: an institutional work perspective on new sport emergence

Jingxuan Zheng and Daniel S. Mason

ABSTRACT
Research Question: The purpose of this study was to explore the role emotions play in new sport emergence.
Research Methods: A qualitative case study of Mixed Martial Arts (MMA) was undertaken, with content analysis employed to identify emergent themes from an archival database of newspaper articles.
Results and Findings: Negative emotions were institutionalized into the discourse surrounding early MMA that hindered its legitimation; in order to legitimize the sport, discursive institutional work was undertaken by pro-MMA stakeholders to address existing negative emotions, and create positive new ones.
Implications: Emotions play a crucial role in new sport emergence; therefore, institutional work aiming at legitimizing a new sport on cognitive grounds alone might be inadequate for the successful emergence of a new sport, without the specific emotion-focused institutional work to disrupt existing negative emotions, and create new positive emotions for the new sport.

Legitimacy work is an example of institutional work (Nite & Edwards, 2021) which aims at creating, maintaining, or disrupting institutions (Lawrence & Suddaby, 2006); therefore, the institutional work perspective is often implicated in theories explaining new category emergence given the decisive role legitimacy work plays in this process (Helms & Patterson, 2014; Krzeminska et al., 2021). However, despite recent advancements integrating emotions into institutional work studies (Fan & Zietsma, 2017; Mair et al., 2012; Moisander et al., 2016), most extant research studying new category emergence is still cognitively grounded (Hiatt & Park, 2022; Younger & Fisher, 2020), neglecting the role emotions play in (de)legitimizing a new category (Zietsma et al., 2019). In this study, we argue that cognitive factors alone cannot adequately explain the emergence of new market categories, given that emotions can often cloud cognitive judgements and hence hinder or precipitate the legitimation process of new market categories.

In this study we adopt a sociological approach to emotions (Voronov & Vince, 2012; Voronov & Weber, 2016; Zietsma et al., 2019), and define *emotions* as 'one's personal expression of what one is feeling in a given moment, an expression that is structured by social convention, by culture' (Gould Deborah, 2009, p. 20). At the macro level, emotions are collective, relational, and intersubjective (Zietsma et al., 2019), and can enable institutional creation work (Farny et al., 2019). The purpose of this study is to explore the role emotions play in (de)legitimizing a nascent market category, by conducting a qualitative case study of the emergence of Mixed Martial Arts (MMA) as a new sport. In doing so, we describe the function of emotions in the evolutionary course of MMA's emergence, and how pro-MMA stakeholders engaged in discursive institutional work to legitimize MMA.

We chose MMA as the focal case for two reasons: first, MMA is arguably the most successful story of new sport emergence over the past three decades – from combat tournaments banned in almost every state in the US, MMA emerged as one of the most popular, fastest growing sports in the world (Bishop et al., 2013; Smart, 2022; Stan, 2019). Yet its early savage imagery threatened its legitimacy as a sport (Andreasson & Johansson, 2019; Jennings, 2021; Thomas & Thomas, 2018; Williams, 2018). Second, it is evident that emotions played a crucial role in the emergence of MMA, to the extent that cognitive judgements may have been skewed by strong emotions (Ball & Dixon, 2011; Bishop et al., 2013; Lim et al., 2010). In this study, we use news articles as our main source of data, and argue that stakeholders not only observe and evaluate, but also directly participate in the construction of the discursive institution of a new market category (Alvarez et al., 2015; Berthod et al., 2018; Galvagno & Dalli, 2014).

Successful emergence of a new market category relies on the establishment of its legitimacy in its nascent stage (Lee et al., 2018; Navis & Glynn, 2010). MMA's legitimation occurred amid a decade-long regulatory and legal battle (Jennings, 2021; Williams, 2018). MMA was delegitimized and stigmatized in its early stages due to its brutal and violent nature (Helms & Patterson, 2014). Therefore, corresponding institutional work was carried out to regulate the sport and address the stigma since 2001 (Helms & Patterson, 2014). By engaging in production work, safety work, and rule work, MMA successfully reduced the stigma and obtained further legitimacy as a participatory sport activity in the eyes of martial arts practitioners, gym participants, and even politicians (Helms & Patterson, 2014). However, the status of MMA as a legitimate professional sport was continuously questioned. This was due to an ongoing ban on hosting professional MMA fights across the US (Williams, 2018) – even though MMA had already been heavily regulated and institutionalized as a sport (Jennings, 2021; Williams, 2018) – as well as the emergence of scientific evidence suggesting MMA to be a safer sport than other combat (e.g. boxing) or even contact (e.g. football) sports (McClain et al., 2014; Sánchez García & Malcolm, 2010; Slowey et al., 2012). This prevailed in numerous states before MMA was fully legalized in the US in 2016 (Williams, 2018).

Extending the work of Helms and Patterson (2014), we argue that emotions played a crucial role in the ongoing view of the sport as extremely dangerous and violent where cognitive evidence suggested this was changing. To address the significant role of emotions in the emergence of MMA, institutional work was employed by pro-MMA stakeholders to influence these emotions, in order to precipitate MMA's legalization and legitimation. Before we go on to review the relevant literature, we would like to define some key concepts first. *Institutions* are broadly defined as 'more-or-less, taken-for-granted repetitive social behavior that is underpinned by normative systems and cognitive understandings that give meaning to social exchange and thus enable self-reproducing social order' (Greenwood et al., 2008, pp. 4–5). *Categories* can be perceived as particular types of institutions, 'providing taken-for-granted boundaries within which actors, action and objects need to fit in order to gain legitimacy' (Greenwood et al., 2017, p. 15). Furthermore, in this study we considered legitimacy to be an ongoing dynamic process – legitimation – rather than a static outcome (Suddaby et al., 2017). Legitimation is defined as the 'process by which cultural accounts from a larger social framework in which a social entity is nested are construed to explain and support the existence of that social entity' (Berger et al., 1998, p. 380). Therefore, our focus was not on empirically investigating whether MMA had achieved an ultimate state of legitimacy or not, but rather on the legitimation process itself and the impact of emotions on said process. This definition of legitimation shows its close linkage to new category formation since 'social entities are nested within social systems at different levels, the legitimation of a single entity requires legitimacy work not only at the organizational level, but also at the level of the category' (Suddaby et al., 2017, p. 461).

This study contributes to the institutional work literature as well as research on new category emergence. For the new category emergence research, emotions play a significant role to hamper or facilitate new category emergence, to the extent that stakeholders' cognitive judgements might be heavily influenced. For the institutional work literature, this study examines how emotions can be specifically addressed and shaped through divergent institutional work during new category emergence.

Theoretical background

New category emergence is an important yet understudied topic in organizational theory research (Durand & Boulongne, 2017; Kennedy & Fiss, 2013). One specific type of institutional work is crucial to new category emergence – legitimacy work (Nite & Nauright, 2020) – 'considering that legitimacy is the desired end state of efforts towards institutionalization, efforts to create, maintain, and disrupt or change institutions are all aimed at establishing the legitimacy of institutions' (Nite & Edwards, 2021, p. 827)

The concept of institutional work, which was defined as 'the purposive action of individuals and organizations aimed at creating, maintaining and disrupting institutions' (Lawrence & Suddaby, 2006, p. 215), was developed under the broad *agentic turn* of institutional theory (Abdelnour et al., 2017) that challenges the structural determinism of neo-institutionalism. Institutional work research focused on *embedded agency* (Battilana & D'Aunno, 2009; Lok & Willmott, 2019), where 'thoughts and action are constrained by institutions are nevertheless able to work to affect those institutions' (Zietsma & Lawrence, 2010, p. 189). In contrast to the structuralist perspective of neo institutionalism, the institutional work perspective bridges the macro and micro components of institution by embedding it in the daily practices of change agents (Hampel et al., 2017), and attributes institutional change to a wide array of causes such as changes in external institutional environments, institutional entrepreneurship, or changes in daily practices (Micelotta et al., 2017).

Departing from the *cognitive turn* (DiMaggio & Powell, 1983) of institutional research that viewed 'people as cognitive "carriers" of taken-for-granted institutional "schemas" or "scripts"' (Lok et al., 2017, p. 591), scholars have started to pay greater attention to the development of institutional theory's micro foundations and the pivotal role emotions play in maintaining, creating, and disrupting institutions (Lawrence & Suddaby, 2006). Thus, integrating emotions into institutional work research is important given that cognitive factors alone are sometimes insufficient to explain institutional creation, maintenance, and disruption (Voronov & Vince, 2012). For example, Voronov and Weber (2016) contributed to literature examining the micro foundations of institutions by revealing the role of individual and structural emotions in conditioning and fermenting institutional stability and change. Toubiana and Zietsma (2017) showed that disruptive events can lead to the violation of expectations, causing emotional turmoil salient enough to destabilize the institution 'through the emotion-laden influence activities of shaming and shunning' (p. 922). In conclusion, institutional work research began to examine how emotions were mobilized to facilitate institutional reproduction and change from a strategic perspective (Fan & Zietsma, 2017; Mair et al., 2012), but leaving how emotions can be manipulated through institutional work understudied (for exceptions, see Moisander et al., 2016).

(Negative) emotions and institutions

Although individual-level psychological emotions might be volatile, a sociological approach to emotions suggests that emotions are structured socially and relationally by cultural conventions and norms – 'emotions are often collectively produced in interactions, socially contagious, and easily amplified' (Zietsma et al., 2019, p. 2). In this study, we propose that emotions can not only animate and complement cognitive institutions (Zietsma et al., 2019), but can also influence cognitive decision-making to the extent that institutional maintenance or change might be accomplished through emotion-focused institutional work (Zietsma & Toubiana, 2018). Additionally, the negativity bias (Baumeister et al., 2001; Rozin & Royzman, 2001) suggests that human beings have the propensity to be more strongly influenced by negative emotions than positives ones (Vaish et al., 2008), especially with strong stimuli such as stigma (Haack et al., 2014). This results in negative emotions being more contagious and convincing, and hence more easily disseminated widely and ingrained in peoples' minds than positive ones (Etter et al., 2019)

However, little research has explored emotions' role in new category emergence driven by legitimacy work since 'the category literature has deep cognitive roots and unsurprisingly has not engaged deeply with emotions' (Zietsma et al., 2019, p. 52). Our research interest was to study negative emotions' influence on cognitive legitimacy assessments of the new category, rather than pinpointing specific emotions. Therefore, we adopted a model of emotions that views emotions as a dimensional spectrum rather than discrete categories advocated by the discrete model of emotions (Harmon-Jones et al., 2017; Sreeja & Mahalakshmi, 2017). The dimensional model of emotions suggests that emotions can exist on a continuum, with various degrees of intensity, valence (positive or negative), and other dimensions. Therefore in this study, we focused specifically on the valence dimension of emotions (positive and negative emotions) (Barrett, 2006; Bowen et al., 2018; Haack et al., 2014; Rasmussen & Berntsen, 2009).

The institutional work (legitimacy work) in this study particularly refers to discursive institutional work, which is 'based on the understanding that institutions are largely constituted through language, and that consequently efforts to sustain and disrupt institutions typically involve discourse' (Goodrick et al., 2020, p. 735). Discursive techniques such as framing and rhetoric contribute significantly to the creation, maintenance, and disruption of institutions (Goodrick et al., 2020). News articles constitute a valuable source to study discursive institutional work and social evaluation of divergent stakeholders given that the mass media provide a common place for journalists, politicians, entrepreneurs, and other important stakeholders to engage in ongoing conversations and negotiations regarding the construction of social reality (Deephouse, 2000; Starr, 2021). Therefore, in this study, discursive institutional work was examined through analyzing newspaper articles which reflect the aggregation of discourse and narratives derived from multiple stakeholders to stigmatize or legitimize MMA. More specifically, pro-MMA stakeholders such as journalists, MMA promoters, MMA practitioners and enthusiasts or even sports and culture study scholars engaged in discursive institutional work for the purpose of legitimizing MMA as a sport.

Method

Research context

Modern Mixed Martial Arts (MMA) was first introduced to North America by the Gracie family from Brazil who sought to promote and popularize grappling fighting techniques called Brazilian Jiu-Jitsu (BJJ) (Jennings, 2021; Souza-Junior et al., 2015; Whiting, 2009). The first MMA event in North America, the Ultimate Fighting Championship (UFC) 1, was held in Denver, Colorado in 1993 (Gentry, 2011). The extremely violent, no holds barred nature of early MMA brought promoters instant financial success (Gentry, 2011). However, the brutality of early MMA also incurred widespread criticism from the public and politicians, with U.S. Senator John McCain being the most notable example (Snowden, 2008). As a result, the sport of MMA was at one time banned in most parts of the United States (Gentry, 2011; Helms & Patterson, 2014).

Starting in 2001, new UFC management began to create rules and introduce weight classes, rounds and time limits to the sport, in order to make MMA more palatable to mainstream audiences (Gentry, 2011; Gullo, 2013). With the Ultimate Fighter reality TV show (first airing in 2005) gaining popularity, MMA gradually became a mainstream sport in North America and globally (Parfitt, 2010). However, MMA did not gain its full regulatory approval across the US until 2016, when New York became the last state in the US to legalize MMA (Gentry, 2011; Gullo, 2013; Jennings, 2021; Williams, 2018). Today, the sport of MMA is heavily regulated under the supervision of state athletic commissions and directed by the Unified Rules, which stipulate the fundamental regulations and norms of MMA (Gentry, 2011).

Data collection

First, we undertook a qualitative content analysis of the evolutionary history of MMA. Qualitative content analysis is defined as 'a research method for the subjective interpretation of the content of text data through the systematic classification process of coding and identifying themes or patterns' (Hsieh & Shannon, 2005, p. 1278). In order to accomplish this, two main sources of data were collected. The first included books (Gentry, 2011; Gullo, 2013; Jennings, 2021; Snowden, 2008; Whiting, 2009; Williams, 2018) and peer-reviewed journal articles (Andreasson & Johansson, 2019; Brett, 2017; Helms &

Patterson, 2014; Smith, 2010) written on the history of MMA and the UFC. Collectively, these materials provided an overview of the historical evolution of MMA as a newly emerged sport, which we used to develop a three-phased timeline.

Our second source of data was newspaper articles relating to MMA or the UFC from five major US dailies – *The New York Times, Washington Post, Los Angeles Times, Chicago Tribune*, and the *Wall Street Journal*. The reason that we focused on these five particular newspaper outlets is twofold. First, we were interested in the historical development of MMA, and the US provided an ideal context for studying the legitimation process with regard to a stigmatized and emerging sport (Gentry, 2011; Smith, 2010); second, these five US major dailies are the five most respected US national and regional newspapers (US Major Dailies, n.d.) that likely played an impactful role in (de)legitimizing MMA. We collected these newspaper articles from ProQuest – All News & Newspaper Databases by searching key words 'MMA', 'Mixed Martial Arts', 'UFC' and 'Ultimate Fighting Championship'. We used the latter two given that the UFC was and still is the most dominant promoter of MMA, and the major driving force of the development of MMA as a new sport (Gentry, 2011; Smith, 2010). All the data were systematically collected from 1993 – when the first MMA tournament was held – to 2016, when New York became the last state in the US to legalize MMA.

Data analysis

After collecting relevant articles, we carefully read books documenting the developmental history of MMA from 1993–2016, which can be categorized into three phases: 1). Sport formation and stigmatization (1993–2000), marked by the financial success of the early UFC tournaments and the no holds barred nature and violence that characterized early competitions; 2). Gravitating towards rules and regulations, gradually transitioning toward a more accepted sport (2001–2004), marked by the creation and enactment of the Unified Rules of MMA, and the acquisition of the UFC by Zuffa; and 3). Transformation from a niche sport to mainstream sport, and achieving the state of complete legalization across the US (2005–2016), marked by the debut of the reality TV show the *Ultimate Fighter*, legalization of the sport in New York (the last state to legalize MMA), and the acquisition of the UFC by WME/IMG for 4 billion USD in the largest financial transaction for any sport organization in history (Rovell & Okamoto, 2016).

Newspaper articles were first screened to exclude advertisements, articles mentioning MMA or the UFC but not as the main subject of the story, and reports or analysis of MMA fights, narrowing the initial data set down to 438 newspaper articles. Our interest was in understanding (1). How emotions affected MMA legitimation (2) how emotions were addressed through institutional work. To answer the first question, we tried to uncover the influence of negative emotions on cognitive evaluations of MMA legitimation. We chose to focus on negative emotions in particular since a negativity bias of negative affect is most effective to strong stimuli and a positivity bias of positive affect is most effective to weak stimuli pertaining to emotions' influence on legitimacy assessment (Haack et al., 2014). We considered the core stigma of MMA (Helms & Patterson, 2014) being violent and dangerous as a strong stimulus inducing predominantly negative emotions that took precedence over positive emotions in influencing MMA legitimation.

We first examined the newspaper articles looking for text related to MMA legitimation – including both text segments endorsing MMA and those criticizing MMA. We extracted 3,778 excerpts of such text. We then categorized the excerpts according to the three developmental phases that we identified above. Next we reviewed all the excerpts closely, looking for key words and expressions that were highly emotive (Toubiana & Zietsma, 2017). Krippendorff (2004) suggested that 'meanings do not reside in words but rather in how words relate to their linguistic environment and capture social actors' focus of attention' (p. 290); therefore, we identified emotions not only by key words such as 'fascinating' 'riveting' or 'disgusting' 'repugnant', but also by the tone of expression. We coded the emotions into two categories – positive and negative emotions. We then looked for the transformation in the relative proportion of negative VS positive emotions in different stages (See Figure 1). In stage 1, approximately 87% of the excerpts were negative emotion laden (466 out of 537). Stage 2 witnessed a decrease in the percentage of negative excerpts to around 63% (228 out of 362). In stage three, the proportion featuring negative emotions further dropped to approximately 44% (1266 out of 2879). The fluctuation in the sheer amount of negative and positive emotions can be primarily attributed to the divergent volumes of data collected over different stages. For example, stage one and two respectively spanned 8 and 4 years, whereas stage 3 constituted 12 years of data. In addition, in stage 1 MMA was still a relatively niche topic featuring fewer mainstream reports than in stage 3 when MMA had become a heatedly discussed media topic. Therefore, we consider percentage change to be a better indication of the dynamics of negative and positive emotions.

Next, we extracted all the excerpts associated with negative emotions, coding them according to the cognitive reasoning of endorsing or opposing MMA legitimation embedded in the excerpt. We identified three major categories: positive cognitive legitimacy assessments (endorsements), negative cognitive legitimacy assessments (oppositions), and excerpts appealing to no cognitive reasoning (pure affective excerpts). We then identified three patterns of interrelationship between negative emotions and cognitive legitimacy evaluation that we coded respectively *enhancement*, *diminution*, and

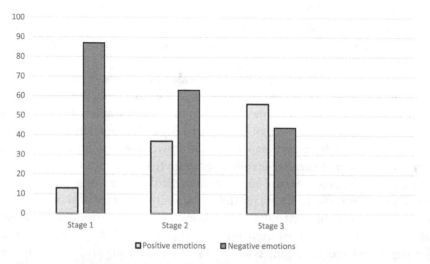

Figure 1. Changes in percentage of positive/negative emotions over different stages.

replacement – excerpts were coded *enhancement* when negative emotions added onto negative cognitive assessments; excerpts were coded *diminution* when negative emotions detracted from positive cognitive assessments; while excerpts were coded *replacement* when negative emotions became the primary source of legitimacy assessment. Examples are later presented in the results section.

Then, we returned to the original newspaper articles by highlighting all the emotive texts we identified from the first step. We obtained five second-order codes or themes (Gioia et al., 2013; Pratt, 2009) by coding the newspaper articles revolving around two central issues: 1) The downturn in the percentage of negative emotions; and 2) The relative growth of positive emotions. We uncovered that negative emotions were addressed (and reduced) through a) alleviation (coded as *emotional pacification*); b) undermining the legitimacy of the negative emotions (*emotional disruption*); and c) replacing negative emotions with positive ones (*emotional substitution*). Positive emotions were generated (and augmented) through a) evoking instantaneous emotional response (coded *emotional stimulation*); b) nurturing long term emotional attachment (*emotional cultivation*); and c) replacing negative emotions with positive ones (*emotional substitution*). We want to clarify that emotion-focused institutional work can be cognition-based. In other words, insofar as we deemed that the text segment was beneficial to alleviate negative emotions, whether it was emotion-based or reason-based, we coded them *emotional pacification*; the rest of the coding followed the same rule.

Furthermore, we noticed similarities between some of our coding and those of Helms and Patterson (2014)'s. We acknowledge that although all our coding were yielded independently, Helms and Patterson (2014) may have influenced the use of some of our terms. With that being said, we also want to point out the different denotations and connotations of our codes from theirs despite ostensible similarities. For instance, *enticement* was a strategy of luring stakeholders to participate in the sport of MMA through cognitive temptation such as monetary rewards or special treatment (Helms & Patterson, 2014), while *emotional stimulation/cultivation* in our study aims to bring stakeholders closer to MMA emotionally through either short-term provocation or long-term bonding. Additionally, *pacification* in Helms and Patterson (2014) was specifically about 'adopting norms, rules, and requests to gain the acceptance of powerful actors' (p. 1476), whereas *emotional pacification* in our study refers to any means through which negative emotions relating to MMA were appeased.

We then coded all the above mentioned second order themes to identity two aggregate dimensions (Gioia et al., 2013; Pratt, 2009): *addressing existing negative emotions*; and *creating new positive emotions*. Finally, we applied these two aggregate dimensions to the original newspaper data to see if any new codes and themes emerged. We went back and forth between the original data, our first order concepts, second order themes, and aggregate dimensions multiple times in order to reach theoretical saturation (Gioia et al., 2013; Glaser & Strauss, 2017).

Results and discussion

Emotions played a pivotal role in the historical course of MMA stigmatization and legitimation, influencing cognitive evaluation to an extent that has not been theorized in prior literature. In this section, we show how persistent negative emotions affect cognitive legitimation of MMA at both the individual level as well as the collective level, and develop five propositions that reflect this discussion. We then identify the institutional work pro-MMA stakeholders employed to offset negative emotions' influence, including addressing existing emotions and creating new positive emotions.

(Negative) emotions and MMA legitimation

Successful emergence of a new market category hinges on its legitimation (Lee et al., 2018; Navis & Glynn, 2010). MMA's legitimation revolved around the transformation of the sport from a nascent ruleless violent spectacle to a highly regulated professional sport with stringent safety measures (Jennings, 2021; Williams, 2018). Before 2001, early MMA was delegitimized and stigmatized due to its scary (aesthetic-based stigma), no holds barred (lawlessness-based stigma), and brutal (harm-based stigma) nature (Helms & Patterson, 2014). Consequently, early MMA coverage was rife with negative emotions in its formative stages (see Figure 1). In this stage, newspaper articles featured negative cognitive assessments of MMA from divergent stakeholders as well. For instance, in the infamous letter 'Extreme Dangers' that Senator John McCain sent to *New York Times*, he wrote:

> I have not had the displeasure of viewing extreme fighting, but I have seen segments of its reprehensible predecessor, the 'Ultimate Fighting Championship.' These repugnant events should be banned because they pose unacceptable risks of severe injury to the participants, and for their glorification of cruelty. (McCain, 1995)

Here the cognitive reasoning for banning the Ultimate Fighting Championship was because it posed risks of injury to the participants; however, terms 'repugnant,' 'reprehensible,' 'unacceptable,' and 'severe' implied emotions such as disgust and worry. All these negative emotions might resonate with, and be infectious among, like-minded stakeholders (Etter et al., 2019; Giorgi, 2017), making banning the sport more urgent and imperative. Negative emotions derived from, and grounded in, negative cognitive judgements, made stakeholders not only cognitively but also emotionally invested in de-legitimizing and stigmatizing MMA (Voronov & Vince, 2012), hence accelerating the institutionalization and diffusion of such process (Etter et al., 2019). This leads to the following proposition:

> Proposition 1: Negative emotions may magnify the effects of stakeholders' negative cognitive judgements on new category legitimation

Despite progress made toward legitimation of MMA as a participation sport since 2001 (Helms & Patterson, 2014), the legitimacy of MMA as a professional sport was continuously questioned due to its illegal status in states that continued to ban MMA as a spectator sport (Williams, 2018). An odd dynamic even emerged where MMA was banned as a professional spectator sport, but legal as a participation sport in states such as New York (Vilensky, 2016). As Ball and Dixon (2011) and Bishop et al. (2013) argued, these bans were largely emotion-based rather than evidence based. However, early negative emotions were so entrenched in the discourse regarding MMA that it exerted lasting influence on cognitive judgements:

> The 'banned in New York' stigma was long an impediment to the kind of respectability the sport has craved. It kept the UFC from holding events in what it calls the largest and most

important media market in the world. It also prevented major companies from signing sponsorship deals. 'A couple have said, "MMA has become a profitable mainstream sport,"' said Lawrence Epstein, a UFC lawyer. 'But our compliance guys are scaring us, asking us how can we sponsor a company that is illegal in New York.' (Segal, 2016)

In this example, as important resource providers of professional sports, the potential sponsors of the UFC acknowledged the mainstream sport status of MMA, yet still refused to sponsor the UFC. This was despite the fact that they cognitively understood the commercial value of the UFC even without being legalized in New York. The negativity bias suggests that, with strong stimuli (such as stigma), cognitive judgements are more susceptible to be clouded and skewed by negative emotions than positives ones (Etter et al., 2019; Haack et al., 2014; Ito & Cacioppo, 2000; Kahneman & Tversky, 2019), leading to 'tarnished' positive cognitive evaluations. Thus:

Proposition 2: Negative emotions may diminish the effects of stakeholders' positive cognitive judgements on new category legitimation.

Furthermore, we noticed that negative emotions can sometimes substitute for cognitive judgements completely as the underlying mechanism for stakeholders to reach their legitimation decisions:

For three hours on Tuesday afternoon, Albany legislators touched on everything from 'fight clubs' to violent videogames, to slavery, to traumatic brain injuries. The topics of discussion incorporated even pornography. 'You have two nearly naked, hot men trying to dominate each other,' said Assemblyman Daniel O'Donnell, a Manhattan Democrat who is openly gay. 'That's gay porn with a different ending.' (Kanno-Youngs & Orden, 2016)

This newspaper excerpt shows that one of the Albany legislators, Assemblyman Daniel O'Donnell, tried to base the decision of (not) legalizing MMA on the similarity between MMA and pornography, which bears little cognitive weight; yet stands as a manifestation of his strong negative affect towards MMA, as well as his employment of said negative emotions as the primary source of his decision making. This supports institutional theorists who have argued that emotions can sometimes act as an alterative means to cognitive evaluation through which social approval decisions are reached (Giorgi, 2017; Haack et al., 2014). Therefore:

Proposition 3: Negative emotions may substitute for stakeholders' rational, cognitive judgements when assessing new category legitimation.

Negative emotions influence cognitive legitimacy evaluations at the individual level by magnifying the effects of negative cognitive judgements, diminishing the effects of positive cognitive judgements, and/or replacing cognitive judgements entirely. At the collective level, evaluations that appeal to emotions influence collective legitimacy judgements by being more persuasive and contagious than cognitive reasoning 'even if factually inaccurate or incomplete' (Etter et al., 2019, p. 40), thus impacting a larger scale of population. Due to the negativity bias (Baumeister et al., 2001; Rozin & Royzman, 2001), negative emotions might be even more contagious and persuasive at the collective level (Etter et al., 2019; Haack et al., 2014). Therefore, we argue that negative emotions will have a harmful effect on collective legitimacy evaluations by not only influencing more people, but also making more individual evaluations appeal to affect rather than cognitive reasoning. Thus:

Proposition 4: Negative emotions may have a destructive influence on collective legitimacy evaluations greater than the sum of its effects at the individual level, thus hindering new category legitimation.

Nevertheless, collective legitimation decisions are not simply the sum of each individual's legitimation judgements but depend on individual evaluators' prediction of others' appraisals as well: '"It's a terrible, nasty, violent sport," said Michael Benedetto, a Democrat from the Bronx, explaining his highly ambivalent "yes" vote on the Assembly floor. "But it is everywhere else"' (Segal, 2016). In this example, despite Benedetto's strong negative emotional view of MMA (a terrible, nasty, violent sport), he still voted 'yes' (albeit ambivalently) to legalizing MMA due to the fact that 'it is everywhere else', indicating consensus under social pressure (Bitektine & Haack, 2015; Haack et al., 2021). When evaluators perceive their own evaluations to be a minority opinion, or when they anticipate the futility of their assessments to make any desired change, they tend to suppress their deviant judgements, whether cognitively or emotionally oriented, and conform to a consensus judgement of the majority (Bitektine & Haack, 2015; Haack et al., 2021; Noelle-Neumann & Petersen, 2004). Therefore,

Proposition 5: The effects of negative emotions on new category legitimation may be moderated by suppressed individual legitimacy evaluations.

Institutional work and (negative) emotions

The above analysis revealed that negative emotions have significant influence on stakeholders' cognitive legitimacy judgements and might hinder new category emergence. These negative emotions need to be addressed specifically through emotion-focused institutional work given that 'appeals to cognition or the pursuit of social approval cannot fulfill the audience's emotional needs' (Giorgi, 2017, p. 725). Helms and Patterson (2014) showed implicitly how negative emotions associated with MMA's early stigma such as fear and worry were dampened by MMA practitioners through institutional work so that MMA as a participatory sport activity was further legitimized. In this study, we explicitly identified two forms of discursive institutional work employed by pro-MMA stakeholders that specifically addressed and manipulated negative emotions, contributing to the ongoing legitimation of MMA as a banned professional sport: *addressing existing negative emotions* and *creating new positive emotions* (see Table 1).

Addressing existing negative emotions

Pro-MMA stakeholders engaged in emotional *disruption*, emotional *substitution*, and emotional *pacification*, to address pre-existing negative emotions associated with MMA. Emotional disruption was used to undermine the legitimacy and validity of negative emotions, while emotional substitution was employed to replace negative emotions with positive ones. In the early stages of sport formation and stigmatization (1993–2000), emotional substitution was complemented with emotional pacification and emotional disruption to address existing negative emotions associated with MMA. For instance, stakeholders such as journalists tried to educate and explain exactly what Ultimate Fighting and MMA was, by highlighting the exciting parts of the sport. Given that those exciting elements were also the ones drawing criticism and triggering negative emotions, by

Table 1. Data structure.

First order concepts	Second order themes	Aggregate dimensions
* It's the same people who want to censor TV, who want to get boxing outlawed, who think hockey is too violent * The reason people don't like it is because it's not politically correct * But he left the Assembly last year after a conviction on corruption charges. Then, a UFC triumph was only a matter of time.	emotional disruption: undermining the legitimacy and validity of negative emotions	addressing existing negative emotions
* The sinister-looking chain-link is actually a safety measure, preventing fighters from tumbling into the crowd * There are no moves allowed anymore that aren't allowed in other sports * My research on televised mixed martial arts has yet to support the notion that it is any more harmful to adult viewers than such prime – time fictional programs * The Nevada Athletic Commission has sanctioned the once-banned sport now that it has agreed to certain rules	emotional pacification: negative emotion alleviation	
* To the average person, 'extreme fighting' may sound unappetizing, but to the promoters, it sounds like a cash register jingling * It is to boxing what snowboarding is to skiing: faster and more extreme and more dangerous * 'This is a fair street fight,' he said. 'When I was a kid, we had street fights, but this reminds me of a street fight that's fair.' * The lack of rules as a means of rendering the fights more real, with less interference from referees and outside forces	emotional substitution: replacing negative emotions with positive ones	addressing existing negative emotions and creating new positive emotions
* If boxing is like shooting a 9-millimeter, imagine adding in a bazooka and machine gun. With the more weapons we have, the interest will come around * U.F.C. isn't a sport, it's war * The energy, the excitement – you have never been to a sporting event like this	emotional stimulation: triggering immediate emotional responses	creating new positive emotions
* The amount of technique that is involved in the sport is incredible * This is literally a chess match in motion * I wanted to know every move and countermove. It was so strategic, like playing a game of chess * If anybody got to meet some of us outside the ring, they'd see I treat people with respect. I consider myself a nice guy * You're going to find the true meaning of, of … Of life * Even a casual observer at the fight would have a hard time missing the through line of personal betterment and triumph over adversity reflected in the apparel in and out of the cage * I love to fight, and I enjoy it in there. It's like I'm free, and I'm really expending myself and competing and trying to be victorious in the sport	emotional cultivation: fostering long-term positive emotional bonds	

accentuating the attributes of the sport in a positive tone, the exact same content could be framed to elicit positive emotions such as excitement or joy, hence supplanting negative emotions with positive ones: 'this was action, oh man, it hammered you right in the gut–like a violent playground brawl. It was primitive, more elemental than any other sport in how it measured a man' (Ferrell, 1997).

In addition to emotional substitution, emotional pacification was also carried out in stage one of MMA emergence to mitigate the magnitude of negative emotions felt by the public and other stakeholders of early MMA. In particular, emotional pacification conveyed the notion that MMA was a very safe sport.:

> He [UFC executive, David Isaacs] argued that the sinister-looking chain-link is actually a safety measure, preventing fighters from tumbling into the crowd. His fighters are safer than boxers because unpadded fists get hurt before they can strike enough blows to cause brain injuries. No one has ever been seriously injured. (Ferrell, 1997)

Furthermore, emotional disruption work, which aimed at weakening the legitimacy and credibility of the sources of negative emotions, was also employed to target negative emotions. As explained by fighter Steve Jennum: 'It's the same people who want to censor TV, who want to get boxing outlawed, who think hockey is too violent' (Brooke, 1995).

In the second stage of MMA emergence, rules and regulations were created aiming at transforming the sport into a fully regulated, state-governed professional sport (2001–2004). During this phase, emotional *pacification* was employed to combat ongoing negative emotions that demonized MMA. Specifically, pro-MMA stakeholders emphasized the all-around safeness of the sport to address fighters' as well as the general public's concerns about the danger of the sport: 'Fighters would undergo neurological exams and be tested for diseases, including HIV and hepatitis B and C... State-sanctioned doctors would be on hand for every fight... There are no moves allowed anymore that aren't allowed in other sports' (Pasco & Allison, 2003).

Additionally, emotional *pacification* work in this phase also aimed to engender faith in regulators as well as appeal to the general public by emphasizing the advancement of the sport itself. As shown in an interview with new UFC owner, Lorenzo Fertitta:

> Back in 1993... fighters were mismatched, rules lax and events organized under a scary 'last man standing' rubric. But he says that in the past three years he has been trying to make the sport legitimate, working with state commissions to institute regulations. (Stephen, 2003)

In the third phase of the sport's emergence and development – where MMA transitioned to a mainstream sport and had become more legitimized, emotional *disruption* work was complemented by emotional pacification to overcome institutionalized negative emotions. Emotional disruption not only questioned the validity of the negative emotions, but also attempted to dismantle the underlying foundation of the negative affect towards MMA by exposing the lack of trustworthiness of the sources said feelings stemmed from. For example, Assembly Speaker Sheldon Silver, a Democrat who refused to pass the bill to legalize MMA for years, was depicted as 'expelled from the legislature after being found guilty of honest-services fraud, extortion and money laundering in Manhattan federal court' (Orden, 2016); while Deborah Glick, a Manhattan assemblywoman, Mr. Silver's successor, was said to continue the ban on MMA not to protect the citizens, but for her own political interests (Vilensky, 2016).

Furthermore, emotional *pacification* was perpetuated to appease the negative emotions and build faith for the sport's safeness not only from the athletes' perspective, but also from a cultural perspective regarding the negative impact of violence on the general public:

> Although children should certainly be shielded from the spectacle of cage fighting, my [Nancy Cheever, an assistant professor of communications at Cal State Dominguez Hills] research on televised mixed martial arts has yet to support the notion that it is any more harmful to adult viewers than such prime – time fictional programs as 'Law & Order' or 'CSI.' (Cheever, 2007)

Creating new positive emotions

Pro-MMA stakeholders employed emotional *stimulation*, emotional *cultivation*, and emotional *substitution* to create new positive emotions for the legitimation of MMA. Emotional stimulation aimed at triggering immediate emotional responses, while emotional cultivation was utilized to foster long-term positive emotional bonds with the sport. By replacing negative emotions with positive ones, emotional substitution not only reduced existing negative emotions, but also created new positive emotions. In stage one of sport formation and stigmatization (1993–2000), emotional stimulation was not only exploited to evoke excitement towards the fights themselves, but also to expose what an exciting business opportunity MMA had become. Emotional *substitution* was employed to create new positive emotions as well. For example, similar excitement was engendered by leveraging emotional substitution work, with the emphasis on replacing negative emotions with positive ones: 'to the average person, "extreme fighting" may sound unappetizing, but to the promoters, it sounds like a cash register jingling' ("Packaging and selling savagery," 1995).

The second developmental phase of MMA, as the sport gradually transitioned into a more legitimized professional sport (2001–2004), was marked by the employment of emotional cultivation work, where stakeholders attempted to establish a long-term emotional bond with MMA: '"I love to fight, and I enjoy it in there. It's like I'm free, and I'm really expending myself and competing and trying to be victorious in the sport," said Bonnar, 27, a Munster, Ind.-born personal trainer at Gold Coast Multiplex in Chicago' (Johnson, 2004). In the meantime, emotional cultivation was perpetuated to keep endowing higher order values and meanings on the sport: 'As to the cage's cool factor, [MMA fighter, Mark] Smith agreed. "You're going to find the true meaning of, of … " 'Of life," [Fight promoter, Darrin] Dotson interjected. "Yeah," said Smith … "Of what your body's capable of"' (Verini, 2002).

Additionally, emotional *stimulation* was carried out to create more excitement about MMA:

> A volatile mix of wrestling, kick-boxing and martial arts popularly known as 'ultimate fighting,' the sport is a hit with crowds in Las Vegas and on pay-per-view television. A match in Las Vegas in November drew more than 13,000 spectators – including celebrities such as actor Vin Diesel and former Dodger Steve Garvey. (Pasco & Allison, 2003)

In the last phase of MMA emergence, where it achieved legalization across the US (2005–2016), emotional *cultivation* was implemented to not only accentuate the culture and history of the sport, but also emphasize the multidimensionality of the sport – as a spectator sport, as an athletic training discipline, as a fitness program, as film and TV series content, as game themes, even as tools for military recruitment, or therapeutic regimen – to resonate with a broader array of stakeholders emotionally: '... those who spoke to RedEye said training in MMA techniques boosts their fitness and confidence levels, as well as their self-defense skills. Fans of the sport say the workouts also give them insight into the TV bouts they watch' (Hines, 2008). In addition to the employment of emotional cultivation to build multi-dimensional emotional values of the sport, it was also exercised to highlight the transcendent meaning of practising MMA beyond the boundary of the sport itself, such as personal betterment over adversity, self discipline, or responsibility to take care of family:

> Even a casual observer at the fight would have a hard time missing the through line of personal betterment and triumph over adversity reflected in the apparel in and out of the cage. This is a sport, after all, with stars that have been drawn from the ranks of math teachers, security guards and veterans. (Tschorn, 2008)

In summation, addressing existing negative emotions and creating new positive ones worked synergistically to mitigate the impact of negative emotions on MMA emergence in the sense that emotional disruption and pacification might facilitate emotional stimulation and emotional cultivation, and vice versa. Likewise, emotional substitution both reduced existing negative emotions and induced positive new ones.

Conclusions

In this study, we found that negative emotions had a significant impact on new market category legitimation; therefore, in order to facilitate new category legitimation, institutional work of emotional disruption, substitution, and pacification were employed by pro-MMA stakeholders to address existing negative emotions, while emotional stimulation, cultivation and substitution were utilized to create new positive emotions. This study contributes to institutional work research, especially those focused on studying the interrelationship between institutional work and emotions. Most existing emotion-related institutional work research considered emotions as the fuel and catalyst of institutional change, rather than the objective of institutional work and the consequence of institutional change. Even with the structuralist perspective of emotions in institutional theory, emotions were still perceived as supportive and complementary to the cognitive components of institutional orders (Lok et al., 2017; Zietsma & Toubiana, 2018). This study demonstrated that emotions are an integral part of institutions that might be more resistant to change than cognitive reasoning, hence influencing institutional creation, maintenance and change. Future scholarly attention should focus on investigating not only how emotions animate institutions and make them more 'live' and relatable (Friedland, 2018), but also how emotions are integral constituents of institutions that need to be worked on (instead of worked with) to drive either institutional maintenance or change (Zietsma & Toubiana, 2018).

In addition, we argue that *embedded agency* (Battilana & D'Aunno, 2009; Lok & Willmott, 2019) is rooted in both cognitive and emotional components of institutions; emotions are not only complementary and supportive of the cognitive ones, but might oftentimes take precedence due to their direct and heuristic nature (Haack et al.,

2014), to the extent that *evaluators* (e.g. medical professionals, legislators, journalists), who are supposed to harness their stock of expertise to make deliberate and rational social approval assessments, might let emotions cloud their cognitive judgment (Giorgi, 2017; Haack et al., 2014). Therefore, institutional work that narrowly focuses on maintaining or changing institutionalized rules, norms, or protocols which speak to the cognitive facet of institutions might not be sufficient to facilitate institutional maintenance or change, necessitating the employment of emotion-specific institutional work. We explored in this study particular emotion-focused institutional work aiming at invalidating negative emotions and building positive ones; future research should investigate types of emotion-focused institutional work that dismantle incumbent positive emotions in order to expedite institutional change. Moreover, further studies are needed to examine under what circumstances *evaluators*, who are supposed to appraise institutions based on reason and logic, switch to emotions as a primary source of judgement making.

This study also contributes to category research by incorporating emotions into new category emergence. Category research was dominated by strong cognitive traditions (Zietsma et al., 2019) with limited attention paid to emotions' crucial role in delaying or precipitating new category emergence. This study revealed the role emotions play in the course of new category emergence; more specifically, how negative emotions might be an impediment to new category emergence. Nonetheless, some market categories are inherently more controversial than others (Durand & Vergne, 2015; Hudson, 2008), such as the pornography industry (Trouble, 2016; Voss, 2019) or the arms industry (Vergne, 2012); yet they have survived widespread stigmatization by obtaining some form of legitimacy (Ashforth, 2019; Helms et al., 2019). Likewise, new category legitimation might not necessitate the eradication of negative emotions. As a matter of fact, our empirical data indicated that even in the final stage before MMA was fully legalized in the US, there still existed a considerable proportion of negative emotions concerning MMA (roughly 56–44 positive–negative). The insight gained from this observation is that negative emotions might not always be a threat to new category legitimation, especially when a certain level of legitimacy is established to suppress deviant judgements derived from negative emotions. Future research is needed to explore the 'tipping point' or the threshold (Fisher et al., 2016; Soublière & Gehman, 2020; Zimmerman & Zeitz, 2002) across which negative emotions will no longer be a significant impediment to new market category emergence. In conclusion, emotions play a crucial role in new category emergence, which calls for emotion-specific institutional work to establish legitimacy necessary for the nascent category.

Disclosure statement

No potential conflict of interest was reported by the author(s).

References

Abdelnour, S., Hasselbladh, H., & Kallinikos, J. (2017). Agency and institutions in organization studies. *Organization Studies*, *38*(12), 1775–1792. https://doi.org/10.1177/0170840617708007

Alvarez, S. A., Young, S. L., & Woolley, J. L. (2015). Opportunities and institutions: A co-creation story of the king crab industry. *Journal of Business Venturing*, 30(1), 95–112. https://doi.org/10.1016/j.jbusvent.2014.07.011

Andreasson, J., & Johansson, T. (2019). Negotiating violence: Mixed martial arts as a spectacle and sport. *Sport in Society*, 22(7), 1183–1197. https://doi.org/10.1080/17430437.2018.1505868

Ashforth, B. E. (2019). Stigma and legitimacy: Two ends of a single continuum or different continua altogether? *Journal of Management Inquiry*, 28(1), 22–30. https://doi.org/10.1177/1056492618790900

Ball, C. G., & Dixon, E. (2011). The consensus statement on mixed martial arts: Emotion, not evidence-based. *Canadian Journal of Surgery*, 54(1), E1–E2.

Barrett, L. F. (2006). Valence is a basic building block of emotional life. *Journal of Research in Personality*, 40(1), 35–55. https://doi.org/10.1016/j.jrp.2005.08.006

Battilana, J., & D'Aunno, T. (2009). Institutional work and the paradox of embedded agency. In T. B. Lawrence, R. Suddaby, & B. Leca (Eds.), *Institutional work* (pp. 31–58). Cambridge University Press.

Baumeister, R. F., Bratslavsky, E., Finkenauer, C., & Vohs, K. D. (2001). Bad is stronger than good. *Review of General Psychology: Journal of Division 1, of the American Psychological Association*, 5(4), 323–370. https://doi.org/10.1037/1089-2680.5.4.323

Berger, J., Ridgeway, C. L., Fisek, M. H., & Norman, R. Z. (1998). The legitimation and delegitimation of power and prestige orders. *American Sociological Review*, 63(3), 379. https://doi.org/10.2307/2657555

Berthod, O., Helfen, M., & Sydow, J. (2018). Institutional work for value co-creation: Navigating amid power and persistence. In S. L. Vargo & R. F. Lusch (Eds.), *The SAGE handbook of service-dominant logic* (pp. 317–335). SAGE.

Bishop, S. H., La Bounty, P., & Devlin, M. (2013). Mixed martial arts: A comprehensive review. *Journal of Sport and Human Performance*, 1(1), https://doi.org/10.12922/jshp.v1i1.6

Bitektine, A., & Haack, P. (2015). The "macro" and the "micro" of legitimacy: Toward a multilevel theory of the legitimacy process. *Academy of Management Review*, 40(1), 49–75. https://doi.org/10.5465/amr.2013.0318

Bowen, H. J., Kark, S. M., & Kensinger, E. A. (2018). Never forget: Negative emotional valence enhances recapitulation. *Psychonomic Bulletin & Review*, 25(3), 870–891. https://doi.org/10.3758/s13423-017-1313-9

Brett, G. (2017). Reframing the 'violence' of mixed martial arts: The 'art' of the fight. *Poetics (Hague, Netherlands)*, 62, 15–28. https://doi.org/10.1016/j.poetic.2017.03.002

Brooke, J. (1995, December 10). Modern-day gladiators head for Denver, but the welcome mat is rolled up. *New York Times*, 1.22.

Cheever, N. (2007, January 17). A mixed reaction to machismo. *Los Angeles Times*, A.16.

Deephouse, D. L. (2000). Media reputation as a strategic resource: An integration of mass communication and resource-based theories. *Journal of Management*, 26(6), 1091–1112. https://doi.org/10.1177/014920630002600602

DiMaggio, P. J., & Powell, W. W. (1983). The iron cage revisited: Institutional isomorphism and collective rationality in organizational fields. *American Sociological Review*, 48(2), 147–160. https://doi.org/10.2307/2095101

Durand, R., & Boulongne, R. (2017). Advancing research on categories for institutional approaches of organizations. In R. Greenwood, C. Oliver, T. B. Lawrence, & R. E. Meyer (Eds.), *The SAGE handbook of organizational institutionalism* (2nd ed., pp. 647–668). SAGE.

Durand, R., & Vergne, J.-P. (2015). Asset divestment as a response to media attacks in stigmatized industries: Asset divestment as a response to media attacks. *Strategic Management Journal*, 36(8), 1205–1223. https://doi.org/10.1002/smj.2280

Etter, M., Ravasi, D., & Colleoni, E. (2019). Social media and the formation of organizational reputation. *Academy of Management Review*, 44(1), 28–52. https://doi.org/10.5465/amr.2014.0280

Fan, G. H., & Zietsma, C. (2017). Constructing a shared governance logic: The role of emotions in enabling dually embedded agency. *Academy of Management Journal*, 60(6), 2321–2351. https://doi.org/10.5465/amj.2015.0402

Farny, S., Kibler, E., & Down, S. (2019). Collective emotions in institutional creation work. *Academy of Management Journal, 62*(3), 765–799. https://doi.org/10.5465/amj.2016.0711

Ferrell, D. (1997). A brutal sport fights for its life; ultimate fighting at first succeeded wildly. *Los Angeles Times, A*, A, 1:1.

Fisher, G., Kotha, S., & Lahiri, A. (2016). Changing with the times: An integrated view of identity, legitimacy, and new venture life cycles. *Academy of Management Review, 41*(3), 383–409. https://doi.org/10.5465/amr.2013.0496

Friedland, R. (2018). Moving institutional logics forward: Emotion and meaningful material practice. *Organization Studies, 39*(4), 515–542. https://doi.org/10.1177/0170840617709307

Galvagno, M., & Dalli, D. (2014). Theory of value co-creation: A systematic literature review. *Managing Service Quality, 24*(6), 643–683. https://doi.org/10.1108/MSQ-09-2013-0187

Gentry, C. (2011). *No holds barred: The complete history of mixed martial arts in America*. Triumph Books.

Gioia, D. A., Corley, K. G., & Hamilton, A. L. (2013). Seeking qualitative rigor in inductive research: Notes on the Gioia methodology. *Organizational Research Methods, 16*(1), 15–31. https://doi.org/10.1177/1094428112452151

Giorgi, S. (2017). The mind and heart of resonance: The role of cognition and emotions in frame effectiveness: The mind and heart of resonance. *Journal of Management Studies, 54*(5), 711–738. https://doi.org/10.1111/joms.12278

Glaser, B. G., & Strauss, A. L. (2017). *Discovery of grounded theory: Strategies for qualitative research*. Routledge.

Goodrick, E., Jarvis, L. C., & Reay, T. (2020). Preserving a professional institution: Emotion in discursive institutional work. *Journal of Management Studies, 57*(4), 735–774. https://doi.org/10.1111/joms.12535

Gould Deborah, B. (2009). *Moving politics: Emotion and ACT up's fight against AIDS*. University of Chicago Press.

Greenwood, R., Oliver, C., Lawrence, T. B., Meyer, R. E. (2017). Introduction: Into the fourth decade. In R. Greenwood, C. Oliver, T. B. Lawrence, & R. E. Meyer (Eds.), *The SAGE handbook of organizational institutionalism* (pp. 1–23). SAGE.

Greenwood, R., Oliver, C., Sahlin, K., & Suddaby, R. (2008). Introduction. In R. Greenwood, C. Oliver, & R. Suddaby (Eds.), *The SAGE handbook of organizational institutionalism* (pp. 1–46). SAGE.

Gullo, N. (2013). *Into the cage: The rise of UFC nation*. Fenn-M&S.

Haack, P., Pfarrer, M. D., & Scherer, A. G. (2014). Legitimacy-as-feeling: How affect leads to vertical legitimacy spillovers in transnational governance. *Journal of Management Studies, 51*(4), 634–666. https://doi.org/10.1111/joms.12071

Haack, P., Schilke, O., & Zucker, L. (2021). Legitimacy revisited: Disentangling propriety, validity, and consensus. *Journal of Management Studies, 58*(3), 749–781. https://doi.org/10.1111/joms.12615

Hampel, C. E., Lawrence, T. B., & Tracey, P. (2017). Institutional work: Taking stock and making it matter. In R. Greenwood, C. Oliver, T. B. Lawrence, & R. E. Meyer (Eds.), *The SAGE handbook of organizational institutionalism* (pp. 558–590). SAGE.

Harmon-Jones, E., Harmon-Jones, C., & Summerell, E. (2017). On the importance of both dimensional and discrete models of emotion. *Behavioral Sciences, 7*(4), 66. https://doi.org/10.3390/bs7040066

Helms, W. S., & Patterson, K. D. W. (2014). Eliciting acceptance for "illicit" organizations: The positive implications of stigma for MMA organizations. *Academy of Management Journal, 57*(5), 1453–1484. https://doi.org/10.5465/amj.2012.0088

Helms, W. S., Patterson, K. D. W., & Hudson, B. A. (2019). Let's not "taint" stigma research with legitimacy, please. *Journal of Management Inquiry, 28*(1), 5–10. https://doi.org/10.1177/1056492618790896

Hiatt, S. R., & Park, S. (2022). Shared fate and entrepreneurial collective action in the U.S. wood pellet market. *Organization Science, 33*(5), 2065–2083. https://doi.org/10.1287/orsc.2021.1532

Hines, M. (2008, March 22). Workout fanatics have discovered that there's more to mixed martial arts than bloody cage matches. *Chicago Tribune*, 6.

Hsieh, H.-F., & Shannon, S. E. (2005). Three approaches to qualitative content analysis. *Qualitative Health Research*, 15(9), 1277–1288. https://doi.org/10.1177/1049732305276687

Hudson, B. A. (2008). Against all odds: A consideration of core-stigmatized organizations. *Academy of Management Review*, 33(1), 252–266. https://doi.org/10.5465/amr.2008.27752775

Ito, T. A., & Cacioppo, J. T. (2000). Electrophysiological evidence of implicit and explicit categorization processes. *Journal of Experimental Social Psychology*, 36(6), 660–676. https://doi.org/10.1006/jesp.2000.1430

Jennings, L. A. (2021). *Mixed martial arts: A history from ancient fighting sports to the UFC*. Rowman & Littlefield.

Johnson, A. (2004, January 30). Mixed martial arts can get very ugly. *Chicago Tribune*, 9.

Kahneman, D., & Tversky, A. (Eds.). (2019). *Choices, values, and frames*. Cambridge University Press (Virtual Publishing).

Kanno-Youngs, Z., & Orden, E. (2016, March 23). New York moves to allow martial arts. *Wall Street Journal (Eastern Ed.)*. https://www.wsj.com/articles/new-york-moves-to-allow-martial-arts-1458694700.

Kennedy, M. T., & Fiss, P. C. (2013). An ontological turn in categories research: From standards of legitimacy to evidence of actuality: An ontological turn in categories research. *Journal of Management Studies*, 50(6), 1138–1154. https://doi.org/10.1111/joms.12031

Krippendorff, K. (2004). *Content analysis: An introduction to its methodology* (2nd ed.). SAGE Publications.

Krzeminska, A., Lundmark, E., & Härtel, C. E. J. (2021). Legitimation of a heterogeneous market category through covert prototype differentiation. *Journal of Business Venturing*, 36(2), 106084. https://doi.org/10.1016/j.jbusvent.2020.106084

Lawrence, T. B., & Suddaby, R. (2006). Institutions and institutional work. In S. R. Clegg, C. Hardy, T. B. Lawrence, & W. Nord (Eds.), *The SAGE handbook of organization studies* (2nd ed., pp. 215–254). SAGE.

Lee, B. H., Struben, J., & Bingham, C. B. (2018). Collective action and market formation: An integrative framework. *Strategic Management Journal*, 39(1), 242–266. https://doi.org/10.1002/smj.2694

Lim, C. H., Martin, T. G., & Kwak, D. H. (2010). Examining television consumers of mixed martial arts: The relationship among risk taking, emotion, attitude, and actual sport-media-consumption behavior. *International Journal of Sport Communication*, 3(1), 49–63. https://doi.org/10.1123/ijsc.3.1.49

Lok, J., Creed, W. E. D., DeJordy, R., & Voronov, M. (2017). Living institutions: Bringing emotions into organizational institutionalism. In R. Greenwood, C. Oliver, T. B. Lawrence, & R. E. Meyer (Eds.), *The SAGE handbook of organizational institutionalism* (2nd ed., pp. 591–617). SAGE.

Lok, J., & Willmott, H. (2019). Embedded agency in institutional theory: Problem or paradox? *Academy of Management Review*, 44(2), 470–473. https://doi.org/10.5465/amr.2017.0571

Mair, J., Martí, I., & Ventresca, M. J. (2012). Building inclusive markets in rural Bangladesh: How intermediaries work institutional voids. *Academy of Management Journal*, 55(4), 819–850. https://doi.org/10.5465/amj.2010.0627

McCain, J. (1995, December 10). Extreme dangers. *New York Times*, 8–9.

McClain, R., Wassermen, J., Mayfield, C., Berry, A. C., Grenier, G., & Suminski, R. R. (2014). Injury profile of mixed martial arts competitors. *Clinical Journal of Sport Medicine: Official Journal of the Canadian Academy of Sport Medicine*, 24(6), 497–501. https://doi.org/10.1097/JSM.0000000000000078

Micelotta, E., Lounsbury, M., & Greenwood, R. (2017). Pathways of institutional change: An integrative review and research agenda. *Journal of Management*, 43(6), 1885–1910. https://doi.org/10.1177/0149206317699522

Moisander, J. K., Hirsto, H., & Fahy, K. M. (2016). Emotions in institutional work: A discursive perspective. *Organization Studies*, 37(7), 963–990. https://doi.org/10.1177/0170840615613377

Navis, C., & Glynn, M. A. (2010). How New Market categories emerge: Temporal dynamics of legitimacy, identity, and entrepreneurship in satellite radio, 1990–2005. *Administrative Science Quarterly, 55*(3), 439–471. https://doi.org/10.2189/asqu.2010.55.3.439

Nite, C., & Edwards, J. (2021). From isomorphism to institutional work: Advancing institutional theory in sport management research. *Sport Management Review, 24*(5), 815–838. https://doi.org/10.1080/14413523.2021.1896845

Nite, C., & Nauright, J. (2020). Examining institutional work that perpetuates abuse in sport organizations. *Sport Management Review, 23*(1), 117–118. https://doi.org/10.1016/j.smr.2019.06.002

Noelle-Neumann, E., & Petersen, T. (2004). The spiral of silence and the social nature of man. In L. L. Kaid (Ed.), *Handbook of political communication research* (pp. 357–374). Lawrence Erlbaum Associates Publishers.

Orden, E. (2016, March 18). Mixed martial arts set to be legalized in New York. *Wall Street Journal (Eastern Ed.)*. https://www.wsj.com/articles/mixed-martial-arts-set-to-be-legalized-in-new-york-1458329933.

Packaging and selling savagery. (1995, December 20). *Chicago Tribune*, 30.

Parfitt, G. (2010, September 23). *UFC 119: A heavyweight sleeper, Matt Mitrione vs Joey Beltran*. Bleacher Report. https://bleacherreport.com/articles/471124-ufc-119-a-heavyweight-sleeper-matt-mitrione-vs-joey-beltran.

Pasco, J. O., & Allison, S. (2003, February 19). The state: "Ultimate Fighting" seeks state's ok to move of the shadows; Promoters want the underground sport sanctioned. Foes say it is too dangerous. *Los Angeles Times*, B.6.

Pratt, M. G. (2009). From the editors: For the lack of a boilerplate: Tips on writing up (and reviewing) qualitative research. *Academy of Management Journal, 52*(5), 856–862. https://doi.org/10.5465/amj.2009.44632557

Rasmussen, A. S., & Berntsen, D. (2009). Emotional valence and the functions of autobiographical memories: Positive and negative memories serve different functions. *Memory & Cognition, 37*(4), 477–492. https://doi.org/10.3758/MC.37.4.477

Rovell, D., & Okamoto, B. (2016, July 11). *UFC sold for unprecedented $4 billion, Dana White confirms*. ESPN. https://www.espn.com/mma/story/_/id/16970360/ufc-sold-unprecedented-4-billion-dana-white-confirms.

Rozin, P., & Royzman, E. B. (2001). Negativity bias, negativity dominance, and contagion. *Personality and Social Psychology Review: An Official Journal of the Society for Personality and Social Psychology, Inc, 5*(4), 296–320. https://doi.org/10.1207/S15327957PSPR0504_2

Sánchez García, R., & Malcolm, D. (2010). Decivilizing, civilizing or informalizing? The international development of Mixed Martial Arts. *International Review for the Sociology of Sport, 45*(1), 39–58. https://doi.org/10.1177/1012690209352392

Segal, D. (2016, March 27). The cage match: [Money and business/financial desk]. *New York Times*, BU.1.

Slowey, M., Maw, G., & Furyk, J. (2012). Case report on vertebral artery dissection in mixed martial arts: Stroke and mixed martial arts. *Emergency Medicine Australasia, 24*(2), 203–206. https://doi.org/10.1111/j.1742-6723.2011.01496.x

Smart, R. (2022, January 24). *MMA is the fastest growing sport financially in the last five years*. SPORF. https://www.sporf.com/mma-is-the-fastest-growing-sport-financially-in-the-last-five-years/.

Smith, J. T. (2010). Fighting for regulation: Mixed martial arts legislation in the United States. *Drake Law. Review, 58*, 617.

Snowden, J. (2008). *Total MMA: Inside ultimate fighting*. ECW Press.

Soublière, J.-F., & Gehman, J. (2020). The legitimacy threshold revisited: How prior successes and failures spill over to other endeavors on kickstarter. *Academy of Management Journal, 63*(2), 472–502. https://doi.org/10.5465/amj.2017.1103

Souza-Junior, T. P., Ide, B. N., Sasaki, J. E., Lima, R. F., Abad, C. C. C., Leite, R. D., Barros, M. P., & Utter, A. C. (2015). Mixed martial arts: History, physiology and training aspects. *The Open Sports Sciences Journal, 8*(1), 1–7. https://doi.org/10.2174/1875399X01508010001

Sreeja, P. S., & Mahalakshmi, G. S. (2017). *Concept identification from poems*. 2017 s International Conference on Recent Trends and Challenges in Computational Models (ICRTCCM).

Stan, S. V. (2019). Strategic management in sports. The rise of MMA around the world-The evolution of the UFC. *Ovidius University Annals, Economic Sciences Series, 19*(1), 540–545.

Starr, P. (2021). The relational public. *Sociological Theory, 39*(2), 57–80. https://doi.org/10.1177/07352751211004660

Stephen, B. (2003, November 28). Taste: A night at the fights. *Wall Street Journal*, W.13.

Suddaby, R., Bitektine, A., & Haack, P. (2017). Legitimacy. *Academy of Management Annals, 11*(1), 451–478. https://doi.org/10.5465/annals.2015.0101

Thomas, R. E., & Thomas, B. C. (2018). Systematic review of injuries in mixed martial arts. *The Physician and Sportsmedicine, 46*(2), 155–167. https://doi.org/10.1080/00913847.2018.1430451

Toubiana, M., & Zietsma, C. (2017). The message is on the wall? Emotions, social media and the dynamics of institutional complexity. *Academy of Management Journal, 60*(3), 922–953. https://doi.org/10.5465/amj.2014.0208

Trouble, C. (2016). Stigma and the shaping of the pornography industry. *Porn Studies, 3*(2), 197–200. https://doi.org/10.1080/23268743.2016.1184484

Tschorn, A. (2008, September 7). Outside the cage, surfing isn't the only sport with a "lifestyle" to sell – mixed martial arts want a piece of that too. *Los Angeles Times*, 6.

US Major Dailies. (n.d.). Proquest.com Retrieved September 29, 2023, from https://about.proquest.com/en/products-services/US-Major-Dailies/.

Vaish, A., Grossmann, T., & Woodward, A. (2008). Not all emotions are created equal: The negativity bias in social-emotional development. *Psychological Bulletin, 134*(3), 383–403. https://doi.org/10.1037/0033-2909.134.3.383

Vergne, J.-P. (2012). Stigmatized categories and public disapproval of organizations: A mixed-methods study of the global arms industry, 1996–2007. *Academy of Management Journal, 55*(5), 1027–1052. https://doi.org/10.5465/amj.2010.0599

Verini, J. (2002, November 14). Their world of hurt; Almost anything goes in new extreme fighting league. *Los Angeles Times*, E.16.

Vilensky, M. (2016, February 23). Mixed martial arts face fierce Albany foe. *Wall Street Journal (Eastern Ed.)*. https://www.wsj.com/articles/mixed-martial-arts-faces-fierce-albany-foe-1456189941.

Voronov, M., & Vince, R. (2012). Integrating emotions into the analysis of institutional work. *Academy of Management Review, 37*(1), 58–81. https://doi.org/10.5465/armr.2010.0247

Voronov, M., & Weber, K. (2016). The heart of institutions: Emotional competence and institutional actorhood. *Academy of Management Review, 41*(3), 456–478. https://doi.org/10.5465/amr.2013.0458

Voss, G. (2019). *Stigma and the shaping of the pornography industry*. Routledge.

Whiting, J. (2009). *A new generation of warriors: The history of mixed martial arts*. Capstone Press.

Williams, M. S. (2018). *Mixed martial arts and the quest for legitimacy: The sport vs. Spectacle divide*. McFarland.

Younger, S., & Fisher, G. (2020). The exemplar enigma: New venture image formation in an emergent organizational category. *Journal of Business Venturing, 35*(1), 105897. https://doi.org/10.1016/j.jbusvent.2018.09.002

Zietsma, C., & Lawrence, T. B. (2010). Institutional work in the transformation of an organizational field: The interplay of boundary work and practice work. *Administrative Science Quarterly, 55*(2), 189–221. https://doi.org/10.2189/asqu.2010.55.2.189

Zietsma, C., & Toubiana, M. (2018). The valuable, the constitutive, and the energetic: Exploring the impact and importance of studying emotions and institutions. *Organization Studies, 39*(4), 427–443. https://doi.org/10.1177/0170840617751008

Zietsma, C., Toubiana, M., Voronov, M., & Roberts, A. (2019). *Emotions in organization theory*. Cambridge University Press (Virtual Publishing).

Zimmerman, M. A., & Zeitz, G. J. (2002). Beyond survival: Achieving new venture growth by building legitimacy. *The Academy of Management Review, 27*(3), 414–431. doi:10.2307/4134387

Agency in institutionalized sport organizations: examining how institutions suppress agency

Brent D. Oja , Calvin Nite , Minjung Kim and Jasmine Hill

ABSTRACT
Research question: This study was designed to better understand how institutionalized work practices in sport organizations influence employee agency. We fill a gap in the literature by reaffirming the roles of institutional structures and the agents themselves when examining how institutions suppress agency and resist change from within.
Research methods: Semi-structured interviews were conducted with 13 full-time sport employees working in the U.S. collegiate sport industry, which is a highly institutionalized sport environment. Thematic analysis was employed to gain insight into agency experiences in institutionalized sport organizations.
Results and findings: Two themes were identified that detailed how institutionalized sport organizations impacted agency. Influential workplace prioritization norms and a bureaucracy effected participants' agency to enact change. Participants enabled these conditions as they preserved their standing within the institution despite its constraining effect on their agency.
Implications: From a theoretical standpoint, the results offer a nuanced understanding of embedded agency in sport by demonstrating how sport institutional maintenance work occurs through the 'silent work' of institutionalized routines and practices. Further, this study relied on agents' perspectives of institutional constraints, which aids the understanding of micro perspectives of embedded agency in sport. From a practical perspective, the results indicate that the status quo of institutionalized sport organizations may not be sustainable and could be difficult to modify and improve. This calls into question the viability of current work arrangements in sport.

The circumstances and conditions of employment in the sport industry have gained considerable attention among scholars (e.g. Huml et al., 2021; Kim et al., 2019; Paek et al., 2022; Schuetz et al., in press; Taylor et al., 2019; Weight et al., 2021). These relationships, or more broadly work arrangements, are important considerations when evaluating labor conditions in sport organizations because of their influences on employee well-being (Oldham & Fried, 2016; Schuetz et al., in press). Work arrangements within sport organizations have been criticized as rigid and overly controlling (e.g. Paek et al., 2022; Schuetz et al., in press). More specifically, sport employees often experience micromanagement and strict structures that limit their creative behaviors (Paek et al., 2022), despite sport employees' desires for greater autonomy and flexibility (Schuetz et al., in press). Yet, difficult work arrangements persist despite their propensity to limit creativity and reduce well-being of sport employees (Paek et al., 2022; Schuetz et al., in press). In fact, it seems these arrangements may have become institutionalized within many sport organizations (e.g. Koustelios, 2001; Lee & Woo, 2017; Weight et al., 2021). These work arrangements seem to endure, no matter their effectiveness or inefficiencies, because they become routinized and unquestioned (see Meyer & Rowan, 1977).

The presence of institutionalized work arrangements or practices does not mean that actors (i.e. individuals within an institutionalized environment) do not want or seek change, but they often struggle to do so because institutions develop overtime to withstand challenges (Micelotta et al., 2017; Nite et al., 2019). Indeed, institutions have been defined by their endurance, self-perpetuation and the manner in which they provide meaning (Greenwood et al., 2008). Institutionalized actors tend to maintain institutions through unchallenged adherence to embedded social structures (Berger & Luckman, 1967) and/or via strategic action (i.e. institutional maintenance work; Lawrence & Suddaby, 2006). However, different interests stemming from the multiple logics within institutionalized settings can destabilize institutions and open the door for change (Seo & Creed, 2002). This creates a situation where incumbents who benefit the most from current institutional structures may be at odds with those seeking change (Micelotta et al., 2017). Whereas research has shown that actors can work towards changing institutions (see Lawrence & Suddaby, 2006), agents could struggle to enact change because their *agency* (i.e. human actions to shape and change institutions; Holm, 1995) may be suppressed by institutional structures or practices that are protected and reinforced by incumbents and even the agents themselves. In conjunction with structure, agents are thought to contribute to the creation and maintenance of institutions, even those that do not serve their interests (Cardinale, 2018; Lok & Willmott, 2019) and agency (intended or otherwise) is a requisite condition for institutions to continue to exist (Giddens, 1984). While agency and concerted action (i.e. institutional work) have received increased attention within sport management (see Nite & Edwards, 2021; Robertson et al., 2022), there is not a clear understanding of how the 'mutually constitutive relationship' (Seo & Creed, 2002, p. 224) between institutional structure and agency impacts the expression of agency within sport organizations. As research and institutional understandings have evolved in this space, scholars have paid less attention to how institutions may suppress agency and have minimized the theoretical foundations of neo-institutionalism's structural roots in favor of the concerted action of institutional work. The current study seeks to return to examining the influence of structure (and participants' endorsement) on agency by examining how institutionalized work orientations are associated with institutional maintenance.

We examined the experiences of sport employees concerning their ability to enact changes to practices and work structures within their organizations. In sum, we found that work prioritization norms, and a bureaucracy that maintained institutional stasis, impacted participants' agency to alter their work orientations. Ascertaining how the interplay between structure and agency among sport employees impacts organizational dynamics can contribute to institutional work literature by learning how sport institutions resist change from internal pressures to maintain their current state. As such, we show how institutional structures and institutionalized actors may work to limit non-executive or managerial employees' ability to change the institution. Our work provides a greater understanding of the dichotomy of structure and agency within sport institutional research by, in essence, reasserting the role of institutional structures within understandings of agency as a form of institutional maintenance. Further, we offer insights into how the rigid and bureaucratic work structures of many sport organizations (see Paek et al., 2022) remain intact and privilege institutionalization over well-being among sport employees (Schuetz et al., in press).

Institutions and agency

Although there have been numerous definitions, most conceptions of institutions have been captured by Greenwood and colleagues' (2008) definition of 'more-or-less taken-for-granted repetitive social behavior that is underpinned by normative systems and cognitive understanding that give meaning to social exchange and thus enable self-reproducing social order' (p. 4–5). The point of emphasis in this definition is the notion of self-reproduction which reflects Micelotta and Washington's (2013) description of 'silent' work whereby institutionalized routines and practices are perpetuated and endure without overt enforcement. However, the emergence of the institutional work perspective moves beyond this neo-institutionalist view that privileges structuration as the primary diffusion mechanism of institutions and incorporates the concepts of agency and concerted action (Lawrence & Suddaby, 2006; Nite & Edwards, 2021). Institutional work presupposes that human activity, along with embedded structures, is instrumental in the institutional processes of perpetuation, disruption and creation (Hampel et al., 2017; Lawrence & Suddaby, 2006; Nite & Edwards, 2021).

It is important to note, however, that institutional work does not completely abandon structuralism and, instead, builds from the notion of embedded agency. Embedded agency describes how people are simultaneously influenced by and influencers of institutions (Battilana & D'aunno, 2009; Seo & Creed, 2002). Embedded agency embodies the work of Granovetter (1985) who discussed the challenges of theorizing the under- and over-socialization as related to action within organizational settings. On one hand, adopting perspectives of under-socialization would prove problematic for understanding how people impact institutional structures (Granovetter, 1985). On the other hand, adopting over-socialization would theorize people as 'cultural dopes' (Garfinkel, 1967) who are incapable of independent thought and action (Granovetter, 1985). Seo and Creed (2002) offered a dialectical perspective to explain how agents are influenced by existing institutional arrangements, and how conflicts and tensions within and adjacent to institutions 'reshapes the consciousness of institutional inhabitants, and they [agents] … act to fundamentally transform the present social arrangements and themselves' (p. 225).

Institutional work has emerged within the sport management literature (Nite & Edwards, 2021; Robertson et al., 2022) with various authors detailing how sport institutions are maintained and disrupted. For instance, Nite et al. (2019) showed how the National Collegiate Athletics Association (NCAA) expanded its boundaries and practices to gain control of most college athletics in the U.S.A. Agyemang et al. (2018) theorized how institutions are maintained when institutional disruptors are neutralized by other institutional actions. Woolf et al. (2016) detailed how members of the mixed martial arts community would police itself in ways that both further developed the sport but also erected entry barriers. Dowling and Smith (2016) outlined how actors created new initiatives in Canada to increase athlete success in international sport events. Despite the increasing popularity of institutional work in sport management, there is still much we do not understand about embedded agency and how it is realized within sport institutions.

One area that has not received much attention and seems particularly well-suited for studying embedded agency within institutional work is institutionalized work arrangements. For example, difficult job structures in sport organizations (see Paek et al., 2022; Schuetz et al., in press) have likely been perpetuated and reinforced through active structuration from superiors *and* from acceptance by employees. Studying work arrangements in sport would seemingly provide new insights into embedded agency by studying the microfoundations of institutionalization within sport organizations. If, indeed, 'institutions are sustained, altered and extinguished as they are enacted by collections of individuals in everyday situations' (Powell & Rerup, 2017, p. 311) then it seems prudent to garner a better understanding of how those everyday actions and work arrangements influence institutional processes. With this inquiry, we are particularly interested in understanding how the structure of sport organizational work arrangements and employee agency interact with institutional maintenance practices. That is, we explore how sport employees experience agency based on active structuration from administrators and their enablement with the following research questions (RQ):

RQ 1 – How do sport employees experience agency within institutionalized sport organizations?

RQ 2 – How is sport employee agency influenced by institutional maintenance work dynamics?

Method

This study was designed within the philosophical assumptions of the constructivism/interpretivism paradigm (Tamminen & Poucher, 2020). In line with these assumptions, we relied on relativism (i.e. multiple interpretations of reality; ontology) to guide the study, which informed the decision to utilize a transactional/subjectivist epistemology. This belief insinuates that knowledge is co-created through interactions between researchers and participants and endorses researchers' past experiences (Denzin & Lincoln, 2011). These beliefs led to the use of a phenomenological methodology based in hermeneutics (Denzin & Lincoln, 2011), specifically Heidegger's hermeneutic phenomenology (Laverty, 2003). This specific form of phenomenology proposes that escaping one's prior knowledge of a phenomenon is impossible and instead argues that one's knowledge of the studied phenomenon is a valuable element in co-constructing meaning (Crotty, 1998). Hermeneutic phenomenology includes both a depiction of the phenomenon and the researchers' interpretation of the various meanings offered by participants (van Manen, 1990).

Research context

The context of the study was the U.S. collegiate sport industry. Athletics departments are non-profit organizations nested within higher education institutions (Hutchinson & Bouchet, 2014) and are governed by the NCAA. Individual athletics departments are free to organize and structure themselves as they see fit, but they must follow NCAA guidelines (e.g. standardized participant and coach numbers for each team). The NCAA provides various classifications that require, among other elements, explicit amounts of sports to be offered, but no specific sports are mandated. Athletics departments include a conglomerate of professional employees (i.e. administrators, marketers, equipment personnel, ticket salespeople, athletic trainers and coaches) that work for the various teams of an athletics department. Various professions create their standards of professionalization (e.g. equipment personnel and athletic trainers have their own certification processes as well as professional trade conferences). Collegiate sport employees are often paid based on market value, with rare instances of trade unions. Although some employees may be assigned to a single team, many employees provide support for multiple teams within the athletics department. This support often includes office work as well as labor on the field or pitch to organize practices or competitions. Intense involvement with multiple teams and demanding labor in the office and on the field constitute a unique setting whereby collegiate sport employees require emotional and physical aptitudes (Oja et al., 2023) to appease various organizational factions. However, the current working conditions (i.e. industry burnout, low pay, job insecurity, funding reductions) have led to athletics departments having issues retaining staff as their turnover rate is worse than similar industries (Huml & Taylor, 2022). The college sport industry is also an appropriate setting to answer the research questions, as it is a highly institutionalized sport environment as demonstrated by past scholarship (e.g. Nite, 2017; Nite et al., 2013; Nite et al., 2019; Nite & Bopp, 2017; Nite & Nauright, 2020; Nite & Washington, 2017). Furthermore, scholars have portrayed working in collegiate athletics departments as institutionalized (e.g. Cunningham, 2015; Cunningham & Nite, 2020). In all, the college sport industry is an ideal laboratory setting to examine agency among employees.

Participants

A purposeful sampling approach was used to gather experiences pertaining to agency in highly institutionalized sport organizations. The researchers purposely selected participants based on their having experienced the phenomenon to be studied (agency in sport organizations; Jones, 2015). The qualification criteria consisted of being a full-time, non-coaching sport employee in an American collegiate sport organization, as they are highly institutionalized (e.g. Cunningham, 2015; Cunningham & Nite, 2020; Nite et al., 2013; Nite & Washington, 2017). We interviewed non-coaching employees to better elucidate the dynamics that exist between those with less agency (i.e. managerial employees) and their supervisors (i.e. administrators). Thirteen participants from separate universities were interviewed. Author One previously knew seven of the participants (i.e. insiders) and six had no previous relationship with the research team (i.e. outsiders). The use of both insiders and outsiders strengthens the study as insiders provide improved rapport and depth, while interviewing outsiders is a 'checking mechanism'

(p. 15) to avoid undesirable bias or favoritism when collecting and interpreting data (Taylor, 2011). Participant demographics can be found in Table 1.

Procedures

Institutional Review Board (IRB) approval was granted before collecting data. After agreeing to participate, the participants engaged in semi-structured interviews and were asked questions concerning their work experiences within sport organizations. The interviews were completed using video conferencing applications. Upon completion, the interviews were transcribed, and participants were assigned pseudonyms. This form of qualitative data collection enables participants to provide their unique experiences with a phenomenon thereby offering previously unknown perspectives to the researcher (Jones, 2015). Participants were asked a series of questions that Kvale (1996) refers to as thematic (i.e. related to the research theme–embedded agency and institutional maintenance) and dynamic (i.e. interpersonal interaction between interviewer and interviewee). Thematic questions included: 'Would you mind describing the norms of the sport workplace?,' 'What changes or agreements have you made with your supervisor (subordinate) in terms of assigned work tasks? Is this an easy process?,' 'Is working in sport more "old school" or bureaucratic or is it more flexible?' and 'Is employee flexibility valued in the sport workplace? Why or why not?' Dynamic questions consisted of sharing similar stories from the interviewer's experiences of working in sport and asking for similarities or differences, and clarification questions. Semi-structured interviews were conducted until ample 'experientially rich accounts … of powerful experiential examples or anecdotes' (van Manen, 2016, p. 353) were collected that enabled a thick and rich description of the experiences of the participants (Braun & Clarke, 2021). Interviews ranged from 45 min to over 2 hours, with most of the interviews lasting over 90 min.

Researcher positionality

Several members of the research team had previous work experience in the collegiate sport industry. Author One worked in the collegiate sport industry for over 5 years which supports the 'critical representation of ourselves within our research' (Misener

Table 1. Participant demographics.

Pseudonym	Age	Gender	Department	Experience
Renae	27	Female	Compliance	3 years
Sally	29	Female	Event Management	8 years
Molly	28	Female	Compliance	5 years
Keith	43	Male	Administration	17 years
Faith	26	Female	Marketing	5 years
Theodore	30	Male	Development	8 years
Tom	36	Male	Compliance	11 years
Marie	33	Female	Marketing	10 years
Lisa	31	Female	Academic Support	4 years
Paul	39	Male	Development	15 years
Megan	35	Female	Academic Support	12 years
John	34	Male	Development	13 years
Danielle	53	Female	Administration	34 years

Note: All participants worked at the Division I level of American intercollegiate sport, which emphasizes competition.

& Doherty, 2009, p. 466). Author One used self-reflexivity to engage with his past status within college athletics to gather a rich understanding of the meanings that participants prescribed to their experiences with agency in their sport workplace (Rich & Misener, 2017). With the use of self-reflexivity, Author One was able to bring forth his voice and by doing so aided the credibility and trustworthiness of the data analysis (Kerwin & Hoeber, 2015).

Trustworthiness

We followed a relativist approach to demonstrate the trustworthiness of the study (Burke, 2017; Smith & McGannon, 2018). In doing so, we selected criteria from Tracy (2010) that were relevant to the study including: a worthy topic in that sport employees' experiences are a growing concern (e.g. Huml et al., 2021; Taylor et al., 2019); the significant contribution of learning how agency interacts with institutional maintenance practices in sport organizations; sincerity via self-reflexivity; rich rigor by using an appropriate sample and detailed descriptions of the research context, data collection and analysis; credibility through thick descriptions and member checks that occurred during the data analysis; retaining meaningful coherence within the purpose, methods and results; and adhering to ethical considerations by following IRB protocols.

Data analysis

Braun and Clarke's (2006, 2012, 2021) thematic analysis procedure was employed to better understand sport employees' experiences with agency in institutionalized sport organizations. Within Braun and Clarke's inductive-deductive continuum, our coding process was largely inductive, which emphasizes interpretations of the raw data when forming the codes and themes as opposed to using previous theory or scholarship to develop codes and themes (Braun & Clarke, 2006). In line with our philosophical assumptions, our interpretation was guided by our past experiences and knowledge to interpret participants' responses to co-construct meaning during the coding process. Our knowledge of institutional theory literature when coding and developing the interview protocol signifies the deductive elements of our coding process, although it was the data that influenced code generation as opposed to past studies or frameworks. Furthermore, it is assumed that thematic analysis will include both inductive and deductive elements (Braun & Clarke, 2012).

Thematic analysis is 'a method for identifying, analyzing and reporting patterns (themes) within data' (Braun & Clarke, 2006, p. 79). This process was not linear in that researchers returned to the elements of thematic analysis as necessary to create an in-depth, rich description of the phenomenon. The thematic analysis process included (a) repeated readings of the interview transcriptions to become familiar with the data, (b) systematic data coding by organizing data into meaningful groups known as codes (e.g. work is important, focus on work and be available), (c) generating initial themes from the coded data via a central organizing concept of shared meaning (e.g. bureaucracies in action, primacy of work, a singular focus on work), (d) developing and reviewing the two final themes that focus on the norms of the institution (i.e. work prioritization) and how bureaucracies sustained stability (i.e. statis supporting bureaucracies) with internal homogeneity (i.e. coherent pattern) and external heterogeneity (i.e. distinct), (e) refining, defining and naming themes to maintain coherence and solidify boundaries of each theme, and (f) writing the final report that included analytic narratives to interpret and expand on vivid data extracts. Table 2 provides an illustration of this process.

Results

Two themes were identified that encapsulate the state of work orientations in this institutional setting: work prioritization and stasis supporting bureaucracies. Employees in administrative positions (i.e. executive decision-makers) are referred to henceforth as administrators. Employees in managerial positions (i.e. full-time employees, but not those who can make organizational level decisions) are referred to as managerial employees.

Work prioritization

This theme describes how participants prioritized work ahead of personal obligations (i.e. employees worked rather than attend momentous occasions such as family weddings) and being available to work as much as possible (i.e. participants were compelled to be present at work as much as possible and 'show face' which resulted in an unofficial competition to be in the office the most and/or longest). The work prioritization norm meant that participants were obligated to work long hours and be available for work. Participants were willing to work long hours during the 'off season', and even greater hours during the 'in-season'. The truncated nature of sport seasons meant that most work obligations and tasks took place during a few months of the year. A function of the seasonality factor was that the public facing features of participants' jobs occurred during others' leisure time (i.e. evenings and weekends). Participants also were available for their coaches and student-athletes during almost all hours. It was expected that employees answered their phones if coaches or student-athletes called late in the evening or early in the morning. Keith, an administrator, summarized these expectations as

Table 2. Example illustrations of theme construction.

Codes	Empirical examples	Theme
Work is important	'My best friend from high school and growing up, she got married my first year here. I didn't even ask to go. It's the expectation [to be at work].'	Work Prioritization
Working hours	'I think you have to understand that it's long hours, certainly longer than a traditional corporate job. There's an expectation that you certainly keep your phone on when you go home and you're on call.'	Work Prioritization
Be available	'I don't have an 8:30 to 5 job. I don't have a Monday to Friday job. I have a Monday to Sunday, 12am to 12am job. It's 24/7, 365.'	Work Prioritization
Desire for the status quo	'If you start doing something that's different, you might start losing your fans, and I think that is where the nervousness comes from.'	Stasis Supporting Bureaucracies
Focus on work	'I think it's a lot of the mentality of 'get it done" and 'be seen and not heard''	Stasis Supporting Bureaucracies
System limits change	'There's so much red tape, you have to cut through that, it just becomes so tiring. People start to realize it's just not worth it to go through all this trouble for something that may not happen.'	Stasis Supporting Bureaucracies

> I think you have to understand that it's long hours, certainly longer than a traditional corporate job. I think flexible hours as well, like nights and weekends and depending on the position, there's an expectation that you certainly keep your phone on when you go home and you're on call.

These conditions had the effect of limiting participants' time away from work in that they were expected to stay or be present at work during the off season but also had to work grueling hours during the in-season. Even when participants were able to leave the office, they were still tethered to their workplace as they were available for coaches or student-athletes. While participants attempted to place boundaries on their availability, the powerful expectation that participants needed to move their schedule to accommodate coaches and/or student-athletes or at minimum answer their calls no matter the prevailing circumstances. Thus, participants were resigned to 'surviving' the season of the team(s) they were associated with, and once a season was completed, they had to contend with exhaustion from the grueling work hours of in-season responsibilities.

The expectation of prioritizing work was reinforced by employees' enablement of these conditions. For example, participants willingly worked roughly 80–100 hours in a week, which sometimes included sleeping in an office. Danielle explained her perspective,

> I don't have an 8:30 to 5 job. I don't have a Monday to Friday job. I have a Monday to Sunday, 12am to 12am job. It's 24/7, 365. Monday night I got home and it's 10 o'clock at night and I had four different coaches call me because they all had issues with something. This was after being in the office all day.

Participants also chose not to attend weddings if they occurred during the seasons of their teams. This was a result of such a request being viewed as pointless as their boss would likely not approve it, and the value participants placed on their specific knowledge of their jobs and the established trust and familiarity with coaches (e.g. Sally and Marie). Marie elaborated on her experience,

> My best friend from high school and growing up, she got married my first year here. I didn't even ask to go; I was so upset. I was so sad. My family went. I felt so guilty. [The sport organization] just invested in me; I've been here like four months. I didn't have the courage to ask, just because of what I've experienced in [the past], it's the expectation [to be at work].

Put differently, working was acknowledged by participants as a priority that took precedence over their personal lives.

Another component of prioritizing work was the willingness of participants to be physically at work, which is part of why being away from work to attend a wedding was nearly unthinkable for participants. There was a perceived need for there to be 'boots on the ground' and to maximize time in the office and not following this norm could induce emotional distress and pressure. Theodore felt anxiety at the prospect of missing work or coming in late,

> I've always gotten anxiety over this because it's that 'be here, no matter what' sort of thing. If I [miss work] once, what's the statute of limitations? Getting anxiety for walking in at nine or nine-thirty and then feeling like someone's going to come in my office and shut the door and be like, 'Hey, so we need to talk about the time that you're getting to work.' That's always been in the back of my mind.

Participants also involved themselves in unofficial competitions to be in the office longer than any other employee and to stay in the office as long as one's supervisor was in the office, irrespective of one's work tasks having already been completed. Such an experience was that of Megan who felt pressure to stay as long as other employees, even if her work was done. Failure to adhere to these unspoken guidelines could result in a perception of being lazy or lacking the same degree of commitment as their fellow coworkers. Megan provided a first day at work story where she was late because she got lost in her new building,

> I was 15 minutes late and the first thing that was said to me was 'I don't mean to be an asshole, but when I say 8:30, I mean 8:30.' There was some underlying pressure, unwritten pressure, because everybody else was in the office on time, if you weren't then you're lazy.

Theodore relayed a similar experience,

> There was this attitude of we don't leave until our direct supervisor leaves. We're just sitting there, like, 'can I just go home?' You're there just to be there. If I leave early and just say, 'I'm going home. Sorry guys, my wife needs me.' Does that get held against you?

Theodores' experience of physically remaining at work to demonstrate a commitment to the job represented how managerial employees enabled the work prioritization norm, as they were willing to remain at work to validate their status within the organization as an employee. Participants understood that part of the expectations of their job was to be constantly available to support coaches and athletes and to demonstrate a commitment to their organization. In sum, the first theme consists of structural workplace pressures and participants willingness to enact or enable such norms, which included being consistently available to work, prioritizing their work schedules over personal and family obligations, and being at work as much as possible.

Stasis supporting bureaucracies

This theme describes the participant perceptions of bureaucracies that maintained the stasis of the institution. Within the bureaucracies, structural determinants, aided by participants' enablement, reinforced traditional hierarchies that were circumspect of change, held tepid support from leadership for workplace modifications, and preserved cumbersome reporting processes.

The overall environment participants experienced was viewed as unyielding and traditional. Faith described her setting as 'there is a little bit of rigidity and bureaucracy. This is what works; this is how things should stay'. Molly expanded,

> You were just part of a machine, and the expectation was 'hey, this is how we do it. We don't need to change it; it has worked before. It has worked in very high-intense situations for us in the past. So, this is what we're going to keep doing.'

These hierarchies were traditional in the sense that they reflected a top-down organizational landscape that reinforced notions of 'an old boys club' (e.g. Lisa, Paul and Danielle) or a fraternity. Furthermore, changes threatened the traditions of college athletics that were important to universities' fans, boosters and alumni. Faith succinctly explained that 'if you start doing something that's different, you might start losing your fans, and I think that is where the nervousness comes from'. One example was the use of non-traditional school colors on uniforms and its ramifications as upset fans were likely to complain to administrators. It was believed to be more advantageous for administrators to maintain traditional customs or processes, for example, avoiding new marketing plans with updated uniforms or colors, which consequently maintained the status quo of the institution.

Within the bureaucracies, participants were expected to concentrate on their work tasks as a means to avoid task-boundary intrusions and increase productivity. Thus participants focused their efforts on the job tasks assigned by their supervisor as opposed to having autonomous workplace orientations. 'I think it's a lot of the mentality of "get it done"' noted Faith. Megan offered concepts such as 'be seen and not heard' when working and having 'territory' over work responsibilities and needing to demonstrate production within those territories, as completing tasks was highly valued. Lisa explained the importance of just doing one's job, 'in my experience, it's "go and get the job done" and do it well.' This system precluded meaningful engagement in anything other than formal workplace tasks, which impeded participants, such as Renae, from implementing new systems. Renae had been wanting to work on a project for months but did not have the proper resources to engage with the idea because she was overwhelmed with the basic or traditional elements of her job. Instead, she focused her energies on the formal job tasks that were assigned to her. Renae explained

> This idea came up in like February, and it's June and I still haven't gotten to it because even though it's a good idea, it's just not a priority. I just simply do not have the time or brain capacity to implement it.

These bureaucracies limited opportunities to develop autonomous workplace orientations as participants chose not to experiment with alternative task completion strategies and instead focused on their prescribed work tasks.

Another element of the bureaucracy that contributed to the limitation of autonomous workplace orientations was the influence of leadership as managerial sport employees were dependent on their supervisors to approve such orientations. Participants' experiences revolved around leaderships' limitations on or willingness to support their ability to attempt new work strategies. In some instances, leaders were viewed as being overbearing and micromanagers when it came to managerial employees going 'off script'. Theodore described a negative experience from a previous sport organization where his supervisor was concerned about him emailing donors, 'He told me, "Don't do that. If you have something like that, just go through me, and then we'll take it up the line". I was like, "Oh my God, are we really doing this?" How am I supposed to do anything … this is pretty basic stuff'. Moreover, direct supervisors were only one component of the need for support from leadership to change workplace orientations. Theodore experienced working in a 'culture of no empowerment' where administrators were viewed as not wanting their employees to do anything other than what was prescribed in their formal job tasks. Participants were acutely aware of the conservative nature of their organizations' hierarchical structure in that the 'old guard' was often not supportive of change. Paul explained, 'they're very careful with any type of change, they're very aware of how people view their brand. I think that's a reason why they're so resistant to change and they know there's so many processes you have to go through to implement any kind of change'. Keith, as an administrator, acknowledged the lack of flexibility,

'Across the industry [there is] a little more of an old school mentality; just rolling up your sleeves and getting the job done'.

Those viewed as the 'old guard' were thought to be comfortable with the current system and any changes brought forth represented a challenge to their way of doing things. Lisa provided a clear example when discussing having the autonomy to work from home, 'You almost prove to yourself that you can do a lot of things over Zoom and you don't necessarily need to be a "body in the building", but [leaders] feel comfortable having a body in the building'. Although administrators would offer encouragement to their employees to provide new ideas, there was rarely, if ever, administrator support for the actual implementation of managerial employee driven ideas or innovations. There were compelling stories of employees who attempted to offer new programs and systems that would have improved organizational functionality, but these ideas fell on the 'deaf ears' of administrators. Faith lamented 'We'd always bring [ideas] up and it always kind of fell on deaf ears. It was always like "Oh yeah, great idea" but nothing happened with it. Everyone would kind of just keep quiet because there was no point for us'. Paul, after describing his idea that would have improved organizational efficiency by enabling open seating as opposed to assigned seating for free admission events,

> It didn't happen. I think the reason was, [my supervisor] is just like 'that's just the way it's always been done.' I'm not saying [my ideas] have to be implemented all the time, but I don't think they were ever really taken seriously. As nice as my boss was and as smart as he was, he's just really used to doing things his way.

Despite demonstratable improvements for the organization, participants perceived that they were turned away from implementing these ideas and concepts.

Beyond the need for support from leaders to implement managerial employee-led changes, a strict reporting structure existed, which deterred change initiatives with complex and cumbersome bureaucratic practices. Participants had to have their new processes or systems approved at many levels of the organizational hierarchy. Paul offered his acceptance that the current system was unlikely to change, 'There's so much red tape, you have to cut through that, it just becomes so tiring. People start to realize it's just not worth it to go through all this trouble for something that may not happen'. This process was slow and frustrated participants, yet they continued to complete their standard work tasks as assigned, which enabled the bureaucracy to perpetuate the expectation of completing work tasks without devoting effort to modify or improve their workplace orientations. Faith also acknowledged that she accepted a limited capacity for change,

> There was never really a way for us to say this is how we'd like to do things. It was always 'we can do things this way.' So, it was always asking for permission and usually being shut down, rather than just experimenting on our own. We always had to go up the chain for [approval].

Managerial sport employees' ability to introduce changes appeared to be restrained (a) by a traditional, change-resistant bureaucracy, (b) a lack of empowerment from their supervisors and (c) having to maneuver through complicated and bureaucratic reporting structures that slowed down and impeded change.

In sum, the agency of managerial employees was influenced by the prioritization of work over employees' personal lives and maximizing one's time at work, and bureaucracies that maintained institutional stasis by slowing down change and limiting opportunities for managerial employees to alter their workplace orientations. Institutional norms compelled employees to prioritize their work responsibilities over personal interests and to focus their efforts on their assigned job tasks, which resulted in a firmly structured workplace environment whereby participants willingly worked many long hours and provided near continuous availability. Lastly, bureaucracies were seemingly maintained by administrators seeking to preserve a traditional hierarchy that supported institutional stasis (i.e. limiting autonomous workplace orientations) and participants' willingness to comply with the norms of the institution.

Discussion

The results of the study answer the research questions by detailing how agency is experienced among managerial sport employees and implications for institutional maintenance practices. Some of the limitations of participants' agency could be explained by Micelotta et al. (2017) whereby administrators as incumbents, or fully institutionalized actors, seemingly desiring to maintain the status quo and constraining the agency of managerial employees by purporting norms which produced limited opportunities to experiment with innovation and instead prioritized their labor by normalizing long hours that often occurred during most individuals' leisure time. To further preserve this dynamic, administrators ostensibly maintained strict bureaucracies that emphasized a clear top-down hierarchical system. Specifically, bureaucracies had the effect of constraining agency among managerial sport employees by isolating the institution from new ideas or advancements from agents by maintaining an ordered hierarchical system of supervision for administrators to closely coordinate managerial employees' tasks with administrative regulations and an unwillingness to deviate from said regulations. Thus bureaucracies offered control and coordination for the administrators and their athletics departments but limited the agency of their managerial employees.

Participants' willingness to continue to engage with their work orientations can be explained by embedded agency in that actors play a role in prolonging institutions by enabling structural determinism with their active participation (Seo & Creed, 2002). In this study, participants noted their concern that failure to subscribe to the institutional norms and bureaucracies would result in the belief that they were lazy or were not as committed as other employees. While it is evident that participants' willingness to accept work orientations that prioritized their jobs and precluded autonomous workplace orientations is likely rooted in their desire to avoid such labels, this phenomenon can also be explained with literature that has explored the psycho-social experiences of sport employees. For instance, sport employees' agreeableness for such conditions could be a product of their held identities as sport employees have been found to identify with their sport organizations because they offer an opportunity to remain engaged with sport and competition (e.g. Oja et al., 2015, 2020, 2023). Thus participants' need to fulfill identities that are centered on ideals that can be realized through membership with sport organizations could be a source of their willingness to perpetuate norms that seemingly defy their own interests.

Theoretical contributions

This study was devised to better understand embedded agency's influence on institutional maintenance in sport institutions by examining the experiences of institutional actors. Thus the theoretical contribution of this study is grounded in advancing knowledge concerning individuals' embedded agency experiences, as opposed to organizational or societal perspectives (Battilana, 2006). Investigating agents' perspectives enables a deeper understanding of how to operationalize embedded agency in sport, which answers the call of recent sport institutional scholars (e.g. Nite & Edwards, 2021; Robertson et al., 2022; Washington & Patterson, 2011). This study also represents a critical step toward understanding how institutions are maintained – through everyday job structures and agents' complicity in enabling structure (Giddens, 1984) in sport organizations. Considering 'institutions are reproduced through the routine activities of ensembles of individuals' (Powell & Rerup, 2017, p. 311), we demonstrate how institutionalized routines may hinder employees' ability to alter their work environment. We detailed how incumbents and the employees themselves idealized the value of work and preserved a bureaucracy which maintained the status quo and suppressed the agency of managerial employees to enact change. In other words, employees were simply unable to develop innovative processes or work designs because their work structures were embedded so deeply and required such effort to navigate that employees did not perceive that innovations or enhancements to their work orientations were likely to occur. We also found that participants endorsed these working conditions by continuing to remain employed in the sport industry (all participants are current sport employees), and by their desire to avoid being labeled as lazy or uncommitted. In this setting, institutional maintenance work was a process whereby participants accepted and facilitated an institutional structure which preserved their institutional standing despite its adverse effects on their working conditions. This follows Giddens (1984) assertion that structure does not solely constrain but instead constrains *and* enables, as participants' willingness to endure the bureaucracy and prioritization of work empowered the system. However, it was evident that participants were not 'cultural dopes' as they attempted to offer and implement alterations to their workplace orientations despite working in an environment where the institution was firmly set in stasis. Instead, participants accepted that their desire to improve their workplace arrangements was unlikely to be realized but persisted in attempting to break through all while perpetuating the current system. Thus we offer greater insight into how sport institutions impact agency and institutional maintenance. These sport-specific challenges of agency can enable targeted examinations to explore how actors can use their agency to enact change within institutions (Battilana, 2006; Battilana & D'aunno, 2009). For example, identifying successful innovation processes of sport employees could shed light on how sport institutions endorse change. Doing so could also pinpoint existing gaps that represent opportunities to further expand agency and consequently innovation in the sport workplace.

Our work adds a nuanced perspective of embedded agency within sport institutions by showing how embeddedness may actually suppress agency. We detail how sport administrators (i.e. incumbents) and the managerial employees themselves maintained institutions by perpetuating work arrangements that ultimately suppress employee agency. We found that highly institutionalized work structures were robust defense mechanisms of the current institutional order considering participants in our study seemed to struggle gaining traction with innovative work dynamics. Indeed, agency was stalled by robust institutional structures (i.e. bureaucracies), individual cognitions (i.e. norms), and agents propagating current work arrangements to maintain their standing in the institution (i.e. not being labeled as lazy or uncommitted). Our work shows the 'silent' work of institutional maintenance wherein cognitively institutionalized routines and practices both suppressed innovative work arrangements and also supported the perpetuation of current arrangements (see Micelotta & Washington, 2013).

Further, we offer insight into agency positioning within sport institutions. In our study, we recognized clear demarcations between administrators (i.e. incumbents) and managerial employees in terms of agentic authority. Our findings suggested that incumbents would encourage employees to be innovative but stop short of supporting innovation. Sally's supervisors claimed they valued innovation, and Paul described being asked about innovation on job interviews. Yet, the way incumbents would structure the work environment would actually suppress employees' ability to enact innovative job features. Even in those instances where granting autonomy to employees could result in improved effectiveness, incumbents instead favored the status quo of current institutional arrangements (see DiMaggio & Powell, 1983; Meyer & Rowan, 1977). In reality, the propagation of the bureaucratic norms and resulting outcomes and behaviors seemingly served the interests of incumbents seeking to maintain the current power dynamics (see also Micelotta et al., 2017; Nite & Washington, 2017).

Finally, we offer further nuance for understanding embedded agency. Often, it seems that institutional scholars, particularly those favoring institutional work, tend to overly emphasize *agency* and ignore the *embedded* aspect of embedded agency. Our research offers a stark reminder that institutions and their embedded structures are reproduced by routine activities that may or may not be concerted (see Powell & Rerup, 2017). Whereas Nite and Edwards (2021) advocated for greater attention to agency and concerted action within sport institutional research, our work offers a cautionary tale of overly privileging rational action outside of institutional dynamics.

Practical implications

This study has several practical implications for the sport industry. The study included the identification of several strongly entrenched structures and norms, which were compounded by two elements that have unique impacts on the sport industry: the seasonal nature and importance of traditions within sport. The seasonal aspect of sport forced most work processes to occur within tight timeframes, which limited the amount of time participants had to conceptualize or engage with new practices. The prominence of traditions within sport reinforced the status quo by incentivizing risk averse practices that strengthened traditions. This meant that new ideas or concepts were met with immediate skepticism. Despite these unique circumstances that limited agency, participants sought to use their agency to inspire change. Thus increasing agency among managerial sport employees (and the resulting changes from their agency) is feasible. However, participants were afforded few opportunities to engage with problem-solving or change initiatives. This indicates an institution that has limited potential for growth and advancement due to controlling practices.

Sport has been previously described as rigid and controlling (e.g. Paek et al., 2022), and this study's results are similar in that strong structures and norms curtailed the agency of managerial sport employees. This suggests that organizational change is more likely to occur from those positioned at the top of a hierarchy (i.e. incumbents), as predicted by Battilana (2006). Although managerial sport employees are not devoid of agency to enact change, it appears to be limited by administrators and their own endorsement of an environment that is resistant to change. This means that for significant innovation to occur it would have to be initiated by incumbents, which presents two problems. The first being that incumbents are more likely to resist change because the current system is beneficial to them (Micelotta et al., 2017), and the second is that incumbents are more likely to be removed from the day-to-day activities and have less knowledge of institutional problems as evidenced by the data. As such, the current status quo may not be sustainable and unsurprisingly has begun to face new challenges from agents (e.g. Schuetz et al., in press). This rigid setting also has implications for the well-being of sport employees and the sustainability of the industry at large given its high degree of turnover (e.g. Huml et al., 2021; Taylor et al., 2019). This study alluded to how bureaucratic structures may play a role in the well-being of the participants. As well-being in the sport workplace continues to gain popularity among scholars (e.g. Anagnostopoulos et al., 2016; Kim et al., 2019; Kim et al., 2023; Oja et al., 2019; Svensson et al., 2021), job designs appear to play an important role (Oja et al., in press; Schuetz et al., in press) and this study expands this approach by underscoring the influence of institutional dynamics.

Limitations and future directions

There are limitations to this study that offer promising areas of future directions for this line of research. The first being a limited understanding of how the administrative layers (i.e. managers, athletics administrators, university administrators) interact and influence organizational dynamics, as most participants were managers as opposed to administrators. Future studies that explore layers of administration would add to the understanding of how agency is experienced in sport organizations. This study did not specifically incorporate innovation, but innovation and change can be viewed as outcomes of individual agency (Battilana, 2006). Examining the outcomes of agency and the organizational and individual ramifications of innovation would provide pathways for actors to justify the need for expanded agency. Lastly, the highly controlled setting described in this study could have implications for the well-being of sport employees (see Schuetz et al., in press) and should be examined to fully understand its impact on the psycho-social experiences of sport employees.

Disclosure statement

No potential conflict of interest was reported by the author(s).

ORCID

Brent D. Oja http://orcid.org/0000-0002-2848-0486
Calvin Nite http://orcid.org/0000-0002-3095-8987

References

Agyemang, K., Berg, B., & Fuller, R. (2018). Disrupting the disruptor: Perceptions as institutional maintenance work at the 1968 Olympic Games. *Journal of Sport Management*, *32*(6), 567–580. https://doi.org/10.1123/jsm.2017-0268

Anagnostopoulos, C., Winand, M., & Papadimitriou, D. (2016). Passion in the workplace: Empirical insights from team sport organisations. *European Sport Management Quarterly*, *16*(4), 385–412. https://doi.org/10.1080/16184742.2016.1178794

Battilana, J. (2006). Agency and institutions: The enabling role of individuals' social position. *Organization*, *13*(5), 653–676. https://doi.org/10.1177/1350508406067008

Battilana, J., & D'aunno, T. (2009). Institutional work and the paradox of embedded agency. In T. B. Lawrence, R. Suddaby, & B. Leca (Eds.), *Institutional work: Actors and agency in institutional studies of organizations* (pp. 31–58). Cambridge University Press.

Berger, P. L., & Luckman, T. (1967). *The social construction of reality: A treatise in the sociology of knowledge.* Doubleday.

Braun, V., & Clarke, V. (2006). Using thematic analysis in psychology. *Qualitative Research in Psychology*, *3*(2), 77–101. https://doi.org/10.1191/1478088706qp063oa

Braun, V., & Clarke, V. (2012). Thematic analysis. In H. Cooper (Ed.), *APA handbook of research methods in psychology* (pp. 57–71). American Psychological Association.

Braun, V., & Clarke, V. (2021). Can i use TA? Should i use TA? Should i not use TA? Comparing reflexive thematic analysis and other pattern-based qualitative analytic approaches. *Counselling and Psychotherapy Research*, *21*(1), 37–47. https://doi.org/10.1002/capr.12360

Burke, S. (2017). Rethinking 'validity' and 'trustworthiness' in qualitative inquiry. In B. Smith & A. C. Sparkes (Eds.), *Routledge handbook of qualitative research in sport and exercise* (pp. 330–339). Routledge.

Cardinale, I. (2018). Beyond constraining and enabling: Toward new microfoundations for institutional theory. *Academy of Management Review*, *43*(1), 132–155. https://doi.org/10.5465/amr.2015.0020

Crotty, M. (1998). *The foundations of social research: Meaning and perspective in the research process.* Sage.

Cunningham, G. B. (2015). Creating and sustaining workplace cultures supportive of LGBT employees in college athletics. *Journal of Sport Management*, *29*(4), 426–442. https://doi.org/10.1123/jsm.2014-0135

Cunningham, G. B., & Nite, C. (2020). LGBT diversity and inclusion, community characteristics, and success. *Journal of Sport Management*, *34*(6), 533–541. https://doi.org/10.1123/jsm.2019-0338

Denzin, N. K., & Lincoln, Y. S. (2011). *The Sage handbook of qualitative research.* Sage.

DiMaggio, P. J., & Powell, W. W. (1983). The iron cage revisited: Institutional isomorphism and collective rationality in organizational fields. *American Sociological Review*, *48*(2), 147–160. https://doi.org/10.2307/2095101

Dowling, M., & Smith, J. (2016). The institutional work of own the Podium in developing high-performance sport in Canada. *Journal of Sport Management*, *30*(4), 396–410. https://doi.org/10.1123/jsm.2014-0290

Garfinkel, H. (1967). *Studies in ethnomethodology.* Prentice-Hall.

Giddens, A. (1984). *The constitution of society: Outline of the theory of structuration.* Univ of California Press.

Granovetter, M. (1985). Economic action and social structure: The problem of embeddedness. *American Journal of Sociology*, *91*(3), 481–510. https://doi.org/10.1086/228311

Greenwood, R., Oliver, C., Sahlin, K., & Suddaby, R. (2008). Introduction. In R. Greenwood, C. Oliver, K. Sahlin, & R. Suddaby (Eds.), *The SAGE handbook of organizational institutionalism* (pp. 1–46). Sage.

Hampel, C., Lawrence, T., & Tracey, P. (2017). Institutional work: Taking stock and making it matter. In R. Greenwood, C. Oliver, R. Lawrence, & R. Meyer (Eds.), *The SAGE handbook of organizational institutionalism* (pp. 558–590). SAGE.

Holm, P. (1995). The dynamics of institutionalization: Transformation processes in Norwegian fisheries. *Administrative Science Quarterly, 40*(3), 398–422. https://doi.org/10.2307/2393791

Huml, M., & Taylor, E. (2022, September 14). Why employees are fleeing the college athletics industry. *Sportico.Com*. https://www.sportico.com/leagues/college-sports/2022/why-employees-are-leaving-college-athletics-1234687903/

Huml, M. R., Taylor, E. A., & Dixon, M. A. (2021). From engaged worker to workaholic: A mediated model of athletic department employees. *European Sport Management Quarterly, 21*(4), 583–604. https://doi.org/10.1080/16184742.2020.1765404

Hutchinson, M., & Bouchet, A. (2014). Organizational redirection in highly bureaucratic environments: De-escalation of commitment among Division I athletic departments. *Journal of Sport Management, 28*(2), 143–161. https://doi.org/10.1123/jsm.2012-0303

Jones, I. (2015). *Research methods for sport studies*. Routledge.

Kerwin, S., & Hoeber, L. (2015). Collaborative self-ethnography: Navigating self-reflexivity in a sport management context. *Journal of Sport Management, 29*(5), 498–509. https://doi.org/10.1123/jsm.2014-0144

Kim, M., Kim, A. C. H., Newman, J. I., Ferris, G. R., & Perrewé, P. L. (2019). The antecedents and consequences of positive organizational behavior: The role of psychological capital for promoting employee well-being in sport organizations. *Sport Management Review, 22*(1), 108–125. https://doi.org/10.1016/j.smr.2018.04.003

Kim, M., Zvosec, C. C., Oja, B. D., & Schuetz, L. (2023). Grit through the grind: Exploring sport employee work grit. *European Sport Management Quarterly, 23*(3), 833–852. https://doi.org/10.1080/16184742.2021.1936114

Koustelios, A. (2001). Burnout among Greek sport centre employees. *Sport Management Review, 4*(2), 151–163. https://doi.org/10.1016/S1441-3523(01)70073-3

Kvale, S. (1996). *Interviews: An introduction to qualitative research interviewing*. Sage.

Laverty, S. M. (2003). Hermeneutic phenomonenology and phenomenology: A comparison of historical and methodological considerations. *International Journal of Qualitative Methods, 2*(3), 21–35. https://doi.org/10.1177/160940690300200303

Lawrence, T. B., & Suddaby, R. (2006). Institutions and institutional work. In S. R. Clegg, C. Hardy, T. B. Lawrence, & W. R. Nord (Eds.), *Handbook of organization studies* (pp. 215–254). Sage.

Lee, Y. H., & Woo, B. (2017). Emotional intelligence, emotional labor, and emotional exhaustion among Korean fitness employees. *Journal of Global Sport Management, 2*(1), 65–78. https://doi.org/10.1080/24704067.2017.1283528

Lok, J., & Willmott, H. (2019). Embedded agency in institutional theory: Problem or paradox? *Academy of Management Review, 44*(2), 470–473. https://doi.org/10.5465/amr.2017.0571

Meyer, J. W., & Rowan, B. (1977). Institutionalized organizations: Formal structure as myth and ceremony. *American Journal of Sociology, 83*(2), 340–363. https://doi.org/10.1086/226550

Micelotta, E., Lounsbury, M., & Greenwood, R. (2017). Pathways of institutional change: An integrative review and research agenda. *Journal of Management, 43*(6), 1885–1910. https://doi.org/10.1177/0149206317699522

Micelotta, E. R., & Washington, M. (2013). Institutions and maintenance: The repair work of Italian professions. *Organization Studies, 34*(8), 1137–1170. https://doi.org/10.1177/0170840613492075

Misener, K., & Doherty, A. (2009). A case study of organizational capacity in non-profit community sport. *Journal of Sport Management, 23*(4), 457–482. https://doi.org/10.1123/jsm.23.4.457

Nite, C. (2017). Message framing as institutional maintenance: The National Collegiate Athletic Association's institutional work of addressing legitimate threats. *Sport Management Review, 20*(4), 338–351. https://doi.org/10.1016/j.smr.2016.10.005

Nite, C., & Bopp, T. (2017). Conflicting prescriptions for 'ethical' leadership in complex institutions: Perspectives from US collegiate athletic administrators. *Leadership, 13*(3), 368–387. https://doi.org/10.1177/1742715015605878

Nite, C., & Edwards, J. (2021). From isomorphism to institutional work: Advancing institutional theory in sport management research. *Sport Management Review, 24*(5), 815–838. https://doi.org/10.1080/14413523.2021.1896845

Nite, C., Ige, A., & Washington, M. (2019). The evolving institutional work of the National Collegiate Athletic Association to maintain dominance in a fragmented field. *Sport Management Review, 22*(3), 379–394. https://doi.org/10.1016/j.smr.2018.05.002

Nite, C., & Nauright, J. (2020). The institutionalization of abuse in sport organizations: Examining the institutional work of U.S. universities in managing sexual abuse scandals. *Sport Management Review, 23*(1), 117–129. https://doi.org/10.1016/j.smr.2019.06.002

Nite, C., Singer, J. N., & Cunningham, G. B. (2013). Addressing competing logics between the mission of a religious university and the demands of intercollegiate athletics. *Sport Management Review, 16*(4), 465–476. https://doi.org/10.1016/j.smr.2013.03.002

Nite, C., & Washington, M. (2017). Institutional adaptation to technological innovation: Lessons from the NCAA's regulation of football television broadcasts (1938–1984). *Journal of Sport Management, 31*(6), 575–590. https://doi.org/10.1123/jsm.2017-0159

Oja, B. D., Bass, J. R., & Gordon, B. S. (2015). Conceptualizing employee identification with sport organizations: Sport employee identification (SEI). *Sport Management Review, 18*(4), 583–595. https://doi.org/10.1016/j.smr.2015.02.002

Oja, B. D., Bass, J. R., & Gordon, B. S. (2020). Identities in the sport workplace: Development of an instrument to measure sport employee identification. *Journal of Global Sport Management, 5*(3), 262–284. https://doi.org/10.1080/24704067.2018.1477521

Oja, B. D., Gordon, B. S., & Hazzaa, R. N. (2023). Navigating psychological membership in sport organizations: Exploring sport employees' identities. *Journal of Applied Sport Psychology, 35*(2), 202–223. https://doi.org/10.1080/10413200.2021.2021563

Oja, B. D., Kim, M., Perrewé, P. L., & Anagnostopoulos, C. (2019). Conceptualizing A-HERO for sport employees' well-being. *Sport, Business and Management: An International Journal, 9*(4), 363–380. https://doi.org/10.1108/SBM-10-2018-0084

Oja, B. D., Zvosec, C. C., & Kim, M. (in press). Reimagining sport/leisure workplace design and management: Conceptualizing sport/leisure employee growth. *Managing Sport and Leisure*, 1–17. https://doi.org/10.1080/23750472.2022.2092537

Oldham, G. R., & Fried, Y. (2016). Job design research and theory: Past, present, and future. *Organizational Behavior and Human Decision Processes, 136*, 20–35. https://doi.org/10.1016/j.obhdp.2016.05.002

Paek, B., Martyn, J., Oja, B. D., Kim, M., & Larkins, R. J. (2022). Searching for sport employee creativity: A mixed-methods exploration. *European Sport Management Quarterly, 22*(4), 483–505. https://doi.org/10.1080/16184742.2020.1804429

Powell, W. W., & Rerup, C. (2017). Opening the black box: The microfoundations of institutions. In R. Greenwood, C. Oliver, T. B. Lawrence, & R. E. Meyer (Eds.), *The SAGE handbook of organizational institutionalism* (2nd ed., pp. 311–337). SAGE.

Rich, K. A., & Misener, L. (2017). Insiders, outsiders, and agents of change: First person action inquiry in community sport management. *Sport Management Review, 20*(1), 8–19. https://doi.org/10.1016/j.smr.2016.08.004

Robertson, J., Dowling, M., Washington, M., Leopkey, B., Ellis, D. L., & Smith, L. (2022). Institutional theory in sport: A scoping review. *Journal of Sport Management, 22*(5), 459–472. https://doi.org/10.1123/jsm.2021-0179

Schuetz, L., Oja, B. D., Zvosec, C. C., Kim, M., & Kerwin, S. (in press). Autonomy in design: Reconciling sport employee experiences with forced job design alterations. *Managing Sport and Leisure*, 1–15. https://doi.org/10.1080/23750472.2022.2092539

Seo, M. G., & Creed, W. E. D. (2002). Institutional contradictions, praxis, and institutional change: A dialectical perspective. *Academy of Management Review, 27*(2), 222–247. https://doi.org/10.2307/4134353

Smith, B., & McGannon, K. R. (2018). Developing rigor in qualitative research: Problems and opportunities within sport and exercise psychology. *International Review of Sport and Exercise Psychology, 11*(1), 101–121. https://doi.org/10.1080/1750984X.2017.1317357

Svensson, P. G., Jeong, S., Shuck, B., & Otto, M. G. (2021). Antecedents and outcomes of employee engagement in sport for development. *Sport Management Review*, *24*(4), 673–696. https://doi.org/10.1080/14413523.2021.1880758

Tamminen, K. A., & Poucher, Z. A. (2020). Research philosophies. In *The Routledge international encyclopedia of sport and exercise psychology* (pp. 535-549). Routledge.

Taylor, E. A., Huml, M. R., & Dixon, M. A. (2019). Workaholism in sport: A mediated model of work-family conflict and burnout. *Journal of Sport Management*, *33*(4), 249–260. https://doi.org/10.1123/jsm.2018-0248

Taylor, J. (2011). The intimate insider: Negotiating the ethics of friendship when doing insider research. *Qualitative Research*, *11*(1), 3–22. https://doi.org/10.1177/1468794110384447

Tracy, S. J. (2010). Qualitative quality: Eight "big-tent" criteria for excellent qualitative research. *Qualitative Inquiry*, *16*(10), 837–851.

van Manen, M. (1990). *Researching lived experience*. State University of New York Press.

van Manen, M. (2016). *Phenomenology of practice*. Routledge.

Washington, M., & Patterson, K. D. W. (2011). Hostile takeover or joint venture: Connections between institutional theory and sport management research. *Sport Management Review*, *14*(1), 1–12. https://doi.org/10.1016/j.smr.2010.06.003

Weight, E. A., Taylor, E., Huml, H. R., & Dixon, M. A. (2021). Working in the sport industry: A classification of human capital archetypes. *Journal of Sport Management*, *35*(4), 364–378. https://doi.org/10.1123/jsm.2020-0070

Woolf, J., Berg, B., Newland, B., & Green, C. (2016). So you want to be a fighter? Institutional work and sport development processes at an elite mixed martial arts gym. *Journal of Sport Management*, *30*(4), 438–452. https://doi.org/10.1123/jsm.2014-0301

The legitimacy work of institutional disruption and maintenance: examining the rivalry between LIV golf and the professional golf association

Calvin Nite, Ajhanai Keaton, Patrick Neff and Craig Fulk

ABSTRACT

Research Question: Research has shown those within sport organizations engage in legitimacy work when innovation is introduced and/or when current institutional arrangements are challenged. However, both legitimacy work and emotions have received limited attention within sport management research. This study sought to answer two questions: How do actors in dominant sport organizations frame messages to influence perceptions of legitimacy? And, how are messages crafted to evoke emotional responses from evaluators of new endeavors?

Research Methods: Using framing theory to guide the analysis, the researchers conducted emotional discourse analysis of 38 mainstream sport media articles to understand how PGA members framed messages to evoke emotional responses from audiences to influence how they perceived LIV Golf.

Results and Findings: The findings showed that the PGA framed itself as true golf and used emotional discourse to show how LIV Golf undermined the PGA's conception. Actors suggested that LIV was eroding the legacy and traditions of golf, destroying the game, and negating the meritocratic structures of golf. The discourses within these themes were rife with emotional syntax that became a means of legitimacy work to maintain the dominant positioning of the PGA.

Implications: This research extends current understandings of legitimacy and institutional work within sport management by showing how emotion can be used as a means of legitimacy work to address/hinder institutional field dynamics, like innovation and competition. This work also shows how subjects of legitimacy work can change from the introduced practices to the introducing actor. Finally, this work shows how challenges can induce institutional evangelism.

Legitimacy has largely been understood as people's perceptions of what are considered correct, desirable, and appropriate behaviors within a given setting (Suchman, 1995). Sport and other organizations tend to adopt operating structures and behaviors that align with expectations of various stakeholders and this, in turn, shields organizations from scrutiny while giving access to resources (broadly conceived) that are needed for survival (Deephouse & Suchman, 2008). Within sport and other industries, organizations must manage new challenges such as innovative product offerings or the emergence of rival organizations, that threaten to alter current institutional arrangements. Those challenges, regardless of utility, presents legitimacy concerns because new practices, structures, and approaches force interrogations of the properness of current institutional dynamics (Nite & Washington, 2017). As such, institutionalized actors, especially when they benefit from current institutional arrangements, will likely defend the current institutional arrangements via the process that has become known as institutional work.

Within the broader institutional work framework, legitimacy work has emerged as a distinct concept wherein actors focus more on influencing perceptions of institutions rather than focusing on institutional structures, practices, and dynamics. In this regard, legitimacy work tends to involve rhetoric and manipulation of discourse to sway opinions surrounding institutional issues (see Lefsrund et al., 2020; Nite, 2017; Nite & Nauright, 2020; Zietsma & Lawrence, 2010). When innovative institutional practices and structures are introduced, institutional defenders can influence perceptions through the manipulation of emotions (Creed et al., 2014), specifically through various forms of media (see Lefsrund et al., 2020; Nite, 2017). For instance, environmentalists produced emotionally charged media messages to garner public support as they pressured those in the logging industry to innovate logging practices in British Columbia (Zietsma & Lawrence, 2010). Despite the emergence of legitimacy work and the utility of emotion within, there is much we do not understand in this space.

Increasingly, institutional scholars have paid attention to the role of emotion within institutional processes (see Lok et al., 2017) and have called for greater attention to emotions within sport institutions (Nite & Edwards, 2021; Robertson et al., 2022). Institutionalists tend to focus on engrained structures of social interaction and tend to dehumanize institutionalization (Lok et al., 2017). However, institutions are *human productions* of collective taken-for-granted behaviors and structures (see Greenwood et al., 2008), and as such, it is important to understand how human emotion influences people's adherence to or rejection of engrained institutions (Lok et al., 2017). Scholars have noted that 'social emotions are likely to be particularly important in institutional processes [because they] are implicated in the ways people make sense of and participate in the interactions that underpin the shared enactment of institutional arrangements' (Creed et al., 2014, p. 279). Further, emotion has been considered a defining feature of sport products as sport organizations often attempt to invoke emotions through marketing efforts (Kwak et al., 2011) as consumers are often emotionally attached to their favorite sport teams (Lee et al., 2018). To fully understand how actors can manipulate sport institutions and perceptions of legitimacy, scholars must account for the influence of human emotion. With this study, we seek to answer calls for developing better understanding of emotions and legitimacy work within sport management.

The purpose of this research is to examine how affiliates of dominant institutions frame media discourses to impact perceptions of legitimacy of emergent rivals. We build upon prior theorizations of legitimacy work to understand how sport actors craft messages that evoke emotional responses to influence perceptions of legitimacy. In doing so, we examine rivalry between the Professional Golf Association (PGA) and the newly founded golf league LIV Golf (LIV). Historically, the PGA has been the dominant governing body of golf and has hosted the PGA Tour as the primary professional golf league, especially within North America. Yet, in recent years, LIV has emerged as an alternative golf league and has drawn several high-profile professional golfers, such as Phil Mickelson and Dustin Johnson, to its league with large guaranteed contracts and reduced number of tournaments. LIV has been a source of controversy given its primary funding source and innovative approaches to golf competitions that deviate from traditional PGA tournament structures. As such, we focus, primarily, on how the PGA and its sympathizers framed various aspects of LIV to influence golf stakeholders' perceptions of LIV's legitimacy. Through emotional discourse analysis (Koschut, 2018), we highlight how organizations, practices, and structures can be framed to invoke emotional responses that were designed to influence perceptions of legitimacy.

Theory: legitimacy work and emotions

Legitimacy is a central concept of institutional theory and is the primary theoretical focus of this research. Deephouse et al. (2017) defined legitimacy as 'the perceived appropriateness of an organization to a social system in terms of rules, values, norms, and definitions' (p. 32). Organizations and other entities seek legitimacy to secure access to resources needed for survival (Meyer & Rowan, 1977). Actions are evaluated by relevant audiences who make judgements on the properness of said actions (Deephouse et al., 2017) and can be influenced by concerted human actions, specifically institutional work (Hampel et al., 2017; Nite & Nauright, 2020). Institutional work has been defined as the 'purposeful, reflective efforts of individuals and collective actors and networks of actors intended to shape a society's ideas, beliefs, values, and assumptions' (Lawrence & Phillips, 2019, p. 189) and draws upon the notion of embedded agency by explicating how actors are simultaneously influencers of and influenced by institutions (Battilana & D'Aunno, 2012).

As institutional work has proven effective for explaining institutional processes, scholars have pointed to new areas of development that may further detail how actors influence institutions. Hampel et al. (2017) suggested scholars move beyond exploring the outcomes of institutional work (i.e. creation, maintenance, and disruption) and develop more insight into the 'means' of achieving institutional objectives. Consequently, the lived experiences of agency are receiving more attention, particularly how the humanized aspect of agency might influence institutions (Lok et al., 2017; Nite & Edwards, 2021). There is a contemporary shift to consider how institutional work is in relationship with other tenets of institutional theory, like logics and legitimacy (Hampel et al., 2017; Nite & Edwards, 2021).

Whereas institutional work focuses on actions that influence institutions and institutionalization, legitimacy work is distinct, as the focus is on influencing perceptions of the properness of institutions. This is an important distinction because the work that influences perceptions of legitimacy, although rooted in and drawing upon institutions, focuses on audience cognitions rather than the activities of institutional work that generally focus on embedding routines, developing regulatory structures, and crafting cognitive schema (see Hampel et al., 2017; Lawrence & Suddaby, 2006; Nite et al., 2019). In effect, legitimacy work tends to be symbolic and focused on influencing actors rather than on institutions.

Although a relatively nascent concept, scholars have recognized various actions of legitimacy work. Research has shown that actors may purposefully obscure institutional processes through collusion and silencing dissenters (Nite & Nauright, 2020). Related, scholars have detailed how strategic alliances may also influence how others perceive the legitimacy of sport endeavors (Byun et al., 2021). Others have shown framing acts and/or actors as 'exemplars' or as 'harmful' may also influence perceptions of legitimacy (Nite, 2017; Nite & Nauright, 2020). Further, Lefsrund et al. (2020) explicated how symbolic text and imagery may be implemented to evoke emotional responses to influence perceptions of legitimacy. Indeed, legitimacy work seems to entail some manipulation of evaluators' emotions. The work of Lefsrud and colleagues (2020) is particularly notable as it addressed the call for more research of symbols and emotions within institutional research (see Hampel et al., 2017). Their work provided evidence of the utility of connecting symbology with human responses to understand legitimation processes.

Emotions

Over the latter part of the 2010s, institutional scholars have recognized the impact of emotions within institutional processes (Lok et al., 2017; Voronov & Vince, 2012). Researching and understanding emotions is important because institutions are products of human activity and emotionality is a defining characteristic of being human (Hampel et al., 2017; Lok et al., 2017). Relevant to the current inquiry, legitimacy work may entail the invocation and manipulation of emotion to influence people's perceptions of properness (Deephouse et al., 2017; Lok et al., 2017). Specifically, emotions may become part of organizational discourse (Koschut, 2018) and may be invoked to influence people's perceptions of properness (Deephouse et al., 2017).

Emotions can be explicit in discourses with authors invoking words like 'fear,' 'shame,' or 'anger.' Emotions can also be *loaded* in words invoking negative connotations such as 'genocide,' 'slavery,' or 'massacre.' Additionally, emotions can be expressed in metaphors and analogies, as these phrases create a mental image/perception to reference that is connected to an emotional sentiment. Examples include, 'Beacon of democracy,' 'heart of a lion,' 'early bird,' or 'He is the biggest fraud since Bernie Madoff.' As such, 'it is emotions that change mere strings of words into meaningful narratives that inform inspired practice' (Lok et al., 2017, p. 595). Whereas people's emotional evaluations may not fully encapsulate evaluations of legitimacy (Deephouse et al., 2017), they are indicative of how people respond to institutional initiatives and/or challenges to institutional processes (Lok et al., 2017). Considering legitimacy is largely a *perception*, it is important to understand how stakeholders' perceptions are influenced by their emotional to challenge institutional field dynamics, like innovation and competition.

Focusing on emotions as integral to legitimacy work seems particularly relevant when new endeavors are introduced that challenge current institutional structures and especially when those challenges are somewhat controversial. Emotions provide insight into people's values and how they make sense of the world (Creed et al., 2014; Voronov & Vince, 2012). When new endeavors are introduced that conflict or even challenge people's values, they will likely experience emotional responses that will impact their perceptions of the properness of the endeavor (Voronov & Vince, 2012). Entities may then take actions to manipulate people's emotions to garner a targeted evaluation of the legitimacy of an endeavor. Often, these actions entail discursive work where an entity may frame messaging around the endeavor to influence people's attitudes (Tewksbury & Scheufele, 2009).

To better understand how discourses may be framed to evoke emotions that influence perceptions of legitimacy, we examine the rivalry between members of LIV Golf and members of the PGA. In the following section, we provide an overview of this rivalry. To study this rivalry, we draw upon framing theory and critical discourse analysis to show how PGA members crafted their messages to evoke negative emotions regarding the emergence of LIV Golf.

The PGA and LIV golf

Our study of legitimacy work was situated within the context of professional golf. The two focal organizations of interest are the Professional Golf Association (PGA) and LIV Golf (LIV). Our research focused men's golf as LIV Golf at the time of this writing was exclusively a men's tour with no female equivalent. It is also important to note that the PGA Tour and LIV announced their merger in June of 2023 (after this research had been completed). The PGA of America was founded in 1916 with 35 charter members (History of the PGA, n.d.). Currently, the organization describes itself as 'one of the world's largest sports organizations, composed of PGA Professionals who work daily to grow interest and participation in the game of golf' (PGA of America, n.d., para. 1). PGA professionals include people working at local golf clubs and touring professional golfers. The PGA is the host organization of the PGA Tour (sponsor title: FedEx Cup) which consists of 47 tournament events that culminates with a Tour Championship tournament. Professional golfers accumulate points throughout the tour season based on how they finish in the different tournaments they play (About us, n.d.). Further, the PGA of America is affiliated with the European Tour (current sponsor title: DP World Tour) that hosts professional golf events throughout the world (What is the DP World Tour?, 2019). In recent years, the PGA Tour and the European Tour (DP World Tour) have developed a close working alliance and have collaborated on popular golf competitions such as the Ryder Cup (Carter, 2020). The PGA provides payment to golfers based on how they place within tournaments (the amounts vary depending on the tournament) and the winner of the 2022 FedEx Cup (Rory McIlroy) earned $18 million (Payday at East Lake, 2022). The typical PGA tournament event is 72 holes played out in four rounds over four days (typically Thursday-Sunday) with a 'cut' after 36 holes that eliminates approximately half of the field who are not within a certain number of strokes of the lead, and, until very recently, PGA tournaments have not provided guaranteed payments to golfers.

LIV Golf emerged in the Fall of 2021 as an alternative league for professional golfers. LIV is funded by Saudi Arabia's Public Investment Fund and is being led by Greg

Norman, a former professional golfer who had been trying to develop an alternative tour to rival the PGA since the mid-1990s (Dethier, 2022). LIV has the stated mission 'to modernize and supercharge the game of professional golf through expanded opportunities for both players and fans alike' (Who we are, n.d., para 1). LIV has touted some revolutionary structural diversions from traditional PGA events. These include shorter durations of competitions (three days, 54 holes), team events within each tournament, guaranteed payments to all participating golfers, fewer golfers per tournament, defined golf seasons, and no cuts during tournaments (How it works, n.d.). Further, LIV offered other perks such as chartered flights to tournaments for golfers and their teams (Zimmer, 2022). The LIV season is comprised of seven regular season tournaments that culminate with a four-day, four-round event that crowns an individual champion who receives $18 million and team champion with first place earning $16 million. Indeed, one of the primary features of LIV has been the amount of money the league offers players. As a *New York Times* article noted, 'The LIV Golf events are the richest tournaments in golf history … The winner's share at each stop is $4 million, and the last-place finisher is guaranteed $120,000. And that is on top of the appearance fees and signing-on payouts individual players have accepted' (Panja & Das, 2022, para 6–7).

However, LIV's emergence was met with substantial backlash from the PGA and other members of the golf and broader sport communities. Specifically, LIV has been heavily criticized as being anti-competitive because of the guaranteed payouts to its golfers. In fact, many PGA affiliates and supporters have labeled defection to the LIV tour as a money grab by players (Panja & Das, 2022). An anonymous player suggested, ' … these guys wanted a quick money grab to go play in an exhibition' and were hurting the sport of golf by playing in LIV events (Schlabach, 2022, para. 28). Others have criticized LIV's 54-hole, no-cut format which is distinct from the PGA Tour's 72-hole with cuts after the first 36 holes offering (Saul, 2022). Tiger Woods even stated, 'I don't understand it … What is the incentive to practice and earn it in the dirt?' (Harig, 2022c, paras. 3 & 7). Further, LIV has been criticized for its reliance on funding from the Public Investment Fund which is directly tied the Saudi Arabian royal family (Warren, 2022). Critics argue that the Saudis' investment in LIV is a form of 'sport-washing' that is meant to distract the public from the nefarious acts committed by Saudi Arabian royals. Sport washing has been defined as 'a means by which a country can deflect audiences' attention away from less favorable perceptions of a country via a program of investment in sport' (Chadwick, 2022, p. 696). The Kingdom of Saudi Arabia and its royal family have been accused of nefarious actions for many years. Specifically, in recent years, the state and royal family of Saudi Arabia was accused of and condemned by leaders of the United Nations for the torturous murder of *Washington Post* journalist Jamal Khashoggi (Khashoggi killing, 2019). Some have also condemned Saudi Arabia's attack on Yemen and accused the Saudis of committing war crimes by bombing civilian homes and other targets such as hospitals (Lee et al., 2022).

Despite the substantial criticism of LIV, numerous high-profile players and members of the mainstream golf and sport community have joined LIV Golf. Notably, LIV has attracted multiple major champions[1] including: Phil Mickelson, Dustin Johnson, Bryson DeChambeau, Brooks Koepka, Patrick Reed, and Sergio Garcia, among other well-known professional golfers (Rivera, 2022). LIV golfers have pointed to various reasons for leaving the PGA Tour to join LIV, such as increased payouts and more favorable tournament schedules (Rivera, 2022). For instance, Phil Mickelson was allegedly offered $200 million, which was more than double his entire PGA Tour career earnings (Cannizzaro, 2022; Rivera, 2022). Whereas the money was cited as an important factor, Cameron Smith (winner of the 2022 Open Championship) also stated that LIV's tournament schedule was one of the main factors in his decision to join LIV (Priest, 2022). Regardless of each player's individual reasoning, LIV has provided an alternative and lucrative professional golf option for professional golfers. Ultimately, the PGA Tour suspended golfers who participated and became affiliated with LIV Golf and its tournaments (Schlabach, 2022). The backlash to LIV is unsurprising considering challenges to current institutional arrangements are typically met with resistance as people and organizations figure out how to manage the implications of the challenges (Nite & Washington, 2017).

We consider the rivalry between the PGA (and its supporters) and LIV as struggle of legitimacy. Whereas we are not privy to internal dialogs, the public messaging from members and advocates for both entities seems to center around arguments regarding the properness of professional golf competition structures, treatment of players, and who should be considered the primary purveyor of professional golf. A distinct feature of the legitimacy struggles between the PGA and LIV has been the noticeable emotionality of messaging from PGA advocates. In an interview with *Golf Digest* regarding LIV golfers playing in a normal PGA event, professional golfer Billy Horschel stated 'There are mixed feelings out here. Some guys don't think the LIV guys should be here ... When they said they wanted to play less golf. It's pretty hypocritical to come over here ... ' (Huggan, 2022, para. 6 & 9). As our research focuses on understanding how dominant sport governing bodies and affiliated actors respond to newly introduced practices and organizing structures, we examined the public messaging of the PGA and its advocates, focusing on how messages were comprised of emotionality to influence perceptions of legitimacy from golf stakeholders such as players, fans, corporate sponsors, and television networks. Our work was guided by two broad research questions:

> RQ1: How do affiliates of dominant sport organizations frame messages to influence stakeholders' perceptions of an emergent rival's legitimacy?
>
> RQ2: How are messages crafted to evoke emotional responses from evaluators of new endeavors?

Method

This study was guided by framing theory (Frederick et al., 2021; Tewksbury & Scheufele, 2009) and used emotional discourse analysis (EDA) (Koschut, 2018) to examine how affiliates of the PGA sought to establish particular frames laden with emotion to influence perceptions of legitimacy. Framing is a sociological approach for examining how perception is dictated by informational schemes that inform interpretive processes (Frederick et al., 2021). A frame 'unifies information into a package that can influence audiences' (Tewksbury & Scheufele, 2009, p. 19). In this regard, framing theory is concerned with how frames are packaged, constructed, and understood to characterize issues. Gross and D'ambrosio (2004) found that framing affected emotional responses, though this relationship was partially dependent on predispositions of the viewer. One intriguing area of framing research focuses on the relatively irrational nature of individuals and situations where multiple frames are brought into opposition (Spiegler, 2014). De Vreese (2005) explained framing as a process that consists of the frame building by the presenter and then the frame setting with the audience and its effects on processing. Hence, a critical aspect of framing is making sense of how media frames inform interpretative processes based upon what information is shared, emphasized, or excluded.

Scholars implementing framing theory are particularly concerned with *frame building*, which examines how frames become established in societal discourse and how these frames become manipulated by dominant actors within various settings to win a *frame contest* (Tewksbury & Scheufele, 2009). These framing contests can have a winner with one frame becoming dominant or can see offsetting effects that lead to an overall neutral response to the framing (Druckman, 2004; Kaplan, 2008). The purpose of exploring *frame building* is to understand how particular entities engage in a *frame contest*. In a frame contest, 'one interpretative package might gain influence because it resonates with popular culture or a series of events, fits with media routines or practices, and/or is heavily sponsored by elites' (Tewksbury & Scheufele, 2009). This notion of a frame contest finds connection to our investigation of legitimacy work. Like legitimacy work, a frame contest is about influence and how different actors engage in particular tactics to maintain or establish a legitimate position. Thus, we used framing theory as a foundational aspect of our methodological approach for examining how dominant sport organizations frame messages to influence perceptions of legitimacy and craft messages to evoke emotional responses from evaluators of new endeavors.

Data collection

In alignment with framing theory (Tewksbury et al., 2000), we focused on major/mainstream and primarily U.S. based sport news outlets (Sports Illustrated, ESPN, Golf Channel, Golf.com, etc.), to examine how dominant sport organizations frame messages to influence perceptions of legitimacy (see Table 1). To answer the research questions, our inclusion and exclusion criteria included the following: (a) Mainstream sport news media articles, (b) Sport news media articles that centered the commentary of key PGA actors, (c) Sport news media articles that discussed LIV, (d) Sport news media articles that contrasted PGA and LIV and used PGA actors' commentary to do so. We intentionally focused on outlets (i.e. *Golf Monthly, Sport Illustrated, New York Times, ESPN, The Athletic, LA Times*, etc.) because of their influence upon societal discourses and perceptions of an issue (Tewksbury & Scheufele, 2009).

Our approach began with a Google News search of 'LIV golf' and selected sport news media articles dating back to the 'early whispers' of a competing golf organization (i.e. LIV) in October of 2021 until October 2022. Considering our initial searches returned thousands of articles, we were stringent with the following inclusion/exclusion criteria to address our theoretical questions. We excluded articles that we considered to be commentary from non-PGA affiliated affiliates. To clarify, we excluded commentary articles from golf pundits who were not touring PGA members or members of the PGA or LIV executive teams. Given the context of the rivalry between PGA and LIV, we sought to only collect discourses from stakeholders who were either members or executive leaders of the PGA and would feel the need to maintain the historical and contemporary

Table 1. Articles included in Emotional Discourse Analysis.

Doc #	Title	Source
1	Weekly Read: PGA Tour Players Offer Opinions on LIV Golf Invitational Possibilities	Sports Illustrated
2	Tiger Woods Restates Support for PGA Tour, Has 'A Lot of Disagreement' With Phil Mickelson, LIV Golf	Sports Illustrated
3	Dustin Johnson Headlines Field for Inaugural LIV Golf Tournament	Sports Illustrated
4	LIV Golf Received 170 Entries for First Event, Including 19 of World's Top 100	Sports Illustrated
5	Padraig Harrington Believes Outrage Over LIV Golf, Saudi Money, Will Dissipate: 'Time Will Pass'	Sports Illustrated
6	Former PGA Tour Players Now With LIV Have Memberships Revoked for Next Season	Sports Illustrated
7	Federal judge denies LIV golfers bid for PGA Tour postseason	Associated Press
8	Saudi money, blockbuster names and a unique format: everything you need to know about the LIV Golf series	CNN
9	LIV Golf Invitational Series to consist of eight events, offer $255 million in purses	ESPN
10	PGA Tour suspends all players taking part in first LIV Golf tournament	ESPN
11	Source: Bryson DeChambeau joining LIV Golf Invitational Series	ESPN
12	Billy Horschel blasts 'hypocrites' playing LIV Golf series, accuses some of 'lying'	ESPN
13	Tiger Woods turned down offer in 'neighborhood' of $700-$800 million when approached to join LIV Golf, Greg Norman says	ESPN
14	LIV Golf players suing the PGA Tour 'frustrating,' says Scottie Scheffler, No. 1-ranked player in the world	ESPN
15	Phil Mickelson: LIV Golf a 'force that's not going away'	ESPN
16	DP World Tour sends memo warning its players against playing LIV Golf events	Golf Channel
17	As LIV Golf dominates current conversation, fate of fall slate more important for many	Golf Channel
18	Rickie Fowler says he's considering playing in Saudi-backed LIV Golf series	Golf Digest
19	Nick Faldo not interested in LIV Golf, knows he and Greg Norman have no interest in each other	Golf Digest
20	Two more players bail from lawsuit against PGA Tour, but LIV Golf added to complaint	Golf Digest
21	Rory McIlroy can't stop, won't stop daggering LIV Golf lawyers	Golf Digest
22	Trevor Immelman Describes 'Pretty Frustrating' LIV Golf Uncertainty	Golf Monthly
23	'Yeah, you can't compare those': Justin Thomas shuts down Talor Gooch's comments about LIV Golf and Ryder Cup, Presidents Cup	Golf Week
24	'Most exciting golf TV ever': Greg Norman's rumored tour is talking a big game	Golf.com
25	11 burning questions about the future of LIV Golf and the PGA Tour	Golf.com
26	'Everybody, it feels like, is against us': LIV tension surfacing at Open Championship	Golf.com
27	'Complete bulls – ': Pro calls out LIV golfers' hollow justifications for leaving PGA Tour	Golf.com
28	'Brutally difficult': Trevor Immelman talks Presidents Cup headaches caused by LIV Golf	Golf.com
29	'They don't count': What Davis Love III thinks LIV Golf is missing	Golf.com
30	LIV Golf's response to PGA Tour's changes? One sentence – for now.	Golf.com
31	Could LIV Golf and the PGA Tour make peace? Don't count on it	Golf.com
32	'First time I have felt betrayal': Rory McIlroy opens up on LIV defections	Golf.com
33	'This Is Uncomfortable': Saudi Arabia Upends Genteel World of Pro Golf	New York Times
34	One Golfer Not Welcome at the British Open? Greg Norman.	New York Times
35	LIV Golf players ineligible for PGA Tour membership renewal	Reuters
36	Matt Fitzpatrick dishes on LIV Golf, critiques FedEx Cup Playoffs ahead of BMW Championship: 'I don't think it's fair'	USA Today
37	'If Rory was born in the United States, I'd vote him for president': Will Zalatoris dishes on LIV Golf, his U.S. Open close call, Tiger Woods, and tons more	USA Today
38	Golf at St. Andrews is real, which is why it has no room for Greg Norman	Washington Post

standing of the PGA. Consequently, we only selected sport news media articles that centered on or interviewed key PGA actors, like PGA golfers, the Commissioner, Senior Vice Presidents, CEOs of PGA affiliated tours, etc. Given our focus upon legitimacy work, we excluded news media articles from less influential actors, such as blogging sites, because our inquiry focused more upon how a dominant governing body would potentially use dominant media outlets to engage and hopefully win the *framing contest* (Tewksbury & Scheufele, 2009). Next, we identified duplicate articles in the sample as Associated Press releases were found to be republished by numerous outlets. Once the duplicates and commentary articles were removed, we scrutinized each article for duplicate quotes from PGA and LIV affiliates. Finally, we removed articles that we perceived as exclusively descriptive of facts and happenings in professional golf. For instance, and whereas we consulted various 'timeline articles' (e.g. Zak, 2022) to educate ourselves on the events leading up to the creation of LIV, articles of this nature were excluded because we did not view them as framed messages designed to evoke emotion. Based upon our research questions, methodology, and sampling techniques, our study included 38 sport news media articles which we viewed as speaking directly to the theoretical topics of this inquiry.

Analysis

We used Koschut's model of emotion discourse analysis (EDA) to examine how discourses evoke emotional responses from evaluators of new endeavors. EDA is an extension of discourse analysis (DA) (see Keaton, 2021; Sveinson et al., 2021), and like DA, EDA requires researchers to move beyond surface level interpretations of text and language to account for deeper complexities of how language is used to maintain or challenge hegemonic systems and power. EDA perceives 'emotions as socially constructed representations of meaning that are linked to conceptions of identity and power' (Koschut, 2018, p. 278). Thus, EDA considers how particular syntax, words, and phrases are strategically paired to evoke an emotional sentiment and examines the intent of the sentiment. A critical aspect of EDA is centering how emotions are informed by identity and sociocultural structures (Koschut, 2018). Thus, our analysis was attuned to *whose* discourses we examined (i.e. prominent PGA affiliates) and attuned to the sociocultural structures of their discourses (i.e. rivalry with LIV). Koschut's conceptual EDA model (2018) has three criteria: (1) selecting appropriate texts, (2) demonstrating what type of emotional meanings are linked to particular discourses (emotion potential of texts), and (3) contextualizing the intent and purpose of the discourse (emotionalization effects of texts). We used this structure in conjunction with our research methodology (framing) and theoretical framework (legitimacy work) to address the research questions.

Data were analyzed through a multi-step process that commenced with detailed critical readings which entailed the development of descriptive comments and concept codes to analyze how each sport news media article engaged in the *framing*. Using Koschut's (2018) conceptual model of EDA, we used the discourse tool, *Situated Meaning* (Gee, 2014) to consider the emotional potential of texts. *Situated Meaning* is a discourse tool that is used when listeners or readers, 'have to figure out – guess – what a [speaker] means based on what else has been said and other aspects of the context' (Gee, 2014, p. 158). Consequently, when analyzing the emotional potential of texts (Koschut, 2018), we were critically attuned to how particular words *appeared* out of place or unnecessary, but then transitioned to questioning how particular language was relevant to the broader contextual issues between the PGA and LIV. We then debriefed how emotional meaning was covertly and overtly presented in discourses and transitioned to considering the purpose of these discourses, which is level three of EDA. Finally, we engaged the iterative process of merging categories to solidify themes, which led to the authors establishing three themes – legacy and tradition, destroying the game, and golf is a meritocracy – with clear emotional discourses. These three themes supported the frame building efforts of the PGA to proverbially *win* the frame contest to maintain the PGA as *true golf* (Tewksbury & Scheufele, 2009).

Findings

Framing the PGA tour as true golf

There was one overarching frame capturing the legitimacy work of PGA tour members and executives. The PGA and affiliated members framed themselves as *true golf*, meaning any other golf association is an improper and illegitimate organization. Their frame building efforts were layered with emotional discourses captured in three themes arguing LIVs illegitimacy while also defending the PGA the dominant actor: (a) The legacy and traditions of the PGA are sacred, (b) LIV is destroying the game, and (c) golf's meritocratic structures are the norm. In each theme, prominent PGA stakeholders sought to delegitimize LIV through emotional appeal, rather than rationality. The use of emotion discourses to frame the PGA as *true golf* is succinctly captured in commentary from CBS Sports Chairman Sean McManus, as he avowed to be uninterested in LIV because he is focused on 'put[ting] out the best golf product in the world.' Thus, the notion of *true golf* is the overarching frame we identified that is built on the three sub-themes we describe in detail.

Legacy and tradition

To maintain the legitimacy of the PGA, stakeholders drew upon what the PGA has meant and should continue to mean to the golf community by focusing on *legacy and tradition*. These discourses framed those participating in LIV as actors wrongly and unjustly disrupting the history of the governing body and falling out of line with institutionalized practices. For example, Tiger Woods discussed how LIV is harming the legacy of the PGA and how doing so is disrespectful to long standing traditions. He shares:

> I just think what Jack (Nicklaus) and Arnold (Palmer) have done in starting the Tour and breaking away from the PGA of America and creating our Tour (in 1968) ... I just think there's a legacy to that ... I understand different viewpoints, but I believe in legacies. I believe in major championships. I believe in big events, comparisons to historical figures in the past. (Harig, 2022b)

Woods stated 'legacy' multiple times in an effort to communicate the sacredness of the PGA. Legacy is loaded with emotional syntax as it speaks to culture, commitment, and time (Koschut, 2018) and is framing the PGA as *true golf* because legacies have a story, history, and 'historical figures of the past' attached to it. In this regard, the PGA is the true institution in golf that was built upon American ideals of meritocracy. Additionally, there was an 'us v. them' component to his framing of PGA as *true golf* rooted in legacy and tradition. For example, he follows the above quote with, 'But you have to go out there and earn it. You've got to go out there and play for it.' Through the discourse tool of *Situated Meaning* (Gee, 2014), what Woods was really saying is that the tradition and history of PGA (us) is to 'earn it' and 'play for it', and, unlike LIV (them), our legacy is built upon 'not [being] guaranteed' [financial success] 'up front'. Hence, the purpose of the us versus them discourse was to remind the organizational field of the traditions and legacies of the PGA that *should* substantiate their status in the field as *true golf*.

When actors in the organizational field refused to uphold the 'legacy' of the PGA by participating in LIV, they were positioned as being 'defectors' and ' ... a field of guys who weren't really going to make a proper tour'. Matt Kuchar, a PGA golfer, used these loaded emotional discourses to delegitimize LIV and those who perceive LIV as a more prosperous financial opportunity. He asserted:

> I couldn't really see who was going to follow suit with what happened to Phil ... but if they [LIV] actually pulled off two or three events that went smoothly and a guy actually was cashing a $4 million check at the end of the week, I could see there being defectors for sure ... Now I think the fear is if they do get started and if it does go smoothly, I think they'll probably get some defectors. (Harig, 2022a)

A 'defector' is an individual who has abandoned their country, which carries the emotional connotation of being unpatriotic. In our current socio-political context, being perceived as a 'defector' has negative social, economic, and cultural repercussions. Therefore, the figurative weight packed into the discourse of 'defector' transitions to being a good citizen by maintaining PGA legacies and traditions. Lastly, Kuchar's discursive framing of the PGA as *true golf* was less about protecting the sport from expansion and more about re-legitimizing the status quo of the PGA in the organizational field, as his discourses attempt to position earning a '$4 million check' as a negative outcome, when it is only negative because it challenges the legacy and traditions of the PGA.

The PGA Tour Commissioner, Jay Monahan, used emotional discourses to frame the PGA as *true golf* by centering legacy and tradition. His emotional discourses drew upon the legacy of the PGA to argue PGA golfers as achieving their 'dreams' and as actors affiliated with a 'preeminent organization in the world of professional golf'. There is an emotion meaning attached to his discourse of 'dream' and 'preeminent organization', as he states in a memo to the Tour's membership:

> These players have made their choice for their own financial-based reasons ... That expectation disrespects you, our fans and our partners. You have made a different choice, which is to abide by the Tournament Regulations you agreed to when you accomplished the dream of earning a PGA TOUR card and – more importantly – to compete as part of the preeminent organization in the world of professional golf. (Schlabach, 2022)

When considering the emotionalization effect (Koschut, 2018) of 'dream', it seems the purpose was to remind PGA golfers who are considering participating in LIV, that they are currently living out their 'dream'. Meaning, their goal of attaining a PGA Tour card has been achieved and, they are affiliated with the greatest ('preeminent') golf organization in the world. Hence, Monahan used emotion discourses rooted in legacy to attempt to remind the organizational field who is *true golf,* as PGA golfers never dreamt of playing for a competing governing body.

Destroying the game

Discourses from prominent PGA stakeholders framed LIV as destroying *true golf*. Their discourses sought to not only delegitimize LIV as an improper golf association, but specifically frame them as actors who are 'fractur[ing] the game'. Rory McIlory, a four-time major PGA tour champion, shared:

> It's a shame that it's going to fracture the game. If the general public are confused about who is playing where and what tournaments this week [or] 'Oh, he plays there and he doesn't get into these events' it just becomes so confusing. (Schlabach, 2022)

McIlory's usage of 'fracture' was an emotional discourse attempting to position LIV as *breaking, damaging,* or *tearing apart* the sport. Additionally, his use of 'confusion' built upon this notion of destroying golf, as 'confusion' is an explicit negative term to reaffirm how LIV is 'fractur[ing] the game'. Essentially, the emotionalizing effect (Koschut, 2018) of these discourses were attempts to not only maintain normative practices, but to argue that LIV will create chaos and disorder because the public is unaware of which events to follow – which would destroy the game. More importantly, his use of 'shame' was another explicitly negative emotion discourse that attempts to instill guilt upon those who support LIV, as those who participate in LIV should feel guilty (or 'shameful') about what they are upholding (see also Creed et al., 2014).

Mark Hubbard, a PGA professional, perceived LIV as destroying the sanctity of golf. Rather than considering how the financial structure of LIV elevated the status of golfers, Hubbard and others evoked emotional discourses to frame LIV as destroying the game. He asserted:

> There's no way that tour (LIV) – 50 super-rich guys playing a 54-hole event – is growing the game. They're people who have already made their money, they're at the end of their career. That's not growing the game. The Tour already does a good job. (Marksbury, 2022)

Hubbard argued that current LIV golfers are 'rich guys' who are playing less holes, as the PGA standard is 72 holes. His discourses in the above excerpt have two emotionalizing effects (see Koschut, 2018): (a) to frame LIV golfers as lazy players destroying *true golf*, and (b) to frame former PGA members who joined LIV as greedy 'rich guys' who are more focused on financial interests. Hubbard then concludes by stating, 'The Tour already does a good job'. In this regard, drew upon broader institutionalized PGA ideals of hard work and meritocracy.

Lastly, although not explicitly stated, several PGA actors attempted to frame the LIV as a 'sportswashing' operation, which is when nations use sport to stoke nationalism and deflect from bringing attention to inhumane practices, human right issues, and other social inequities (Boykoff, 2022). Web Simpson, a PGA player, proclaimed:

> But what I think they have to look at long term is what does that mean for their brand, right? What do they stand for in life? I'm not going to point a finger at anybody, but I also know there's an awful lot of things that have been said about that group … Some guys are not looking at the source of the money. They are looking at the opportunity. And in this day and age, you can make an argument for that. But there's a lot of unknowns. I feel like there is security on the PGA Tour, it's going to be here for a long time. So, we'll see. (Harig, 2022a).

Emotional syntax is evident in the two questions Simpson poses: How does aligning with LIV impact a golfers' brand and how does the relationship inform their moral compass? Both questions appear to be broad sentiments of concern, but the issue of sportswashing is undergirding these questions, as he goes on to assert, 'Some guys are not looking at the *source* of the money.' Hence, Simpson's discourses are attempting to win the framing contest by loosely reminding the institutional field of *who* is financially supporting LIV (i.e. Saudi Arabia) and covertly reminding the field of *what* they are known for, as 'there's an awful lot of things have been said about that group' (i.e. human rights violations). Essentially, the questions and covert messaging of 'sportwashing' build to Simpson articulating how LIV lacks 'security', as the PGA '[will] be here for a long time'. The use of 'security' is an emotional appeal to frame the PGA as stable, secure, *true golf* – in comparison to the 'unknowns' of LIV.

Golf is a meritocracy

The legitimacy work of PGA affiliates used emotional discourses to argue that their meritocratic structures were essential to maintaining *true golf*. These discourses assisted in the frame building efforts to legitimize the PGA as *true golf* and cast LIV as morally inept, thereby undermining the moral legitimacy of LIV (see Suchman, 1995). Meritocracy represents the fallacy of a 'level playing field', thus, people who ' … choose to break the rules', are not upholding meritocracy and, instead, are a threat to it. Hence, those participating in LIV are golfers who break the rules and are not upholding PGA meritocratic values. This was especially noticed in comments from Martin Slumbers, a Chief Executive of the PGA Tour, who claimed LIV actors are 'driven by money' and 'undermin[ing] the merit-based culture and spirit of open competition that makes golf so special' (Bastable, 2022, para. 5). Additionally, his use of 'undermines' attempted to frame LIV as eroding and hurting the uniqueness of golf, which is the 'spirit of meritocracy'. Slumbers stated:

> I believe the model we've seen at Centurion and Pumpkin Ridge (LIV tournaments) is not in the best long-term interests of the sport as a whole and is entirely driven by money. We believe it undermines the merit-based culture and the spirit of open competition that makes golf so special. I would also like to say that in my opinion the continued commentary that this is about growing the game is just not credible and if anything, is harming the perception of our sport which we are working so hard to improve. (Bastable, 2022)

LIV tournaments at Centurion and Pumpkin Ridge were not structured upon meritocratic values, as these tournaments ensured all tournament golfers were adequately compensated (Panja & Das, 2022), not solely based upon 'the cream […] ris[ing] to the top'. Hence, this structure demonstrates that golf does not have to continue to have meritocratic structures, but Slumbers uses emotional discourses to legitimize PGA structures and argues this (read: more equitable financial payouts) 'is not in the best long-term interests of the sport' because *true golf* has a spirit of meritocracy.

Discussion

Our research provides insight into how emotionally charged discourse can impact perceptions of legitimacy. Through EDA, we analyzed how PGA-affiliated actors crafted emotionally laden discourses in response to the emergence of LIV Golf. We interpreted the evoking of emotion as an instantiation of legitimacy work to defend and maintain the PGA's position of dominance while also attacking the legitimacy of the emergent LIV Golf league. Despite the contextually bound aspects of our research, we address calls to better understand emotions within institutional studies, while also advancing understandings of legitimacy work within sport (see Nite & Edwards, 2021). Our work contributes to more nuanced perspectives of actor positioning and how emotion may be strategically manipulated by dominant sport entities. We also speak to the decoupling of legitimacy work and associated discourses from material practices.

Legitimacy work and emotions

The primary contribution of our research is extending theorizations of how emotions can be utilized within institutional work, specifically legitimacy work. We build on the notion that 'people can strategically use emotions in others to advance certain institutional projects by appealing to the ethos of a particular audience whose support they want to elicit' (Lok et al., 2017, p. 606). Sport management scholars have suggested emotions may be integral in garnering support for new policies (Lu & Heinze, 2020), creating social bonds (Pedras et al., 2020), and may sow seeds of distrust among stakeholders (Kihl & Richardson, 2009). Our research contributes by showing how sport entities can work to strategically manipulate emotions of stakeholders (in our case, players, fans, sponsors, and media affiliates) to both erode support for rivals and reify the legitimacy of dominant sport institutions. We theorize emotive framing as a form of legitimacy work, building on previous institutional work research in sport management (see Nite, 2017; Nite & Nauright, 2020). Specifically, Nite and Nauright (2020) outlined a process of legitimacy work in response to internal abuse scandals. Their work largely focused on material actions whereby university officials manipulated internal processes and collaborated with externalities to maintain universities' perceived legitimacy. The current study builds upon this work to show how discourse and emotions may be strategically employed as legitimacy work. By framing LIV's efforts as being harmful to golf and the PGA propping itself up as the protector of golf, PGA stakeholders used negative-laden discourse (i.e. defector) to discourage support for LIV. Thus, LIV would be deemed illegitimate at an emotional level.

Considering a key differentiator of sport products is the emotions ascribed to them (Kwak et al., 2011; Lee et al., 2018), the actions of sport organizations seem particularly attuned to the broader impact of emotions in the evaluation of proper behavior. Our research suggests that dominant sport governing bodies may craft discourses to impact the different forms of legitimacy; pragmatic, moral, and cognitive (see Suchman, 1995). In their responses to the emergent LIV Golf, PGA affiliates used emotion to attack the legitimacy of the new league on each legitimacy front. The pragmatism of LIV Golf was undermined with emotion with the suggestion that it was hurting the game of golf. Related, the cognitive legitimacy was also emotionally attacked by suggesting that LIV was counter to the traditions and legacy of golf. The funding of LIV Golf and by suggesting defecting players were simply chasing money was meant to evoke negative emotions to trigger questions of the morality of the new endeavor. Our findings are applicable to scholars in various sport domains as we demonstrated how emotion can be weaponized to attack the legitimacy of a competing sport endeavor. Future research should seek to establish empirical relationships between emotional discourse and perceptions of legitimacy.

Actor positioning and emotions

Our research also intimates the differentiation of actor positioning and how actors in various roles may implement emotional discourse as legitimacy work. Specifically, our work also intimates how institutional challenges may be catalysts for the emergence of institutional evangelicals. Massa et al. (2017) defined evangelists as 'members of key audiences who build a critical mass of support for new ways of doing things' (p. 461). In this regard, emotion is an integral aspect of institutional evangelism as language may be manipulated to evoke emotional responses of audiences (Massa et al., 2017). Whereas Massa and colleagues connected evangelism with innovation and change (see also Zietsma & Lawrence, 2010), they also pointed toward the possibility of evangelism being used in institutional maintenance. We demonstrate the utility of this concept as our work suggests that attacks on current institutions may result in evangelism in defense of the current institutions. Our findings suggest that by using emotional discourses, like 'driven by money' and 'betrayal', to establish a sense of loyalty amongst institutional actors, the PGA was trying to dissuade professional golfers from joining LIV, rather than using rational arguments to remain a member of the PGA. This emotionally charged language seemed to send a message to fans and sponsors that LIV would hurt the sport.

Our work may be useful for those studying other pertinent sport issues such athlete activism or diversity and inclusion efforts, particularly given the increase of such efforts in sport are in relation with and to issues of violence such as anti-blackness (see Keaton & Cooper, 2022; Singer et al., 2022). For instance, Read and Lock (2022) detailed how the National Football League (NFL) sought to address player protests in a manner that would not damage the league's image. Building on the findings of our study, the NFL could craft emotionally laden discourse to impact fan perceptions. Considering actor roles and identities were not the focus of our research, future research should interrogate how challenges to current institutional structures seem to sort members of the field into different positions such as institutional evangelicals.

Decoupling of legitimacy discourse from material practice

Finally, our research points to an interesting dynamic between emotional discourse and material practice. Considering the totality of our case, we proffer that emotionally charged legitimacy work can be targeted at both practice and actors. Our case suggests that the emotional discourse was aimed at those *who* introduced challenges into sport and less about the challenges themselves. PGA affiliates initially took umbrage with LIV's innovative approaches to professional golf and framed messages to position LIV as antithetical to the institutionalized structures of golf. Yet, despite such emotional rhetoric, the PGA soon adopted similar innovations (e.g. guaranteed payments for top players, PGA-sponsored travel arrangements, and new competition formats; Blinder, 2022). At which point, the PGA's framing shifted toward attacking LIV and defecting

PGA members as being harmful to the sport of golf. Our work complements Nite and Washington's (2017) research of television broadcasting in college sport. They intimated that the NCAA was concerned with both television as a technical challenge that might harm material practice, but their work also showed that control of television was a bigger concern (that is, the concern was not television as practice). We extend this work by showing that emotional discourse may be impactful in shaping perceptions of the legitimacy of new endeavors at the cognitive and moral level. Future research should provide a more nuanced account that specifically interrogates how emotion may impact legitimacy perceptions when material practices are decoupled from perceptions of those who introduce institutional challenges.

Conclusion

With the current study, we sought to further develop the tenets of legitimacy work by garnering a better understanding of how emotion may be incorporated into sport organizations' efforts to influence perspectives of innovations introduced by rivals. We showed how members of a dominant sport organization crafted messages to evoke emotional responses that would impact perceptions of legitimacy. As such, we answered calls to better understand emotions and legitimacy work within sport management research (see Nite & Edwards, 2021). Our work points to new avenues of research that could add further contributions in this space. Specifically, future research could provide insights into the dynamism of impact versus intent. Our work focused on our perceptions of the intent of the messaging, but future work investigating the actual impacts of emotionally laden messages in regard to altering audience perceptions. Additionally, our study pointed to actor positioning as an important aspect of legitimacy work. However, an in-depth investigation of actor positioning was beyond the scope of the current work but would be an important extension as this would better delineate tactics implemented by defenders and challengers of current institutional arrangements.

Finally, it is important to note that after this research was completed, the PGA and LIV Golf announced their merger in June 2023 (see Draper, 2023). Indeed, as we noted in our detailing of the research context, the PGA had already taken steps to incorporate changes similar to those of LIV into some of their events. This lends further credence to our assertion that legitimacy work often entails framing messages to influence perceptions and that material practices may be less consequential in terms of legitimacy perceptions.

Note

1. The professional golf tournaments that are considered 'major championships' include: The PGA Championship, The Masters Tournament, The United States Open Championship, and The Open Championship (i.e. The British Open).

Disclosure statement

No potential conflict of interest was reported by the author(s).

ORCID

Calvin Nite http://orcid.org/0000-0002-3095-8987
Ajhanai Keaton http://orcid.org/0000-0001-5019-9976
Patrick Neff http://orcid.org/0000-0002-2510-248X

References

About Us. (n.d.). https://www.pgatour.com/company/aboutus.html
Bastable, A. (2022, July 15). 'Everybody, it feels like, is against us': Liv tension surfacing at open championship. *Golf.* https://golf.com/news/liv-tension-bubbling-up-old-course/
Battilana, J., & D'Aunno, T. (2012). Institutional work and the paradox of embedded agency. In T. B. Lawrence, R. Suddaby, & B. Leca (Eds.), *Institutional work: Actors and agency in institutional studies of organizations* (pp. 31–55). Cambridge University Press.
Blinder, A. (2022, October 30). LIV Golf threw a sport into chaos. It has also changed it. *The New York Times,* https://www.nytimes.com/2022/10/30/sports/golf/liv-pga-trump-doral.html
Boykoff, J. (2022). Toward a theory of sportswashing: Mega-events, soft power, and political conflict. *Sociology of Sport Journal, 39*(4), 342–351.
Byun, J., Ellis, D., & Leopkey, B. (2021). The pursuit of legitimacy through strategic alliances: The examination of international joint sport event bidding. *European Sport Management Quarterly, 21*(4), 544–563. https://doi.org/10.1080/16184742.2020.1759668
Cannizzaro, M. (2022, June 6). Phil Mickelson bolts to Saudi-backed LIV Tour after months of controversy. *New York Post.* https://nypost.com/2022/06/06/phil-mickelson-joins-liv-tour-after-months-of-controversy/
Carter, I. (2020, November 27). PGA Tour and European Tour reach agreement on closer working alliance. *BBC,* https://www.bbc.com/sport/golf/55098732
Chadwick, S. (2022). From utilitarianism and neoclassical sport management to a new geopolitical economy of sport. *European Sport Management Quarterly, 22*(5), 685–704. https://doi.org/10.1080/16184742.2022.2032251
Creed, W. E. D., Hudson, A. B., Okhuysen, G. A., & Smith-Crowe, K. (2014). Swimming in a sea of shame: Incorporating emotion into explanations of institutional reproduction and change. *Academy of Management Review, 39*(3), 275–301. https://doi.org/10.5465/amr.2012.0074
Deephouse, D. L., Bundy, J., Tost, L. P., & Suchman, M. C. (2017). Organizational legitimacy: Six key questions. In *The SAGE handbook of organizational institutionalism* (Vol. 4, Issue 2, pp. 27–54).
Deephouse, D. L., & Suchman, M. (2008). Legitimacy in organizational institutionalism. In R. Greenwood, C. Oliver, K. Sahlin, & R. Suddaby (Eds.), *The SAGE handbook of organizational institutionalism* (pp. 49–77). SAGE.
Dethier, D. (2022, September 8). The inside story of LIV Golf vs. the PGA Tour: Money, innovation and loyalty. *Golf.com.* https://golf.com/news/liv-pga-tour-inside-story/
De Vreese, C. H. (2005). News framing: Theory and typology. *Information Design Journal+ Document Design, 13*(1), 51–62. https://doi.org/10.1075/idjdd.13.1.06vre
Draper, K. (2023, June 7). The merger of LIV Golf and the PGA Tour: Here's what to know. *The New York Times.* https://www.nytimes.com/2023/06/07/sports/golf/pga-liv-golf-merger.html
Druckman, J. N. (2004). Political preference formation: Competition, deliberation, and the (ir) relevance of framing effects. *American Political Science Review, 98*(4), 671–686. https://doi.org/10.1017/S0003055404041413
Frederick, E., Pegoraro, A., & Sanderson, J. (2021). Sport in the age of trump: An analysis of Donald Trump's tweets. *International Journal of Sport Communication, 14*(3), 356–378. https://doi.org/10.1123/ijsc.2020-0287
Gee, J. P. (2014). *How to do discourse analysis: A toolkit.* Routledge.
Greenwood, R., Oliver, C., Sahin, K., & Suddaby, R. (2008). *The SAGE handbook or organizational institutionalism.* SAGE.

Gross, K., & D'ambrosio, L. (2004). Framing emotional response. *Political Psychology, 25*(1), 1–29. https://doi.org/10.1111/j.1467-9221.2004.00354.x

Hampel, C. E., Lawrence, T. B., & Tracey, P. (2017). Institutional work: Taking stock and making it matter. In R. Greenwood, C. Oliver, T. B. Lawrence, & R. E. Meyer (Eds.), *The SAGE handbook of organizational institutionalism* (2nd ed, pp. 558–590). SAGE.

Harig, B. (2022a, March 21). *Weekly read: PGA Tour players offer opinions on Liv Golf Invitational possibilities*. Sports Illustrated. https://www.si.com/golf/news/weekly-read-pga-tour-players-offer-opinions-liv-golf-invitational-possibilities

Harig, B. (2022b, May 17). *Tiger Woods restates support for PGA Tour, has 'a lot of disagreement' with Phil Mickelson, Liv Golf*. Sports Illustrated. https://www.si.com/golf/news/tiger-woods-restates-support-for-pga-tour-has-a-lot-of-disagreement-with-phil-mickelson-liv-golf

Harig, B. (2022c, July 12). *Tiger Woods disappointed with players joining LIV Golf: 'I don't understand it.'* Sports Illustrated. https://www.si.com/golf/news/tiger-woods-disappointed-players-liv-golf

History of the PGA. (n.d.). https://www.pga.org/history/

How it works. (n.d.). https://www.livgolf.com/format

Huggan, J. (2022, September 6). *Billy Horschel calls out LIV golfers in BMW PGA field: 'Why are you here?'* Golf Digest. https://www.golfdigest.com/story/billy-horschel-liv-golfers-bmw-pga-championship-wentworth

Kaplan, S. (2008). Framing contests: Strategy making under uncertainty. *Organization Science, 19*(5), 729–752. https://doi.org/10.1287/orsc.1070.0340

Keaton, A. C. (2021). A critical discourse analysis of racial narratives from White athletes attending a historically Black college/University. *Qualitative Research in Sport, Exercise and Health, 14*(6), 969–986. https://doi.org/10.1080/2159676X.2021.1944901.

Keaton, A. C., & Cooper, J. N. (2022). A racial reckoning in a racialized organization? Applying racialized organization theory to the NCAA institutional field. *Journal of Issues in Intercollegiate Athletics*.

Khashoggi killing. (2019, June 19). *Khashoggi killing: Executive summary of Callamard's UN report*. Aljazeera. https://www.aljazeera.com/news/2019/6/19/khashoggi-killing-executive-summary-of-callamards-un-report

Kihl, L., & Richardson, T. (2009). "Fixing the mess": A grounded theory of a men's basketball coaching staff's suffering as a result of academic corruption. *Journal of Sport Management, 23*(3), 278–304.

Koschut, S. (2018). Speaking from the heart: Emotion discourse analysis in international relations. In M. Clément, & E. Sangar (Eds.), *Researching emotions in international relations* (pp. 277–301). Palgrave Macmillan.

Kwak, D. H., Kim, Y. K., & Hirt, E. R. (2011). Exploring the role of emotions on sport consumers' behavioral and cognitive responses to marketing stimuli. *European Sport Management Quarterly, 11*(3), 225–250. https://doi.org/10.1080/16184742.2011.577792

Lawrence, T. B., & Phillips, N. (2019). *Constructing organizational life: How social-symbolic work shapes selves, organizations, and institutions*. Oxford Press.

Lawrence, T. B., & Suddaby, R. (2006). Institutions and institutional work. In S. R. Clegg, C. Hardy, T. B. Lawrence, & W. R. Nord (Eds.), *Handbook of organization studies* (2nd ed, pp. 215–254). SAGE.

Lee, J. S., Kelly, M., & Mirza, A. (2022, June 4). Saudi-led airstrikes in Yemen have been called war crimes. Many relied on U.S. support. *The Washington Post*. https://www.washingtonpost.com/investigations/interactive/2022/saudi-war-crimes-yemen/

Lee, S., Kim, Y., & Heere, B. (2018). Sport team emotion: Conceptualization, scale development and validation. *Sport Management Review, 21*(4), 363–376. https://doi.org/10.1016/j.smr.2017.08.007

Lefsrund, L., Graves, H., & Phillips, N. (2020). "Giant toxic lakes you see from space": A theory of multimodal messages and emotion in legitimacy work. *Organization Studies, 41*(8), 1055–1078. https://doi.org/10.1177/0170840619835575

Lok, J., Creed, W. E. D., DeJordy, R., & Voronov, M. (2017). Living institutions: Bringing emotions into organizational institutionalism. In R. Greenwood, C. Oliver, T. B. Lawrence, & R. E. Meyer (Eds.), *The SAGE handbook of organizational institutionalism* (2nd ed, pp. 591–620). SAGE.

Lu, D., & Heinze, L. (2020). Examining institutional entrepreneurship in the passage of youth sport concussion legislation. *Journal of Sport Management, 35*(1), 1–16.

Marksbury, J. (2022, July 28). 'Complete bulls—': Pro calls out Liv Golfers' hollow justifications for leaving PGA Tour. *Golf.com*. https://golf.com/news/pro-calls-out-liv-golfers-leaving-pga-tour/

Massa, F. G., Helms, W. S., Voronov, M., & Wang, L. (2017). Emotions uncorked: Inspiring evangelism for the emerging practice of cool-climate winemaking in Ontario. *Academy of Management Journal, 60*(2), 461–499. https://doi.org/10.5465/amj.2014.0092

Meyer, J. W., & Rowan, B. (1977). Institutionalized organizations: Formal structure as myth and ceremony. *American Journal of Sociology, 83*(2), 340–363. https://doi.org/10.1086/226550

Nite, C. (2017). Message framing as institutional maintenance: The national collegiate athletic association's institutional work of addressing legitimate threats. *Sport Management Review, 20*(4), 338–351. https://doi.org/10.1016/j.smr.2016.10.005

Nite, C., & Edwards, J. (2021). From isomorphism to institutional work: Advancing institutional theory in sport management research. *Sport Management Review, 24*(5), 815–838. https://doi.org/10.1080/14413523.2021.1896845

Nite, C., Ige, A., & Washington, M. (2019). The evolving institutional work of the National Collegiate Athletic Association to maintain dominance in a fragmented field. *Sport Management Review, 22*(3), 379–394. https://doi.org/10.1016/j.smr.2018.05.002

Nite, C., & Nauright, J (2020). Examining institutional work that perpetuates abuse in sport organizations. *Sport Management Review, 23*(1), 117–129. https://doi.org/10.1016/j.smr.2019.06.002

Nite, C., & Washington, M. (2017). Institutional adaptation to technological innovation: Lessons from the NCAA's regulation of football television broadcasts (1938-1984). *Journal of Sport Management, 31*(6), 575–590. https://doi.org/10.1123/jsm.2017-0159

Panja, T., & Das, A. (2022, July 28). What is LIV Golf? It depends whom you ask. *The New York Times*. https://www.nytimes.com/article/liv-golf-saudi-arabia-pga.html

Payday at East Lake. (2022, August 27). *Here's the FedEx Cup prize money payout for each golfer at the 2022 Tour Championship*. Golf Digest. https://www.golfdigest.com/story/final-pga-tour-fedex-cup-prize-money-payout-for-each-golfer-at-the-2022-tour-championship

Pedras, L., Taylor, T., & Frawley, S. (2020). Responses to multi-level institutional complexity in a national sport federation. *Sport Management Review, 23*(3), 482–497. https://doi.org/10.1016/j.smr.2019.05.001

PGA of America. (n.d.). https://www.pga.org

Priest, E. (2022, August 30). *Why did Cameron Smith jump to LIV Golf? It was more than money he says*. Golf Digest. https://www.golfdigest.com/story/cameron-smith-jumps-to-liv-golf-to-spend-more-time-in-australia-home

Read, D., & Lock, D. (2022). Image repair using social identity leadership: An exploratory analysis of the National Football League's response to the national anthem protests. *Journal of Sport Management, 36*, 587–599.

Rivera, J. (2022, September 2). *Who is playing LIV Golf? Updated list of PGA Tour defectors includes Phil Mickelson, Dustin Johnson, Bryson DeChambeau, others*. The Sporting News. https://www.sportingnews.com/us/golf/news/liv-golf-tour-list-mickelson-johnson-dechambeau-pga/rlwprhtsx6uwgq73zq0e7ryc

Robertson, J., Dowling, M., Washington, M., Leopkey, B., Ellis, D. L., & Smith, L. (2022). Institutional theory in sport: A scoping review. *Journal of Sport Management, 36*(5), 459–472. https://doi.org/10.1123/jsm.2021-0179

Saul, D. (2022, July 12). *Tiger Woods rips into LIV Golf: 'I just don't understand it.'* Forbes. https://www.forbes.com/sites/dereksaul/2022/07/12/tiger-woods-rips-into-liv-golf-i-just-dont-understand-it

Schlabach, M. (2022, June 9). *PGA Tour suspends all players taking part in first LIV Golf tournament*. ESPN. https://www.espn.com/golf/story/_/id/34063037/pga-tour-suspends-all-players-taking-part-first-liv-golf-tournament

Singer, J. N., Agyemang, K. J., Chen, C., Walker, N. A., & Melton, E. N. (2022). What is Blackness to sport management? Manifestations of anti-Blackness in the field. *Journal of Sport Management, 36*, 215–227.
Spiegler, R. (2014). Competitive framing. *American Economic Journal: Microeconomics, 6*(3), 35–58. https://doi.org/10.1257/mic.6.3.35
Suchman, M. C. (1995). Managing legitimacy: Strategic and institutional approaches. *Academy of Management Review, 20*(3), 571–610. https://doi.org/10.2307/258788
Sveinson, K., Hoeber, L., & Heffernan, C. (2021). Critical discourse analysis as theory, methodology, and analyses in sport management studies. *Journal of Sport Management, 35*(5), 465–475. https://doi.org/10.1123/jsm.2020-0288
Tewksbury, D., Jones, J., Peske, M. W., Raymond, A., & Vig, W. (2000). The interaction of news and advocate frames: Manipulating audience perceptions of a local public policy issue. *Journalism & Mass Communication Quarterly, 77*(4), 804–829. https://doi.org/10.1177/107769900007700406
Tewksbury, D., & Scheufele, D. A. (2009). News framing theory and research. In J. Bryantand, & M. B. Oliver (Eds.), *Media effects: Advances in theory and research* (pp. 17–33). Taylor & Francis.
Voronov, M., & Vince, R. (2012). Integrating emotions into the analysis of institutional work. *Academy of Management Review, 37*, 58–81.
Warren, M. (2022, July 28). Controversial Saudi-backed golf tournament to begin Friday at Trump golf course. *CNN*. https://www.cnn.com/2022/07/28/politics/trump-liv-golf-tournament-saudi-arabia/index.html
What is the DP World Tour? (2019, June 26). https://www.europeantour.com/dpworld-tour/news/articles/detail/what-is-the-european-tour/
Who we are. (n.d.). https://www.livgolf.com/about
Zak, S. (2022, September 8). LIV Golf timeline: How we arrived at pro golf's civil war. *Golf.com*. https://golf.com/news/timeline-liv-golf-how-we-arrived-pro-golf-civil-war/
Zietsma, C., & Lawrence, T. B. (2010). Institutional work in the transformation of an organizational field: The interplay of boundary work and practice work. *Administrative Science Quarterly, 55*(2), 189–221. https://doi.org/10.2189/asqu.2010.55.2.189
Zimmer, T. (2022, July 7). LIV Golf's charter jet for players, caddies: Looks like a wild scene. *Golf.com*. https://golf.com/news/features/liv-golf-charter-jet-wild-scene/

Index

Page numbers in **bold** refer to tables and those in *italic* refer to figures.

Aboriginal Sport Circle 53
accountability 55, 62–4, 66
ACTIVE2010 Strategy 60
actor positioning 128
agentic turn 74
Agyemang, K. 95
analytic autoethnography 36–7
athletics departments 97
autoethnography 35; analytic 36–7; defined 35; product dimension 36

Ball, C. G. 80
'banned in New York' stigma 80–1
Barberá-Tomás, D. 12
Battilana, J. 108
Bishop, S. H. 80
Block, K. 13
Bourdiuesian Theory 56
Braun, V. 99
Brazilian Jiu-Jitsu (BJJ) 76
Burris, M. A. 14
Burton, L. J. 45

Canada: accountability and responsibilization 62–4; changing role of sport 60–2; methodology 58–9; organizational fields 56–8; policy and multi-level governance 53–5; regional development and governance systems 55–6
Canadian amateur sports system 52
Canadian Sport for Life 52, 53
Canadian Sport Policy (CSP) 53–4
Canadian Women in Sport 53
categories, defined 73–4
Clarke, V. 99
coded emotional stimulation 79
cognitive turn 74
Cohen, A. 27
collective emotions and institutions 26–7
collective legitimation decisions 82
college sport industry 97
collegiate sport employees 97
Comeau, G. S. 55
Community Sport Organizations (CSOs) 52
competitive amateur sport 60
cost-sharing agreements 63
Cousens, L. 57
Creed, W. E. D. 95

D'ambrosio, L. 119
Deephouse, D. L. 115
De Vreese, C. H. 120
DiMaggio, P. J. 2, 5, 56
Director of Goalkeeping (DOCG) 44
Directors of Coaching (DOC) 44
disbursements 63
discrimination 9
discursive techniques 75–6
Dixon, E. 80
DOC Youth Girls (DOCYG) 44
Dowling, M. 10, 96

Edwards, J. 3, 10, 107
Elite Clubs League program 44
Ellis, C. 37
embedded agency 74, 86–7, 95
emotional cultivation 79
emotional discourse analysis (EDA) 119, **121**, 122
emotional disruption 79, 82
emotional pacification 79, 84, 85
emotional stimulation 85
emotional substitution 79, 85
emotions 3, 116–17; actor positioning 128; data collection 14; defined 72; initial open coding 15; institutional work 10–12; pattern coding 15–16; SDP-related institutional work 9–10; and 'sensory experiences' 9; sport for development and peace 12; work and legitimacy 127–8
evaluators 87

Farny, S. 27
field-level contestation 5
field members 58
Fortune, M. 55
frame building 120
framing contest 119, 120, 122

Gérard, S. 57
Giddens, A. 35, 106
Global North hegemony/Global South dependence 10
goalkeepers 41
Greenwood, R. 2, 95
Gross, K. 119

Hampel, C. E. 115
Healthy Kids Panel 61
Heinze, K. L. 11
Helms, W. S. 73, 79, 82
hermeneutic phenomenology 96
Hoffman, A. 52
Howe, P. D. 56

ice hockey 10
innovative product offerings 114
institutional defenders 114
institutional leadership 5
institutional logics: agency and sensemaking 40–1; conform socially logic 41–2; defined 37; 'less than' logic 37–8; micro foundations model 38–40; 'protect girls' logic 42–3; 'vision of value' logic 43–6
Institutional Review Board (IRB) 98
institutional theory 5; agency and structure 35; contributions 47–8; cultural narratives 35; sport-specific logics 35; *see also* autoethnography; institutional logics
institutional work 3; and (negative) emotions 82
institutions: and agency 95–6; defined 73
intercollegiate athletics 10
International Paralympic Committee 57

Jarvis, L. C. 11
Jingxuan Zheng 4

Kitchin, P. J. 56
Koschut, S. 119, **121**, 122
Krippendorff, K. 78
Kvale, S. 98

Lawrence, T. B. 2, 10
Lefsrund, L. 116
legitimacy work: data analysis 77–9, *78*; data collection 76–7; defined 72, 73, 115; discourse from material practice 128–9; institutional work 74; negative emotions and institutions 75–6; new category emergence 74; work and emotions 127–8
'less than' logic 37–8
LIV Golf (LIV) 117–19
LIV golfers 118–19
Lock, D. 128
Lok, J. 11, 12, 15, 25
Long-term Athlete Development Framework 60
Lu, D. 11

Mason, D. S. 4
Massa, F. G. 128
McSweeney, M. 3, 10
Meyer, J. W. 2
Micelotta, E. R. 95, 105
micro foundations model 38–40
Mixed Martial Arts (MMA) 4, 73, 76, 80–2
most valuable defensive player (MVP) 42
multi-level governance system 53–5
multi-level studies 3
municipalities 54

National Coaching Certification Program 60
National Collegiate Athletics Association (NCAA) 10, 41, 95, 97
National Football League (NFL) 128
national sport organizations (NSOs) 53
Nauright, J. 127
negative emotions 75–6, 80–2, 81
Nelund, A. 55
neo-institutionalism 2
neoliberal governmental agendas 55
new category emergence 74
Nite, C. 3, 4, 10, 95, 107, 127, 129
Nols, Z. 12, 25
novel methodological approaches 3

Oja, B. D. 4
Olympic Development Program (ODP) 45
Olympic Games 10
Oncescu, J. 55
Ontario Sport Action Plan 60
organizational accountability 58
organizational fields 56–8, 64–5
Organizational Institutionalism 2

Pan/Parapan American Games 61
Parent, M. M. 54
participatory action research (PAR) 3, 13
Patterson, K. D. W. 73, 79, 82
PGA tour members 123; destroying true golf 125–6; legacy and tradition 123–4; meritocracy 126
photocollaging 14
photovoice 14
pornography industry 87
Powell, W. W. 2, 5, 56
Professional Golf Association (PGA) 4, 117–19
professional golfers 117
pro-MMA stakeholders 76, 82, 84
'protect girls' logic 42–3
provincial and territorial sport organizations (PTSOs) 53

Read, D. 128
regional development and governance systems 55–6
regional policy 65–7
responsibilization 62–4
Rich, K. A. 3
Robertson, J. 3, 58

role of Own the Podium 10
Rowan, B. 2

Saldana, J. 15
Saudi Arabia's Public Investment Fund 117–18
Savoie, D. J. 55
Schaillée, H. 12, 26
Scott, D. S. 12
sensemaking process 40–1
Seo, M. G. 95
Skille, E. Å. 58
Slack, T. 57
Smith, J. 10, 96
social emotions 114
social exclusion 9
social inequality: community tensions, Kampala 17–19; conflict resolution via SDP 23–4, *24*; defined 10; emotional attachment to home 22–3, *23*; emotional toll, forced displacement 16–17, *17*, *18*; SDP-related institutional work 19–20, *20*; stress relief 20–2, *21*
Spaaij, R. 9, 12, 26
sport for development and peace (SDP) organisation 3, 9
sport formation and stigmatization (1993–2000) 77
Sport Funding and Accountability Framework (SFAF) 63
sport news media articles 120
sport policy implementation 65–7
sport-specific logics 35
sports researchers 57
sports scholars 52
sport washing 118
stasis supporting bureaucracies 102–5
Suddaby, R. 2, 10

thematic analysis 99
Thornton, P. 35, 36, 38

Tolbert, P. S. 2, 5
TopFlight goalkeeper camps 41
Toubiana, M. 75
Tracy, S. J. 99
transfer payments 63
trustworthiness 99

Ultimate Fighting Championship (UFC) 76
unemployment 9

'vision of value' logic 43–6
Voronov, M. 75

Wang, C. 14
Washington, M. 95, 129
Weber, K. 75
Welty Peachey, J. 25, 27
Women's United Soccer Association (WUSA) 34
Woolf, J. 96
Woolford, A. 55
Wooten, M. 52, 56
work arrangements: data analysis 99–100, **100**; institutionalized actors 94; institutions and agency 95–6; limitations and future studies 108; mutually constitutive relationship 94; participants 97–8; practical implications 107–8; researcher positionality 98–9; sport organiizations 93–4; stasis supporting bureaucracies 102–5; theoretical contributions 106–7; trustworthiness 99; work prioritization 100–2
work prioritization 100–2
Wright, A. L. 11, 57

Young African Refugees for Integral Development (YARID) 3, 12–13

Zietsma, C. 75
Zucker, L. G. 2, 5

Printed in the USA
CPSIA information can be obtained
at www.ICGtesting.com
LVHW081753041124
795688LV00005B/576